THE
National Pastime

A REVIEW OF BASEBALL HISTORY

CONTENTS

EDITOR: James Charlton **FACT CHECKER:** Scott Flatow **GRAPHIC DESIGN:** Lisa Hochstein
DESIGNATED READERS AND PEER REVIEWERS: Peter Bjarkman, Pete Cava, Larry Lester, Rod Nelson, Jules Tygiel, John Zajc, Scott Flatow, Lyle Spatz, Phil Birnbaum.

COVER PHOTO: Courtesy of Stormy Kromer Mercantile
(Stormy Kromer with his Kaukauna teammates in an undated photograph.
Kromer is on the front cover, far left, with a jacket over his uniform.)

THE NATIONAL PASTIME Number 27. Published by The Society for American Baseball Research, Inc., 812 Huron Road, Suite 719, Cleveland, OH 44115. Postage paid at Kent, OH.

A Note from the Editor

This is the first issue of *The National Pastime* devoted to articles on "individuals in the game." An all-biographical issue, if you will, though this is a leaky umbrella over the subject: there are interviews, slices of players' lives, and write-ups of big games by players. One SABR wag commented to me that he "thought every issue of TNP was all biographical," but that has not been the case. The journal has always published a wide variety of articles on pennant races, pitching tandems, umpire uniforms, Cuban baseball, fair-foul hitting, integration, stadiums, women's baseball, and dozens of other topics. Whew!

It is not, of course, the first dedicated issue of the journal. John Thorn and Mark Rucker put together delightful all-pictorial issues in the 1980s that were on particular topics, such as 19th-century ball. In 1992, the estimable Peter Bjarkman edited an issue of TNP devoted to baseball around the world. These are among my most cherished issues of the journal, and for newer members, these are well worth seeking out and acquiring.

This issue of TNP has some wonderful pieces on some surprising subjects. One is Jeff Obermeyer's profile of major leaguer Jim Riley, who also played in the NHL. Dick Thompson's article on Cannonball Bill Jackman is an illuminating piece on this little-known New England star. James Smith provides a warm portrait of longtime PCL personality Lester Cook, while Pete Bjarkman persuasively speaks to Roberto Clemente's groundbreaking impact on Latin players and baseball. The late Smoky Joe Wood proves to be as outspoken and interesting an observer as he was as a pitcher and hitter. The cover article, by Steve Bennett, introduces us to one of the game's great characters, George Kromer.

One of my favorite pieces is by one of my favorite musicians, jazz pianist and lyricist Dave Frishberg, whose albums have been nominated four times for Grammy Awards. Dave is the composer and singer of the wry and amusing "My Attorney Bernie," Schoolhouse Rock favorites such as "I'm Just a Bill," and the iconic "Van Lingle Mungo." He shares with us the creative steps on the writing of that tribute. You'll be humming by the end.

– Jim Charlton

The Indomitable Stormy Kromer

by Steve Bennett

In his 94 eventful years, George "Stormy" Kromer caught for the Wisconsin All-Stars, worked 54 years on the railroad, invented the railroad engineer's cap, founded a manufacturing empire, and managed a minor league team to 35 straight defeats. And if that's not enough, when he was 75, he managed a minor league team to an embarrassing 40-5 defeat that received national attention, forced an investigation by the minor league governing body, and resulted in the end of Kromer's involvement in Organized Baseball.

Many parts of the Kromer legend are shadowy. A lot was written about him in his native Wisconsin, but the source for much of what was written was Kromer himself. In this regard Kromer was the equal of a more famous baseball storyteller and mythmaker, Bill Veeck. But if this is the story of one man's romance with baseball, then we must hear the story as he wanted us to hear it, for it's not the facts that count here, it's how we tell them. But don't fear: I'll draw distinctions between what is certifiably real and what is likely Kromer embellishing the details.

In 1897, at the insistence of his future father-in-law, 21-year-old George Kromer got a real job, starting as a railroad fireman on the North Western line. Fifty-four years later he retired as an engineer. But to simply say he was a railroad man and leave it at that is to miss most of a delightful tale of a true American original.

STEVE BENNETT's greatest baseball thrill was sitting in the nosebleed seats with his son and SABR members Rod Nelson and Mark Rucker and watching the White Sox win the first game of the 2005 World Series. A SABR member since 1987, Bennett lives in Grinnell, IA with his wife and two children. He enjoys being the public address announcer for his son's high school baseball games.

Stormy Kromer was born in Kaukauna, WI, a town known for the cheese that bears its name. As a boy, he was often found throwing and catching a baseball with a homemade glove, which he crafted out of an old ladies boot and some black string. Stormy eventually quit school and was working delivering groceries when he was pressed into service for his local high school team. He claimed he played so well that he became the regular catcher even though he did not attend school!

In the mid-1890s, Stormy caught for the Wisconsin All-Stars. Kromer took particular pride in associating with players who enjoyed major league success. He said he caught four men who later pitched in the major leagues. One player he definitely caught was Pete Husting, who went on and pitched for Connie Mack's Philadelphia Athletics. As a 24-year-old, Husting won 14 games for the American League champion A's. He was their number three starter that season behind future Hall of Famers Rube Waddell and Eddie Plank. It's hard to imagine in today's world, but Pete Husting retired from baseball after that season and moved back to Wisconsin to practice law.

While catching for semi-pro teams in the Midwest, Stormy was upset that he didn't have a matching cap for his uniform. Unable to afford one, he asked his wife, Ida, to fashion a cap from the sleeves of his "uni." Stormy was always a stickler for neat appearance at the ball park. Little did he know how that would come to profit him.

Railroad men of the period wore regular hats, anything from straw hats to derbies. Kromer came home from a train run one day determined to design a new cap that would not blow away when the winds whipped through the locomotive cab. Using the experience they had gained from making a baseball cap, Stormy and Ida created a canvas and cloth cap that proved so practical other rail men would "steal" Stormy's cap and force money on him. The Kromers decided to manufacture the pieces for sale.

In three weeks Mrs. Kromer and two girls put together 18 caps. That inauspicious beginning led, in just a few years' time, to the Kromer Cap Company and its famous Kromer Klean Kloth Kabin Kap. It also led to a plant in Milwaukee, distribution on three continents, production of 360,000 caps annually, and a healthy bankroll that enabled Stormy Kromer to pursue his real passion—baseball.

Though still working four months a year on the railroad and overseeing a cap empire, Kromer had ample time and financial resources to invest in baseball teams, both semi-pro and professional. During the 1920s he claims to have sunk $60,000 into a total of 11 teams. One of those teams stood out from the rest.

In 1925 Stormy leased the Blytheville, Arkansas Tigers of the old Tri-State League for $2,000. They were a Class D minor league, which was the lowest professional classification. He found some pretty fair ballplayers for this entry level squad. One, Jack Kloza, wound up briefly in the bigs. Another, Bill Lewis, batted .397 in the Western Association in 1930. He claimed six others also scored later successes in higher leagues, though there is reason to believe some of them may have simply had the same last names as players who performed well in higher leagues.

Stormy liked to tell of how he found Lewis. As the story goes, Lewis was a newsboy in Memphis when Stormy saw him playing catch in the street. Stormy offered him a tryout, and the boy made good. The reality is Lewis had already played for three minor league teams by the time he got to Blytheville. It's possible Kromer found some player playing catch on a Memphis street, but it wasn't Lewis. More likely it was a player who was soon back on that same Memphis street playing catch and talking wistfully about when he used to play pro ball.

The 1951 Vincennes Velvets, managed by Stormy Kromer (far right).

Kromer's policy with the 1925 Blytheville Tigers and all their diamonds in the rough was the same one Branch Rickey used so successfully years later: He sold his players when he felt their value to be at its peak. This was a common practice of astute minor league operators in the days before farm systems. Sometimes the practice could backfire when the team was left bereft of talent. In the early 1920s when the Baltimore Orioles were in the middle of a string of seven consecutive International League pennants, owner Jack Dunn chose not to sell his great pitcher, Lefty Grove. He didn't want to damage his team's chances of winning.

Some operators, though, didn't have the luxury of passing up good money from higher leagues. In Blytheville, Stormy wasn't racing toward a pennant, and he had no qualms about moving talent. Kloza was shipped to Birmingham for $1,000. Outfielder Parker Perry went to Chattanooga for the same price. Two other players went at the same time, and between injuries and sell offs, the team was decimated. They went into a tailspin that didn't end until a new standard for futility had been set: 35 consecutive defeats.

The community was outraged. Kromer said the Ku Klux Klan threatened to run him out on a rail. He often recalled how the townsfolk decided the matter for him by staying away from the ballpark. After a series of games when allegedly no spectators showed up, Stormy figured it was time to take his show on the road. Thus was born Kromer's Arkansas Night Riders. They became a road club that actually turned a small profit. The visiting team was guaranteed $100 a game, and Kromer's expenses ran between $75 and $85 a day. Best of all, he was true to his ultimate purpose: developing baseball talent. Toward that end, he kept bringing in rookies for tryouts: 117 by year's end. "Most of them weren't worth much, but it didn't take me long to pick out the good ones," he said. "I released 14 one night and on another occasion canned seven at one time." The circumstances of the Blytheville season make for a great tale. The only problem is there is no evidence that any of it is true, except for the parts about selling off players and losing 35 in a row. The league played a split-season schedule. Blytheville's record in the first half was 27-33. In the second half they dipped to 4-44.

In 1933 Kromer was compelled to defend his record and methods in Blytheville in a letter to the editor of *The Sporting News.* This is telling in that years after the fact, people were still talking and writing about what occurred there.

After years of working with semi-pro teams in Wisconsin, Stormy had one final fling in Organized Baseball. In 1951 he paid the owners of the Class D Vincennes Velvets of the Mississippi-Ohio Valley League for the right to manage the club on the field. The Vincennes club lost $8,000 in 1950, a fact they blamed on a combination of bad weather, a losing team, and out-of-town ownership. Local owners were recruited, but when Kromer came calling with an offer of $10,000 to run the team, of course the new owners accepted. Furthermore, he let them know that developing hitters was his specialty. Even though it had been more than half a century since his days as a catcher for the Wisconsin All-Stars, the 75-year-old man had lost none of his desire to teach youngsters his system of baseball, the "sizzels of baseball" as he called it.

One of Stormy's "sizzels" was his advocacy of good balance for his players. Today balance drills are common practice. High school pitchers and younger practice throwing while standing on a balance beam. They practice maintaining the balance point of their deliveries while standing on a fulcrum. Similar drills exist for hitters.

Some of his other "sizzels" made less sense, then or now. The training camp for the Vels was like no other. There was Stormy with his rum-soaked cigars expounding on his baseball theories. He had players looking into the sun to strengthen their batting eyes. Contrast this with the beliefs of Rogers Hornsby, the seven-time batting champion who refused to read or go to movie houses because he was worried it would damage his vision. Stormy would have been familiar with Hornsby's views. As an older man, Kromer enrolled in Hornsby's baseball school in Hot Springs, AK. He went through the same paces as the 18-year-olds who made up the school's attendees. Hornsby noted, "That guy Kromer is the best example of a player with guts I ever knew." The source for the quote is probably "that guy Kromer."

Stormy had the team practice with sponge rubber balls. Bob Signaigo, his assistant manager and right fielder, explained, "That was to keep you from being afraid of being hit. But by God, we were professionals. We had been hit a thousand times by then!" Kromer's use of rubber balls dates back to at least 1923. An *Appleton Post-Crescent* article mentions him using soft rubber balls for practice with his Wisconsin State League team.

Late in spring training the *Vincennes Sun-Commercial* reported that manager Kromer was "getting ready to get down to his favorite pastime—improving batting averages." It went on to mention a visitor to camp, one of Stormy's players on the 1925 Blytheville team that had won 32 games in a row!

Stormy's most famous theory of all was to "Take two; take all you got coming to you. Then hit the third one where you want." He tried to teach his hitters discipline by commanding them to not swing until they had two strikes. He believed this made them hungrier hitters, though a Dodgers scout countered, "If a Class D team or a high school team will take two strikes, bunt and run, it will win a lot of games. You'd win, though you wouldn't develop any real hitters." Stormy argued his system worked because he produced a number of good minor league hitters during the 1920s such as Lewis, Perry, and Kloza. Kloza may have been quite a hitter anyway. In his first at bat with Blytheville, Kloza disregarded Kromer's advice to "take two" and instead swung at the second pitch, blasting a drive over the center field fence.

Stormy liked to tell the story of a practice game long ago. A young boy ran off with a ball. When he was stopped by one of the players, he explained, "I only got one! Stormy always says, 'Take two.'"

Signaigo often threw batting practice with 75-year-old Stormy catching. "I decided to play a little joke on Stormy," he recounted. "I substituted one of the rubber balls and let loose with a rising fastball that hit him in the mask and bounced away. Was he impressed! I don't think he ever knew it wasn't a real baseball."

It might have been the rising fastball hitting him in the mask that convinced Stormy to use outfielder Bob Signaigo as a pitcher in a game. It ended up being Kromer's last game in Organized Baseball.

Here's what happened: The Velvets traveled to Danville, IL, to take on the Dans in a doubleheader. In the first game Kromer used a patchwork lineup that featured only four players in their regular positions: the pitcher, the second baseman, the shortstop, and the right fielder. When Long George Smith got shelled for seven runs in the first, Stormy chose to live to fight another day. He shifted Smith to right and brought Signaigo, he of the rising fastball, in to pitch. Unfortunately for Vincennes, Signaigo, who was hitting almost .400 at the time, did not have his best stuff. Eight walks, eight hits, 13 runs, and just six outs later, Signaigo was replaced by the center fielder, John Richmond. He was tagged for nine runs in just one inning before giving way to the first baseman, Eddie Garcia. Garcia mopped up admirably, allowing only 11 runs over the last four innings.

It was reported that when Danville got to 39 runs, the fans started clamoring for 40. With a runner on third, a ball was hit to an infielder who had an easy play at the plate. But true to the old showbiz adage, "Give the people what they want," the infielder screamed, "Here's your 40!" and threw the ball into the stands, allowing the fortieth and final run to score. Less than three hours after it started, Danville was victorious by the startling score of 40-5. It was one of the highest scoring games in modern baseball history.

The umpires decided Stormy was making a mockery of the game and ejected him prior to the start of the doubleheader's second game. This decision wasn't entirely fair to Kromer. True, many of the players were in positions they had not played before, and responsibility for the lineup rests with the manager. But when the starting pitcher didn't have his best stuff (or any stuff at all), Stormy chose to rest his real pitchers and save their arms for more winnable games. This is a practice that still occurs today, though usually the faux pitcher enters the game in the eighth or ninth inning, not the second.

Three days later the Illinois House of Representatives passed a resolution commending the Dans for their victory. The resolution claimed the Dans "eked out a 40 to 5 victory" in a "stirring pitchers' battle reminiscent of the classic duels between the immortal Christy Mathewson and Mordecai Brown."

That same day Stormy Kromer resigned and was replaced by his assistant, right fielder Bob Signaigo. Stormy bore no grudges. He continued to show up for Velvets' games. His players liked the man. Lefty Mehringer, the team's best hurler, spoke for his teammates. "We all liked Stormy. He was trustworthy, and he was honest."

Cy Deem, one of the young pitchers on the Velvets, related this story:

> Stormy was in the stands and saw kids chasing the foul balls that went out of the park. I suppose he didn't know they were turning them in to the Danville officials and started paying the kids to bring them to him. The Danville officials caught on and confronted him. When Bob Signaigo went to help him, Stormy was crying and said it was for the good of the league and that he intended to turn them in after the game.

To provide background for the league investigation into the Danville debacle, Robert Rouse, the Velvets general manager, sent a letter to George Trautman, president of the National Association of Professional Baseball Leagues. The letter is presented in its entirety.

Dear Sir:

Your letter to Mr. Horace Parrish, President of the Vincennes Baseball Club, has been handed to me for reply. This letter was regarding a complaint by Mr. George J. Kromer against Mr. Parrish and Mr. Raymond Werner, Secretary of the Club.

In an agreement dated March 28, 1951 Mr. Parrish and Mr. Werner agreed to let Mr. Kromer take over management of the Vincennes Club, on the field, for the 1951 season. Mr. Kromer had stated that he was an old time professional ball player and had managed professional clubs at Blytheville, AK and Blackwell, OK. Kromer further stated that he had a system of play that had developed several major league players and would teach that system to the Vincennes Club. In return for letting him "coach" the club, Kromer agreed to pay the Vincennes Club $5,000 when the agreement was signed and another $5,000 on June 1, 1951. Kromer paid the first $5,000 and arrived in Vincennes in time for spring training. At that time I had my first meeting with him and he sat down to give me what he called the "Sizzels" of baseball. Kromer made it plain at once that baseball had been played all wrong for 75 years. He referred to such men as Cobb, Speaker, Alexander, Hornsby, Ruth, and Musial as "dummies" and stated that none of those men played any better than the average sand lot kid. I was informed that this spring training would be different and would be run the right way. It, in part, consisted of using sponge rubber balls instead of baseballs, always

throwing the ball in the infield to any base on two or more bounces, never using a glove or mitt to catch a ball and to catch with both arms extended rigidly in front of you with all fingers spread apart as far as possible. Never to run, as that would tire you and for pitchers not to throw. To warm up, a pitcher was to hold his arms upraised for 10 minutes. He was then ready to go. To strengthen the eyes, players were asked to look into the sun for 15 minutes. For hitting practice, players went to the plate with a 3-2 count on them. Kromer positioned himself behind the mound as umpire. The pitcher delivered. If the ball was over and the batter took the pitch, he was out and another man came up. If the pitch was bad, the batter walked and a new man came up. If the batter fouled the pitch, he was out. New man. The only way a batter could get more than one pitch was to hit the first one for what Kromer judged to be a base hit. In that event, he stayed up, still with a 3-2 count.

Naturally, after two days of this I knew something had to be done so I started taking Kromer on "scouting trips" every day while one of our veteran players conducted spring training. When the season opened, I was able to convince Kromer, whose age is 75, that the road trips were too hard for him and that he should not make them. At home I could watch him and keep him from causing too much trouble. My task was to keep Kromer happy in order to protect the owners, who know little of baseball and take no part in the operation of the club, because of Kromer's investment, and at the same time see that the players were not subjected to a lot of "hocus pocus" that Kromer believed in.

Things went along well until June 17th. On that day we were playing at Danville. Kromer, unknown to me, had hidden himself on the club bus and made the road trip. This was the chance he had been waiting for. He submitted a lineup for the first game of a double header that found outfielders pitching, pitchers in the infield, and infielders in the outfield. The players tried to show Kromer that this was bad baseball but he replied that if they were ballplayers they could play just as well one place as another. The result was Danville 40, Vincennes 5. After the unbelievable score, Kromer left the park and club and didn't return for three days. When he did arrive, it was to brag about how he made the headlines in papers all over the country as a result of the game at Danville. I tried to explain that things like that were very bad for the game and could only result in causing the club trouble with both the League and the National Association. I was soundly cursed by Kromer and further informed that no one could do a damn thing about it because he had a contract and could run the club the way he wanted to. That same evening, June 20th, one of the players told me that Kromer was again drawing up a lineup with players out of normal position. I went to the players bench and talked with Kromer. He refused to alter his plan. I then called the club president, Mr. Parrish, and he tried to talk with Kromer but Kromer hung up. Mrs. Parrish came to the park to talk with Kromer but he refused to alter his plan and used bad language in her presence. When nothing else would work, I again went to the player's bench, tore up Kromer's lineup and informed him that he could no longer manage the club. He had already broken his contract because he had not paid the second $5,000 that was due on June 1st. Kromer left the field and the next day sent a letter thanking the club owners for the chance they had given him and stating that he was "resigning" and going home. It must have been while he was at home that he wrote your office. I understand that our League President and *The Sporting News* also received a similar letter.

Kromer is now back in Vincennes. He goes to the ball park every night and spends a lot of time with me. He does not, however, try to manage the club. Today, when Mr. Parrish handed me your letter, I asked Kromer when and why he had written your office. He replied, "I don't remember ever writing to Mr. Trautman."

That is the story. I know it sounds unbelievable but it is true. In fact there is much, much more that could be added but I think this is enough to give you some idea about Kromer. If you should desire more information, I can send you a few of Kromer's "sizzel sheets," full of information about the new strike zone, complete information on why a batter should strike out on one strike or walk on two balls, how a ball game should be only four innings or a lot of other things that I'll bet even your office never thought of.

I am not trying to make a joke of this thing but it is hard to keep from seeing some humor in the thing when one knows that Kromer sincerely thinks that baseball is all wrong and that he, alone, has the answer that will save it.

Yours very truly,

Robert M. Rouse

Three years later the Kaukauna Elks threw a testimonial dinner for Stormy Kromer, "the best sport in the world." 125 people showed up to pay tribute to this baseball pioneer and to share their favorite stories about him and his affection for baseball. They told how he would collar people on the train platforms during layovers and make them play catch with him. They told how, as a passenger, Stormy would miss his stops on the train because he was so engrossed in baseball conversations. They told how as a boy in Kaukauna, he would play ball with whatever was available, even corn cobs and bundles of rags. They told of the time he sold a player to the White Sox, even though the player had lost a finger. The Sox figured they wouldn't lose him to the military draft. Instead the boy quit baseball six months later. And they told of the time when, with the bases loaded, Stormy hit 18 foul balls in row, waiting for his pitch. Then he struck out. That one at bat served as a microcosm for Kromer's baseball career. It was in failure that Stormy Kromer was most remembered, but he kept dusting himself off and going back for more. Nothing could quench his passion for baseball, and it was that quality that endeared him to all who knew him.

At 19 he was catching future big leaguers on the sandlots of Wisconsin. At 75 he was still catching batting practice in the minors. Stormy summed up his feelings in four words. "Baseball keeps you young." ■

Retiring Clemente's "21"

True Recognition for Latinos in the Majors

by Peter C. Bjarkman

Most of what I learned about style I learned from Roberto Clemente.

—Filmmaker, John Sayles

A ballplayer's life is rarely if ever finely crafted finish-work carpentry; rather it is almost always rough framing, with all the gaps and gouges exposed to critics and admirers alike. Polishing and puttying and sanding the rough edges while overlooking and/or even hiding the ill-measured angles are the devoted tasks of revisionist historians; eager critics can inevitably expose and exploit the flaws in even the most exemplary heroes. Roberto Clemente, like most of our baseball idols, cobbled together a life on and off the diamond that was as noted for its raw ego and barely controlled rage as it was justly celebrated for its unrivalled artistry and valor in the face of endless setbacks—humiliations that were both real and perceived.

If nothing else, Coopertown's Clemente was an unsurpassed cultural icon in the environs of his Caribbean homeland. Exemplars of this fact are of course legion. Pirates outfielder José Guillén, for one, once proudly posed for his colorful 1998 Topps baseball card below a gigantic monument of Roberto Clemente that briefly graced the entrance to now-fallen Three Rivers Stadium. Guillen's bubblegum card was, to be sure, far more than a clever photo-op for the Dominican-born slugger. It represented a true measure of the way most Latino ballplayers have long felt about their leading idol and the

PETER C. BJARKMAN *is the author of many books including the recent* A History of Cuban Baseball, 1864-2006. *He can be found in cyberspace at* www.bjarkman.com *and* www.bjarkmanlatinobaseball.mlblogs.com. *Bjarkman lives in Indiana and travels extensively in Cuba and Croatia.*

first of their countrymen to reach the hallowed halls of baseball's Valhalla.

Many Latino stars have quietly honored Roberto with their choice of big league uniform number. Guillén, Rubén Sierra, Sammy Sosa, and Mexican hurler Estéban Loaiza are among the dozens of recent Hispanic ballplayers sporting "21" in tribute to Puerto Rico's and Latin America's greatest athletic hero. There is little question that Clemente remains the most significant role model for today's Latino major leaguers. But are these silent personal tributes sufficient? Should there not be a more formal enshrinement for the immortal Clemente—one with some official sanctions from major league baseball itself?

Upon the 50th anniversary of North American baseball's racial integration, now a full decade in the past, major league moguls appropriately decided to honor Jackie Robinson by permanently retiring the number "42" once proudly worn by the one-time Brooklyn Dodgers star. This precedent-setting honor was certainly not a result of Jackie's on-the-field résumé—which consisted of a mere 10 seasons, barely more than 1,500 hits, and a single National League batting crown. Jackie Robinson's tribute came because he was a pioneer—for many, the sport's most significant pioneer. Before Robinson, all African Americans and most Afro-Latinos played in their own league buried deep in the shadows of a North American white man's sport. That Robinson had actually been preceded in circumventing the "gentlemen's agreement" by a small handful of largely unnoticed Afro-Latinos (beginning with Cubans Marsans and Almeida in 1911 and peaking with Hi Bithorn and Tomás de la Cruz in the early 1940s) would remain little more than an intriguing footnote. For after Jackie had symbolically if not literally cracked open the door for athletes of color the game not only witnessed a steady influx of black stars, many of them Latinos, but the sport itself was also radically changed forever.

Clemente in the 50s played much the same role as had Robinson a decade earlier. It was Roberto who paved the way for Latin ballplayers in the big time, especially black Latinos. Cuba's Minnie Miñoso and Venezuela's Chico Carrasquel may have preceded Clemente by a handful of summers, but neither wore the stamp of the superstar or carried the image of crusading pioneer. Puerto Rico's greatest ballplayer not only opened a door to the big league clubhouse, but he was from the first an outspoken and irrepressible champion of his struggling countrymen. Whereas Robinson led silently—letting his bat and glove do all the talking— Roberto led by words as well as by deeds. And sometimes this practice regrettably tarnished his otherwise attractive ball-playing image.

A huge cultural gap dividing Latino ballplayers from many mainstream North American fans during the 50s and 60s often worked to Clemente's distinct disadvantage. Because he was intelligent, intense and always outrageously outspoken, the brash Pirates outfielder was also always a magnet for controversy. Many detractors in the press—as well as among Pittsburgh management and even some teammates—judged him to be aloof, combative, and sullen, often something of a hypochondriac and even a hot dog for his flamboyant playing style. It was the image of hypochondriac that was perhaps Roberto's most damning and also most unjustified battle scar. Teammate and fellow future Hall of Famer Willie Stargell once lamented that too few properly appreciated the fact that Roberto "played every game like his very life depended on it" and thus suffered more than his expected share of injuries as a result. Roberto himself once complained, "When Mickey Mantle says his leg is hurt no one questions. But if a Latin or a black is sick, they always say it is in his head!"

But cultural perceptions change with time, and a long-overdue call has now finally been raised in many quarters across the major league baseball world to retire Clemente's number as was earlier done for Robinson. Surprisingly the idea has not been universally accepted, and even some Latinos seem to object, as do a number of noted former

players of African-American heritage. Hall of Famer Frank Robinson, for one, has recently questioned where it will all end if Clemente is to be honored in a fashion similar to Robinson. "If Clemente, then who will be next?" Robinson recently commented in an ESPN interview. It would seem that Frank Robinson's comments are disingenuous at best, since they parrot the same twisted logic once voiced against racial integration in the first place. In light of Rafael Almeida, Marsans, Bithorn and a handful of other Afro-Latinos it is somewhat of a distortion of history to assume that Jackie Robinson—for all his brave pioneering—broken down baseball's barriers of prejudice entirely by himself. It is a further distortion of racial justice to now claim that Robinson is diminished as a cultural icon by now sharing the stage with other bold and abused pioneers like Doby, Miñoso, Marsans, Clemente, and even Frank Robinson (the first full-time black big league field manager) himself.

One popular New York-area Latino sports broadcaster has recently taken an even less defensible position by raising the claim that Clemente was not the first Latin American in the big leagues, or perhaps not even the most noteworthy Hispanic big leaguer of integrated baseball's first full decade. Roberto's own countrymen Vic

Power and Rubén Gómez preceded him to The Show, as did flamboyant Cuban hurler Dolf Luque and flashy Cuban black outfielder Miñoso. Venezuela's Carrasquel played in the 1951 All-Star Game, three seasons before Clemente arrived on the scene, and Mexico's Beto Ávila had already captured an American League batting title during Roberto's first year in Organized Baseball.

Such arguments seem weak and naive at best in light of Clemente's oversize role in the early days of the sport's full-scale integration. Other pioneers aside, none among the dozens of Latinos cracking the big league barrier before Clemente could be called a true diamond superstar. If he was admittedly not the first Latin big-leaguer, Roberto was easily the biggest Latino star of his generation and arguably the biggest-impact Latino ballplayer of the past century. Robinson, remember, was not technically the first black-skinned big leaguer either. Branch Rickey's hand-picked pioneer had been preceded in the first four decades of the 20th century by a handful of dark-skinned Latinos—Luque and Puerto Rico's Hi Bithorn most prominent among them—all conveniently dismissed at the time by denizens of the press as mere "foreigners" or "Cubans." Robinson was in reality only the first African American big leaguer, and then only the first African American of the 20th century. But this conveniently buried fact never diminished Robinson's remarkable role as racial pioneer. At the time such facts hardly blunted the painful road Robinson had to travel as the "perceived" first modern-era big league black-skinned athlete.

Any head-to-head comparison of Robinson and Clemente suggests that the Puerto Rican star's role as a racial pioneer was every bit as significant. Latinos (Pudge Rodríguez, Tony Pérez, Orlando Cepeda, Juan Marichal, Pedro Martínez, David Ortiz) following in Clemente's footsteps over the past four decades have impacted the game every bit as much as did Robinson-inspired blacks (Hank Aaron, Frank Robinson, Don Newcombe, Willie McCovey) in the 50s and 60s. Today's big-league game is dominated by Latin stars who indisputably owe their prominence in large part to Clemente. If not for the politics surrounding Cuba, or still existing MLB restrictions on allowed visas for international ballplayers, today's Latino domination of the big leagues would be admittedly far greater than it already is. And while many if not most of today's black stars seem to know little of Robinson's role back in the 40s, there are few Latin ballplayers indeed who do not openly acknowledge Clemente as their lasting inspiration.

Acknowledgment of Clemente's pioneering role comes from all quarters among Latinos. Venezuelan idol Luis Aparicio—Latin America's third Cooperstown inductee—remembers his own indebtedness by observing that Clemente "was truly a leader for all Latinos. He was always an advocate for our rights," Aparicio reminds any who will listen to his plaintive testimonials. Recently retired Giants manager Felipe Alou is also an outspoken champion of permanently enshrining Roberto's memory. Alou recently told an ESPN interviewer (during the 2006 All-Star Game weekend) that he's heard stories that many of today's black ballplayers don't even know who Jackie Robinson was. "I don't want Latinos to forget who Roberto Clemente was," Alou justifiably if perhaps unnecessarily cautions.

When it comes to measures of immortality, on-the-field, certainly, comparisons favor Clemente over Robinson by the widest of margins. Roberto was a legitimate Hall of Famer by any measure, whereas Robinson seemingly resides in Cooperstown only due to his considerable stature as racial pioneer. A 10-year .311 career batting average, barely 1500 base hits, less than 150 homers, a single league batting trophy, and a half-dozen All-Star Game appearance hardly seem the key to Cooperstown. Clemente's impact on the game goes far beyond his championing of the Latino cause; had the Puerto Rico star been as understated as Felipe Alou or as retiring and press-friendly as Roy Campanella his image would be just as indelible. An even 3,000 hits, 11 All-Star Games, four NL hitting crowns and an unparalleled reputation as a defender bury Robinson's on-field performances. Clemente may even have been the most exciting baseball player ever to take the field in any league and in any era. The sight of Roberto tearing head-long around the base paths, legging out another extra-base hit, was as thrilling an image as any moment from baseball's long and dramatic history. Billy Jurges, who played against Ruth and managed Ted Williams, once told this writer that Clemente was easily the best all-around

Roberto Clemente, with his wife Vera and two sons, at Roberto Clemente Night in Three Rivers Stadium.

ballplayer he ever laid eyes upon, and the opinion has had numerous seconds down through the decades.

While some fans and historians argue that Clemente was the best natural ballplayer ever, there is almost universal opinion that Pittsburgh's best-ever outfielder was tops among a new and exciting breed of Latin American athletes entering baseball in record numbers during the two decades immediately following World War II. Clemente performed in a manner approaching pure recklessness, yet also with incomparable grace and unmatched style. Only Robinson ran the bases in similar fashion, and perhaps only Willie Mays roamed the outfield with quite the same flair. Certainly Roberto's brilliant achievements lend considerable weight to any such argument for ranking among the game's greatest. Only 10 batters reached the magical level of 3,000 hits before Clemente got there in 1972, and only 14 more have scaled this lofty peak since "Number 21's" untimely death over 30 years ago. At the time his marvelous career tragically ended, he was already the all-time Pittsburgh Pirates leader in at-bats, hits, singles, and total bases. He was tied with Honus Wagner in games and second to

Wagner in RBIs. This in itself was a most remarkable achievement for a storied franchise that had already boasted such Hall of Fame sluggers down through the years as Wagner, Paul Waner, Arky Vaughan, Ralph Kiner and teammate Willie Stargell.

Clemente won four National League batting titles—including the first ever by a Latino—starred in two World Series, and dominated all pitchers in the 1971 fall classic with a scintillating .414 batting average. He played in 11 All-Star Games (he was selected for a 12th but replaced due to injury), and still holds a record for the most putouts by an outfielder, with six in 1967. He also earned a dozen Gold Gloves (tied with Willie Mays for the most ever by an outfielder) and still is the only player in big league history with more than a dozen fall classic appearances to hit safely in all 14 of his World Series contests. Clemente is also universally acknowledged as the greatest defensive right fielder in the game's long annals.

No other Latin American before or since has achieved such career numbers or demanded such lasting recognition, though Clemente himself always thought the fame he achieved was all too slow in coming, as it always seemed to be for those of his race and Hispanic background. A perceived insult in the 1960 NL MVP balloting—when he finished only eighth after leading the Pirates to their first World Series in more than three decades—spurred Roberto on to a string of batting crowns that reached four in the next five seasons. But even in the face of such eventual successes the Pirates superstar remained outspoken about the repeated slights leveled at him and his countrymen by an insensitive and unappreciative North American media.

Roberto never minced words about the perceived plight of his countrymen. "The Latin American player doesn't get the recognition he deserves," he once told a wire-service reporter. "We have self-satisfaction, yes, but after the season is over nobody cares about us." Clemente was himself the very prototype if not the poster boy of such repeated under-appreciation. When stardom finally came in the wake of his string of batting titles and a 1966 league MVP, *Time* magazine was quick to note that still nobody was offering Clemente the chance to do any television shaving cream commercials.

In the end it was these battles for recognition of his fellow Latinos that remain Clemente's greatest legacy. Roberto always maintained, "My own greatest satisfaction comes from helping to erase the old opinions about Latin Americans and blacks." There were also his achievements as one of baseball's most outstanding humanitarians. Roberto died tragically on New Year's Eve 1972 attempting to transport relief supplies in an overloaded plane to Nicaraguan earthquake victims. He left perhaps his greatest living legacy in the form of his Roberto Clemente Sports City serving disadvantaged youngsters of San Juan and the entire Puerto Rican island. Intimate friend and former Clemente Sports City public relations director Luis Mayoral speaks the final word when he reminds us, "He spoke for Latinos and he was the first among us who dared to speak out."

There are many blood-pressure-spiking controversies surrounding today's big league game that seemingly have no easy solutions or bring no unanimity of opinion. Is inter-league play, with its diminishing of traditional rivalries and its destruction of a balanced summer-long pennant race schedule, a boon or a bane for the long-term health of the besieged national sport? Should a stronger stance be taken by the game's moral guardians against players found cheating nature with performance-enhancing steroids? Should something be done to protect cherished records against onslaughts by players who have been physically aided by these illegal substances? We can not expect much accord soon on any such contentious issues.

But one debate seems to lead to quick resolution, and one potential action by big league officials seems to be a clear no-brainer. MLB officials today seek to extend a view that baseball is now truly an international game and that the sport's roots lie just as deeply in the Caribbean and in Latin America as in the byways of North America. MLB's inaugural World Classic was heavily promoted to underscore and celebrate the game's Latino and Asian roots. What better way might there have been to open the March 2006 World Baseball Classic—the sport's first genuine World Series—than with an overdue ceremony permanently retiring number 21 once worn by professional baseball's greatest Latino and international ambassador? And yet the opportunity went begging. Instead pro baseball's top moguls only diminished the game's Latino heritage by hyping an all-time Latino Legends All-Star team (voted on by media-driven fans saturated by hype surrounding current-era stars) which slighted legitimate Hall of Famers like Tony Pérez and Orlando Cepeda and celebrated contemporary favorites like Vladimir Guerrero and Manny Ramirez.

The current 2007 major league season marks six full decades since Robinson's 1947 debut in Brooklyn and the tumbling of racial barrier for baseball-savvy African Americans. It also marks 40 years since Clemente's greatest single season (1967) distinguished by a career-high .357 batting performance and an eighth straight All-Star selection. The time indeed has now come—some would say it has long since passed—for a proper tribute to Latino baseball's greatest lasting icon. ∎

The Wildest Kind of Crank

The Story of Players' League Magnate Al Johnson

by Ethan M. Lewis

At 3:38 on the afternoon of April 19, 1890, Albert Johnson was on top of the world. When Boston's Matt Kilroy threw the first pitch to Brooklyn left fielder Emmet Seery, a revolution in American sports began.[1] The 30-year-old Johnson, who had spent his working life making a fortune in street railway lines in Louisville, Cleveland, and Brooklyn, had been the leading financier of the Players' League (PL). The league, whose teams were stocked with stars from National League and American Association teams, was being run on a cooperative basis, in which players would be co-owners of their teams and would share in the profits of the league. Johnson must have been proud on this Opening Day, especially when he saw the receipts, which showed that the Players' League greatly outdrew the other two major leagues. Opening Day 1890 was the high point in Johnson's career as a baseball man. While many savvy baseball fans recognize the name of John Montgomery Ward (the player most responsible for organizing the league), few today know anything about Al Johnson. A century later, it is time to rescue him from obscurity, and remind baseball fans of his contributions to the game.

Al Johnson was born in Kentucky to a slave-owner father, Albert Johnson, Sr., who fought as a Confederate officer in the Civil War. Al Johnson (1860-1901) was the youngest of three brothers; his eldest brother, Thomas Loftin Johnson, was a prominent businessman, inventor,

ETHAN M. LEWIS *is a history teacher, college counselor and baseball coach at Wyoming Seminary College Preparatory School in Kingston, PA. He has been interested in the Players League for 20 years, since learning about it in a SABR publication about 19th century baseball. His Masters' thesis about the League, "A Structure to Last Forever: The Players' League and The Brotherhood War of 1890," is available online.*

and progressive politician. Tom Johnson's memoir provides interesting background information about the Johnson brothers' upbringing. Tom describes his father's politics, in the process revealing a great deal about the Johnson family's commitment to loyalty and fairness. According to Tom, their father, who had served in the Confederate Army throughout the war:

> …was a great admirer of Lincoln and very much opposed to slavery, and many, many times, even while sectional feeling was most bitter, he told me that the South was fighting for an unjust cause. My own hatred of slavery in all forms is doubtless due to that early teaching which was the more effective because of the dramatic incidents connected with it. Father's sympathies were with the North but loyalty to friends, neighbors and a host of relatives who were heart and soul with the South kept him on that side." [2]

Tom Johnson also described a memory from the first few months of the war, when his father was forced to carry out an order to burn all the cotton in the district.

> The burning of this cotton made a great impression on my mind, especially the sorrow of the negroes who stood around the smouldering bales and cried like children at sight of the waste of what had cost them such hard work to raise."[3]

This early childhood memory, perhaps, became a touchstone to a family whose members later took a great interest in working people.[4]

Postwar attempts to revive the family plantation using free labor resulted in failure, and the Johnsons moved to Louisville, KY, where Tom Johnson (six years older than Albert) took a job on the street railway in Louisville.[5] Streetcars played a major role in the growth of cities, as they greatly increased the distance people could travel in one day. In his early 20s, Tom Johnson invented the coin-operated fare box that is in use on public conveyances to this day.[6] Soon thereafter, with proceeds from the fare box, and a $30,000 loan from the duPont family (who owned the Louisville lines), the Johnsons moved to Indianapolis, where Albert Johnson Sr. became the president of the streetcar company and Tom became "the board of directors." Baby brother Albert took a job in the company to learn the ropes of the business.[7]

The Johnson family continued to pursue opportunities to increase their streetcar ownership holdings, and moved to the larger city of Cleveland. Soon thereafter, Albert Jr. struck out on his own, while maintaining partnerships in his family's enterprises. While Albert's endeavors (a road in East Liverpool, OH, and another connecting Allentown, PA, to surrounding villages) were not the grand successes he sought, he steadily made money. Johnson's biggest success was the Nassau Railroad Company of Brooklyn. Among the features of the line was a five-cent fare to Coney Island, which was the cheapest rail route to "Sodom by the Sea," as New York's favored getaway was called.[8] When all of Brooklyn's lines consolidated some years later, the Johnsons sold for an estimated $4 million, which established them among the truly wealthy of the Gilded Age.[9] The family built adjoining mansions on Shore Road in Brooklyn, overlooking the ocean, and used them as vacation homes for the rest of their lives.

At 6'1" and over 200 pounds, Albert Johnson was a sporting enthusiast and a follower of baseball.[10] Besides harboring a love of the sport, he could not have failed to notice that thousands of spectators traveled to ballparks on streetcar lines in the various cities of the National League and American Association. In Cleveland, a friendly competitor in the street railway business was Frank Robison, who owned the National League Spiders.[11] In his late 20s, flush with an astronomical fortune and looking for new challenges, Albert Johnson was in the right place at the right time to try to recreate the business model of professional sports.

In 1889, major league baseball consisted of two eight-team leagues with clubs in Boston, Chicago, Indianapolis, Kansas City, New York, Philadelphia, St. Louis, Washington, Baltimore, Brooklyn, Cincinnati, Columbus, Kansas City, and Louisville. The term "major league" sprang from the loftily titled "National Agreement" of 1883, in which the National League and the American Association declared their clubs to be major league teams. This agreement established a maximum salary of $2,000, and it also made the reserve rule a mandatory part of each player's contract.[12]

While the maximum salary rule was vexing to some players, many more were opposed to the reserve clause, especially the way that it allowed teams to "sell" players to other teams without giving the player a percentage of the sale. In 1885, New York Giants shortstop John Montgomery Ward and eight of his teammates formed the Brotherhood of Professional Base Ball Players. The Brotherhood's purpose, as stated in its charter (penned by Ward, who was an attorney in the off-season) was "to protect and benefit its members collectively and individually, to promote a high standard of professional conduct, and to advance the interests of the National Game."[13] By the beginning of the 1887 season, the Brotherhood had 107 National League and American Association players on its membership rolls, and had chapters organized in every major league city.[14]

That year Ward wrote an article in *Lippincott's Magazine* called "Is the Base-ball Player a Chattel?" In the piece the Brotherhood leader stated clearly the players' position that "every dollar received by the club in [a sale] is taken from the pocket of the player; for if the buying club could afford to pay that sum as a bonus, it could just as well have paid it to the player in the form of increased salary. The whole thing is a conspiracy, pure and simple, on the part of the clubs, by which they are making money rightfully belonging to the players."[15] When Detroit Wolverines infielder Deacon White was sold to Pittsburgh in 1889, he refused to play, saying, "No man can sell my carcass unless I get half." Wolverines owner Frederick Stearns displayed the typical baseball magnate's attitude when he responded, "He'll play in Pittsburgh or he'll get off the earth!"[16]

Around this time, Pittsburgh player-manager and Brotherhood member Ned Hanlon looked up Al Johnson when on the western swing to Cleveland.[17] According to Johnson:

> One evening…Ed Hanlon called on me and asked if I did not have a ball ground on my streetcar line. He spoke

of how the League had broken faith with them so often, and that he, Ward, [Fred] Pfeffer and [Jim]Fogarty…had thought of getting capital in each city to build the grounds for them, for which they would allow a fair percentage of the risk, the players to receive a portion of the profits, and to try, if such were possible, to liberate themselves from the tyrannical rule of the league….I agreed to lend all the assistance in my power to help them accomplish their aim. So as each visiting club came we held meeting after meeting, until every league player had heard our views and suggested whatever he thought would be best for the best interests of such an organization.[18]

Referring to that heady time later, John Montgomery Ward recalled:

A. L. Johnson was the organizing genius…of the new League. He spent time and money for the benefit of the cause he had espoused, traveled long distances to attend meetings, and give form and encouragement to the various groups out of which the Players' National League was formed. Mr. Johnson's services were of inestimable value to the new League.…Without this aid, the ball players could not have carried out the project started by the Brotherhood.[19]

Johnson was sold on the chance to give the players a better deal, and on the opportunity to make a buck (the new league would need new ballparks, and they would be built along Johnson-owned lines). As a long-time resident of Cleveland, Johnson intended to operate the Players' League franchise in that city. Helping the league succeed would give personal satisfaction and help the Johnson family gain more prominence in Cleveland, a town crucial to the family's future.[20] After all, Tom Johnson later served the city as mayor, running on a platform that included the guarantee of three-cent fares for city streetcars.[21]

Only a generation removed from emancipation, Al Johnson, the son of a former slaveholder, was receptive to the players' arguments that their inability to control where and for whom they worked was akin to involuntary bondage. As always, the Johnson family was united in pro-labor sentiments. Tom, the eldest and richest Johnson, was also committed to fairness. After a street urchin persuaded him to buy a copy of 1880's best seller *Progress and Poverty* by single-tax advocate Henry

George, Tom Johnson decided to enter politics. In 1890, the same year his brother spent running the Players' League, Tom Johnson was elected to Congress, where the "young millionaire street railway monopolist" spent his terms actively opposing any tariffs designed to protect the steel industry that made the rails upon which his fortune depended.[22] Tom Johnson had always encouraged unions among his workers, and was known to settle strikes quickly.[23] The middle Johnson brother, Will, told *The Sporting News* (which was strongly in favor of the Brotherhood):

No man living that I know of feels friendly to the way the League bosses have been running things. This selling and trading of players as though they were so much cattle is all wrong and the time has come when the players must take the bull by the horns and do something for themselves.[24]

Before the 1890 season began, Al Johnson told the *Chicago Tribune:*

I see that [the Brotherhood] are termed "anarchists". I can hardly see how the term fits them, for it is not a division of profits gained in the past that they ask for, nor is it the wild, visionary scheme of Socialism that this struggle is for. …While it may be a bitter pill for the magnates who claim to have the ownership of these men…[the players] believe that they ought to share in that which they earn.[25]

The 1890 season saw three major leagues, the Players' League, the National League, and the American Association, take the field. While total attendance was up, the existing leagues took the aggressive step of scheduling games in direct conflict with the Players' League. Day by day, gate receipts were examined like auguries of the strength of the respective leagues. The tone was set by the *New York Times* in reporting on baseball's Opening Day, when it began its article: "In this city the Players outdrew the League over two to one in attendance, and, in consequence, the backers of the Brotherhood are jubilant. In all other cities the result was the same."[26] *The Sporting News* crowed, "The Brotherhood teams have scored the first blood and the first knock-down."[27]

So much attention was paid to attendance figures in part because they were the barometer of success for the leagues and in part because they were so often lies.

With the exception of Ward's Brooklyn team, every club supplied its turnstile count to the press for publication, and quite naturally the clubs did their best to look good. Years after the Brotherhood War, Albert Spalding (the owner of the National League's Chicago White Stockings) wrote, "If either party to this controversy ever furnished to the press one solitary truthful statement...a monument should be erected to his memory." Spalding gave a humorous example of this:

> I recall being present one day at Chicago when the attendance was particularly light. At the close of the contest I was talking to [club] Secretary Brown, when a reporter came up, asking: "What's the attendance?" Without a moment's hesitation the official replied "Twenty-four eighteen." As the scribe passed out of hearing, I inquired, "Brown, how do you reconcile your conscience to such a statement?" "Why," he answered, "Don't you see? There were twenty-four on one side and eighteen on the other. If he reports twenty-four hundred and eighteen, that's a matter for his conscience, not mine.[28]

Besides the gate, off-field business developments were of great interest to the sporting public all season long. On May 15, 1890, the *Tribune* reported that St. Louis "street railway magnate Will Johnson" was in negotiation to buy a large share of the AA Browns in exchange for Johnson's streetcar line. The article speculated that with Sportsmen's Park's lease coming due soon, eccentric Browns owner Chris von der Ahe would sell and the team would move to the Brotherhood park, which was built along Johnson's line.[29] On July 4, Spalding and other NL owners gave $80,000 to beleaguered New York Giants owner John B. Day to float his floundering franchise.[30] During the first week of September, Al Johnson reportedly chaired a meeting between Players' League and American Association representatives to plan a merger between the two leagues.[31] In the closing days of the 1890 campaign, more financial casualties were reported:

> The owners of Philadelphia's PL franchise bought that city's bankrupt AA Athletics, and Albert Johnson purchased the NL Cincinnati Reds, announcing plans to move that club to the PL for the 1891 season.[32]

Financially, all three leagues failed to make a profit, with estimated losses in the National League ranging

Al Johnson, head of the Players' League, pictured in this 19th Century woodcut, one of the rare images of this early baseball pioneer.

anywhere between $300,000 and $500,000. The Players' League suffered an operational loss of approximately $125,000.[33] *The Sporting News* estimated the losses of both Cleveland franchises at over $50,000.[34] The American Association was even worse off; in addition to the bankruptcy of the Philadelphia ball club, the Brooklyn AA team also went under, and finished the last month of the season in Baltimore. Overall, the Brotherhood War adversely affected every outpost of big league baseball. However, as impetus for a settlement grew, the Players' League seemed to be the circuit least hurt during the season and, by virtue of its control over the game's star players, was in the best position to come out of the peace talks unscathed.[35] Unfortunately, as events transpired, the Players' League, having won the war, proceeded to lose the peace.

In October 1890, the Players' League was in a dominant position. In less than one year from its first public declaration the League had built eight stadiums, signed the leading players of the day, won court decisions invalidating the National League contract, produced an exciting season, and outdrew the venerable National League. Plans were already in high gear for the 1891 Players' League season, and as *The Sporting News* noted, "With all due respect, the Players' League is a pretty healthy yearling."[36] However, within a month the war was over, and the League was dissolved. The demise of the Players' League came rather suddenly, and for the first time Albert Johnson was left on the outside, instead of being the center of the movement.

Accounts of the negotiations between the leagues agree that the Players' League backers (wealthy men, though not on the scale of Johnson) were shocked at the losses they had incurred, and said as much to National League representatives Albert Spalding and Nick Young, who were coy about their own financial bloodbath. Whether the Players' League capitalists were naïve to expect profits in a year in which ballparks had to be built, advertising conducted, and entire teams recruited is hard to judge. Regardless, the plans for the Players' League to make sizable profits (some of which would be given to the players) did not come to fruition, and the backers were nervous. Many league moneymen sought a separate peace with the National League, without consulting with the Brotherhood (with whom they were partners). John Addison, a Chicago contractor and builder, sold his share of the Chicago Players' League unit to Albert Spalding, in exchange for stock in the team, which went on to become the Cubs. Wrigley Field currently sits adjacent to a street named for Addison. Edward Talcott (a New York financier) sold his share of the New York Players' League team, which immediately merged with the National League Giants.[37] Future Hall of Famer Tim O'Keefe, Brotherhood member and pitcher for the New York Players, expressed shock at these machinations:

It looks rather strange to me…I don't know what to think about it all…. The capitalists have all along professed to have our interests at heart, and yet it seems as though they were doing something underhanded…. I still feel that [Talcott] has the players' interests at heart, but I don't like this secret conference business.[38]

In the midst of these defections, Albert Johnson stuck with the Brotherhood and the players who had become his friends. He claimed to want no compromise; he was willing to merge into a unified organization called the "United League," but he wanted the players' interests respected.[39] When asked about this, Ward insisted that the reserve rule was abusive to players, a detriment to the game, and must be abolished.[40] When Ward, Hanlon, and Art Irwin (representing the Brotherhood) came to the Fifth Avenue Hotel in New York to attend negotiations between the leagues, they were turned away. John Ward rose to speak in defense of his fellow players, identifying themselves as stockholders as well as athletes, saying:

I believe I have more money at stake proportionately than any other gentleman on any committee. I have every

dollar I own invested in the Players' League and if I were not a player there could probably be no objection to my presence here. …Mr. Spalding, are you willing to put such a stamp of infamy upon the profession of which for years you were a member and to which you owe your start in life?[41]

After this rebuff the players, along with Al Johnson, walked out on the meeting.[42] A week later, *The Sporting News* reported:

There will be no compromise in Cleveland. That is a positively assured fact. As one of the [National] League officials said the other day, 'Johnson is in the streetcar business and we are in the base ball business.' Al seems determined to have the games played by Willson Avenue or not at all.[43]

Johnson himself, in an interview given after returning triumphantly from his brother's successful campaign for Congress, stated:

As far as the Cleveland situation, we are all right. I will take $25,000 and put it aside to lose next season in holding up my end at the Forest City. I will go broke in my club if necessary, and I think I can carry a club for several seasons before such a catastrophe happens.[44]

Despite his devotion to the cause, Johnson did not have the chance to risk more of his fortune as the League collapsed due to lack of funds, desertion of backers, and a seeming unwillingness on the part of the public to endure another season in which business was the lead in baseball stories. Even *The Sporting News* soured on the Players' League by the end, saying:

the players having shown their complete inability to manage their affairs we see no way out of the difficulty but a return to the old order of things…. It is a pity, but Ward, Ewing et al will have to be slaves once more."[45]

In a final obituary for the League, the paper declared:

Al Johnson's association with the national game has carried with it dignity and honor. His love of base ball has cost him thousands of dollars, and his manly action and nobility of purpose in sacrificing his money and his valuable time will always be to his credit.

He entered the Players' National League firm in the conviction that the cause he espoused was right and just. He made a gallant fight in furtherance of its interests and now that the cupidity of one or two of his associates has precipitated the developments of the past few weeks, he is the last to forsake the organization.

He stood the test like a man, never swerving to the right or left, but unflinchingly standing at his post. He had no scheme with which to "throw anybody down", but he fought against odds to save the organization even to the last….Al Johnson is the soul of honor. He is staunch, true and sincere in all his dealings and he deserves a world of credit for the magnificent fight he made in behalf of the Players' National League.[46]

With the demise of the League, Johnson's interest in baseball ownership seemed to collapse. As the owner of the Cincinnati NL/PL team, he led a movement to defect to the American Association, but that fell apart within weeks, and Johnson sold the Reds to John T. Brush, who, after the Association evaporated in 1892, helped create the National League cartel which dominated baseball until the creation of the American League in 1900.[47]

Al Johnson only survived for another decade after leaving baseball. He stayed engaged in his railroad interests, and spent a great deal of time on grand projects, such as a unified trolley system between New York and Philadelphia which would carry passengers between the two metropolises for forty cents, a tunnel between Brooklyn and New York, and an effort to bring three-cent trolley fares (his brother's pet issue) to New York City.[48] Showing typical loyalty, Johnson hired John Montgomery Ward as company lawyer when suits were filed against the Nassau Railway in Brooklyn, until the family sold its stake in the line.[49] At the young age of 41, Johnson died of a heart attack at his home in Brooklyn on July 2, 1901. The earliest obituaries of Johnson failed to mention his experiences with the national game, but a week later, the *Chicago Tribune,* in a pictorial tribute, wrote:

When the death of Albert L. Johnson of Cleveland, "the Brooklyn trolley magnate" was announced last week, a great many people did not know it was the man who was famous in the winter of 1889-90 as the principal financial backer of the Brotherhood of Baseball Players [sic]…Johnson lost thousands of dollars in the failure of the brotherhood scheme, and lived just long enough to see a second rebellion against National League rule, based on more conservative lines, succeed.[50]

The last line of the *Tribune*'s piece referred to the National League's agreement to finally modify the reserve rule so that it only gave clubs a one-year option to renew player contracts, not a lifetime ownership of a player's services.[51]

Though Al Johnson's services to baseball have been covered by the shifting sands of time, he brought a sense of crusading idealism to the sport at the height of the Gilded Age. Only two years before National League owners formed "The Big League," a cartel operated more for owners' profits than to benefit fans in League cities, Johnson helped spearhead a movement that would have treated players as skilled entrepreneurs instead of unskilled labor. Johnson's loyalty, dedication, and respect for the athletes ran counter to the trend of his time, although it was in keeping with his family's tradition of honoring the common laborer. This made Al Johnson an uncommon man for his time, and one worthy of being remembered for his contribution to the sport of baseball. ■

Notes

1. "'Twas a Beauty," *Boston Daily Globe*, April 20, 1890, 4.
2. Tom L. Johnson. *My Story*, ed., Elizabeth J. Hauser, 1911, 6. Accessed online clevelandmemory.org/ebooks/johnson/index.html.
3. Johnson, *My Story*, 3.
4. James R. Alexander. "Jaybird Geneaologies." http://faculty.upj.pitt.edu/jAlexander/Research archive/ Jaybird/JaybirdGenealogies.htm.
5. Johnson, *My Story*, 12.
6. Johnson, *My Story*, 14. Johnson soon came to hold many patents, including those covering the making of the rails themselves. Eventually he came to own a steel mill at Johnstown, PA, where rails were manufactured. The mill was damaged in the disastrous flood at Johnstown in 1889.
7. "Al. L. Johnson Dead from Heart Disease," *New York Times*, July 3, 1901. 1; John F. Kasson. *Amusing the Million: Coney Island at the Turn of the Century* (New York: Hill & Wang, 1978), 7.
8. "Al. L. Johnson Dead from Heart Disease." The modern equivalent would be over $70 million. The Johnsons experimented with using cables to pull their cars, but horses or mules pulled most of their lines.
9. "Al L. Johnson Dead From Heart Disease." "Al. Johnson Wins a Race," *Washington Post*, June 8, 1890; 14.
10. "Affairs in Cleveland," *The Sporting News*, November 15, 1890.
11. Ethan M. Lewis, "A Structure to Last Forever: The Players' League and the Brotherhood War of 1890." www.ethanlewis.org/pl/ch2.html.
12. John Montgomery Ward. *Baseball: How to Become a Player* (Cleveland: Society for American Baseball Research, 1993), 32; Tim Keefe, "The Brotherhood and Its Work," *Players' National League Guide* (Chicago: W.J. Jefferson, 1890), 7.
13. "A Structure to Last Forever."
14. John Montgomery Ward, "Is the Base Ball Player a Chattel?" *Lippincott's*, August 1887. xroads.virginia.edu/~HYPER/ INCORP/baseball/wardtext.html.
15. "A Structure to Last Forever."
16. "Albert Johnson Talks," *Chicago Tribune;* October 30, 1889, 6.
17. "Albert Johnson Talks."
18. John M. Ward, "The Players' National League," *1890 Players' National League Base Ball Guide* (Chicago: F.H. Brunell, 1890), 5.
19. "A Double Headed President," *The Sporting News*, October 19, 1890.
20. Johnson, *My Story*, xviii.
21. "Tom Johnson Dead—Made Millions in Business, But Fought on the Side of the People," *Boston Daily Globe*, April 11, 1911, 1.
22. Johnson, *My Story*, xxi.
23. "The Brotherhood," *The Sporting News*, September 21, 1889.
24. "Albert Johnson Talks."
25. "The Season of Baseball," *New York Times*, April 20, 1890, 3.
26. "Caught on the Fly," *The Sporting News*, April 26, 1890.
27. Albert Spalding. *Base Ball: America's National Game*, ed. Samm Coombs and Bob West (San Francisco: Halo, 1991), 179-81.
28. "Rumors of a Deal at St. Louis," *Chicago Daily Tribune*, May 16, 1890, 2.
29. "A Structure to Last Forever."
30. "The Latest News-Players and Association Men in Session," *The Sporting News* September 6, 1890.
31. "1890 to 1899." www.redshistory.com/Timeline/1890-1899.htm.
32. David Q. Voigt. *American Baseball: From Gentleman's Sport to the Commissioner System* (Norman: University of Oklahoma, 1966), 166; Harold Seymour. *Baseball: The Early Years* (New York: Oxford, 1960), 238.
33. "Caught on the Fly," *The Sporting News* October 25, 1890.
34. While attendance figures for 1890 are unreliable, those for 1889 are not, and it is indisputable that the National League did not reach its attendance figure of 1889, which was 1,355,468. Equally without question is that the American Association did not draw close to 1889's 1,576,254. Daniel Pearson. *Baseball in 1889: Owners vs. Players.* (Bowling Green, Ohio: Bowling Green State University Popular Press, 1993), 159.
35. "Caught on the Fly," *The Sporting News* October 25, 1890.
36. Lee Lowenfish. *The Imperfect Diamond–A History of Baseball's Labor Wars* (New York: Da Capo, 1991), 48.
37. "News," *New York Clipper*, November 11, 1890.
38. "News from New York," *The Sporting News*, October 18, 1890.
39. "Ward and Spalding," *New York Clipper*, December 20, 1890.
40. "The Tripartite Committee Meets," *New York Clipper*, November 1, 1890.
41. Lowenfish, *The Imperfect Diamond*, 48.
42. "Affairs in Cleveland," *The Sporting News*, November 15, 1890.
43. "Loyal Al Johnson," *The Sporting News*, November 15, 1890.
44. "The Reasons For It," *The Sporting News*, November 8, 1890.
45. "The Players' League," *The Sporting News*, November 29, 1890.
46. "Three Clubs Sell Out," *The Washington Post*, January 17, 1891, 1; "Base Ball Men Revolt," *Chicago Daily Tribune*, February 19, 1891, 6.
47. "Al L. Johnson's Life," *The Hartford Courant*, Jul 4, 1901; 9.
48. *David Stevens, Baseball's Radical for All Seasons: A Biography of John Montgomery Ward* (Lanham, MD: Scarecrow Press) 1998; 186.
49. "Death of the Brotherhood's Backer," *Chicago Daily Tribune;* July 7, 1901, 19.
50. Lowenfish, *The Imperfect Diamond*, 60-65.

Sunny Jim Bottomley's Big Day

St. Louis Cardinals at Brooklyn Robins, September 16, 1924

by David W. Smith

Over the years, baseball fans have often debated which record is the most "unbeatable." At one time it seemed unimaginable that Lou Gehrig's streak of 2,130 consecutive games played would ever be approached, let alone seriously challenged, but of course Cal Ripken topped that by some 500 games. Joe DiMaggio's 56-game hitting streak in 1941 is still intact at this writing, as is Hack Wilson's mark of 191 RBIs, officially revised a few years from the long-standing 190. Jack Chesbro's 41 wins in 1904, the most since the current pitching distance was set in 1893, and Cy Young's career 511 wins have not been threatened. There are many other choices to consider, of course, but most of them deal with career accomplishments, or at least the efforts of a whole season. There is time for anticipation and fan interest to build as the player strives toward the new mark.

Single-game records are very different, since there is no way to predict a record-setting performance on any given day. The topic for the present discussion is the extraordinary achievement of a player on a single afternoon, in a game which took one hour and 55 minutes in mid-September of a hot pennant race. The player is Jim Bottomley (always referred to as "Sunny"), and the record is 12 RBIs in a game. This mark was subsequently tied by Cardinal Mark Whiten in September of 1993.

In addition to his 12 RBIs, Jim was 6-for-6 that day, for the first of two times in his career (Jimmie Foxx and Doc Cramer are the only other players with two 6-for-6 games). Let's recount the at-bats of the left-handed slugging first baseman.

DAVID SMITH *received SABR's highest honor, the Bob Davids Award, in 2005. He is founder and president of* Retrosheet.

1. **1st Inning:** Single to center with bases loaded: **2 RBIs.**
2. **2nd Inning:** Double down left-field line with men on 1st and 2nd: **1 RBI**.
3. **4th Inning:** Homer over right-field fence with bases loaded: **4 RBIs.**
4. **6th Inning:** Homer over the right-field fence with man on third: **2 RBIs.**
5. **7th Inning:** Single to right with men on 2nd and 3rd: **2 RBIs.**
6. **9th Inning:** Single down right-field line with man on 3rd: **1 RBI.**

It is obvious that Bottomley had a substantial amount of help from his friends that day. His teammates also had to hit well, and there were a total of 12 men on base for his six at-bats. He drove in 10 of those 12, in addition to driving himself in twice with home runs.

However, there is more to this story than first meets the eye. Closer analysis shows that Sunny Jim had other kinds of help as well, some of which is a bit strange. For example, Taylor Douthit stole second base in the seventh inning when the score was 9-1. If this were to happen in a game today, we would certainly hear that the runner was "showing up" the opposition. Later in the same inning, with the score now 13-1, Jimmy Cooney stole second.

Even harder to explain than these stolen bases are the bunt plays by the Cardinals. With the score 4-0 in the second inning, men on first and second and no one out, Douthit, the second place batter, fouled out on an attempted bunt, hardly a likely sacrifice situation by today's standards. In the fourth inning, with the score now 5-1 Douthit successfully sacrificed with men on first and second and no outs. But the strangest events of all occur in the seventh inning. With the score now 13-1,

Jim Bottomley

Douthit bunted again, and was credited with a sacrifice when the pitcher was late with his throw to second. This was followed, astonishingly enough, by another successful sacrifice. This one was by Rogers Hornsby, and it set the stage for a two-RBI single for Bottomley, which would have only been a one-RBI single without the sacrifice. Remember that this is the season in which Hornsby batted .424 to set the modern National League mark. It was also the fourth year of a five-year span during which he *averaged* .402, topping the .400 mark three times. As he stood at the plate in the seventh inning that Tuesday afternoon in September, preparing to sacrifice in a 13-1 game, he was batting .425. Imagine the uproar which would result today if a manager ordered bunts in all of the above situations! Can we come to any conclusions about why things may have happened the way they did?

To begin with, let's consider that the manager of that Cardinal team was the famous Branch Rickey. He had a sub-.500 record for his 10 seasons at the helm of the Browns and Cardinals, stepping down from the manager's position the following summer, when Hornsby took over the job. Branch's questionable on-the-field strategy this day may help us understood why his main fame came in the front office.

Something else to remember is that the opposition that day was the Brooklyn Robins, who carried that name for several seasons in honor of their manager, Wilbert Robinson. The newspapers of the time often referred to "the flock" in their stories about the Brooklyn team. The significant point here is that when Bottomley got his 12 RBIs, the record he broke was in fact held by Wilbert Robinson. Uncle Robbie went 7-for-7 with 11 RBIs on June 10, 1892, for the Baltimore Orioles against the St. Louis National League team, then known as the Browns (they didn't get the name Cardinals until 1899).

Robinson was not a well-liked manager, even by his own players. This point is put forward strongly by Frank Graham in his book *The Brooklyn Dodgers,* published in 1945. On page 90, Graham tells a story of the game in 1923 when Brooklyn first baseman Jack Fournier went 6-for-6 against the Phillies (Graham has the date as June 19, but it was actually June 29). The story has Fournier coming to the plate for the seventh time with two outs and a runner on first in the ninth inning. Robinson, coaching first, told the runner on first to steal. The runner was thrown out to end the inning, denying Fournier the chance for a seventh hit which would have tied Robinson's record. Graham tells us that Fournier never forgave Robbie and that he (Fournier) suspected Robinson had maneuvered to deny Jack a chance at a record-tying seventh hit. Of course, this isn't a very nice episode, but the simple truth is that it never happened. On June 29, 1923, the Robins beat the Phillies 14-5 and Fournier was indeed 6-for-6, with his last hit being a single in the ninth inning. In fact, Brooklyn had only 51 men get to the plate that day, and for Graham's story to be true they would have needed at least 58 (6 times around the order plus 4 to get to Fournier, the cleanup hitter). Why would Graham blatantly misrepresent an incident which is refuted so easily (the details of the game are very clear in the *New York Times* of June 30, 1923)? Perhaps this is further indication of the low esteem in which Robinson was held, although it certainly does not reflect well on Graham.

Nonetheless, this story might help us understand why the Cardinals made the extra effort in the seventh inning as Bottomley was within reach of the record. Of course, this doesn't necessarily mean that Rickey ordered Hornsby to bunt. Rogers was a tremendously headstrong person who could very well have made the decision to bunt on his own. As far as I know, neither Rickey nor Hornsby was ever quoted on the matter. This "conspiracy" theory also assumes that the players on the field knew that Bottomley was approaching the record. Today they would certainly be informed by records mavens as the game was in progress, but it is not at all certain that in 1924 they would have this information. Another point to consider is that, if Robinson really were as villainous as Graham portrays, then he could have ordered Bottomley walked in the ninth (first and second bases were open).

NATIONAL BASEBALL LIBRARY, COOPERSTOWN, NY

In its story of the game, the *New York Times* did mention that Robinson was the previous RBI record holder and it noted that Bottomley only batted six times and therefore did not have the opportunity to tie Robinson's hit mark. But there is more to that aspect as well in that the *Times* left out something. After Sunny Jim's last at bat of the game, when he singled for his 12th RBI, Rickey inserted a pinch-runner for Bottomley, a runner who was immediately picked off first. Is it possible that Rickey had not ordered all the bunts and that he was trying to spare Robinson's feelings? Although Rickey has a well-deserved reputation as a sensitive man, I find it hard to believe that he would insert the pinch-runner just to protect a batting record set by the opposing manager 32 years earlier. It is also unlikely that the Cardinals were going to bat around that inning, which would be necessary for Bottomley to have a seventh chance. However, it's hard to understand why Rickey would use a pinch-runner in the ninth inning of a game that was 17-2 at the time. Bottomley was young, only in his second full year in the majors, so it's unlikely that he was being given the bottom of the ninth off, as is still done with older stars. Bottomley also had a good reputation as a fielder, but that doesn't seem to be a very important argument with a 15-run lead in the ninth inning. You probably can't play first base badly enough to give away 15 runs in one inning. One other possibly relevant point is that Rickey also used a pinch-runner for Hornsby in the ninth. Rogers led off the inning with a triple and Blades replaced him, scoring on Bottomley's single. It's possible to interpret this action in two ways also. Hornsby certainly was an established star, and although he wasn't old, it seems reasonable to give him an inning off in a game that was already decided. The other view is that the replacement runner was faster than Hornsby, and therefore more likely to score if Bottomley happened to hit a fly ball. This latter suggestion is highly speculative, and frankly I don't think it is very likely.

Finally, let's briefly consider the larger picture of the pennant race. In 1924 the Robins finished second to the Giants by one and a half games, the only season in the 1920s in which they finished in the first division (except for their pennant-winning season of 1920). As the game of September 16 began, the Giants had a lead of one

game over Brooklyn, which was one and a half games in front of Pittsburgh. With only 13 days left in the season, this game mattered very much to the Robins. On the other hand, the Cardinals were in sixth place, 24 games under .500, 27-and-a-half games behind the Giants. In other words, they were going nowhere. Baseball history is full of instances in which the underdog rises up and knocks the favored team down a peg. In fact, these examples are often cited as evidence of baseball's integrity and add meaning to the victory of the eventual pennant winner.

So, was this game just another one in a close pennant race where the apparently poorer team beat the better one? Were there some hidden motives which led Branch Rickey to make decisions which appear questionable? Did the Cardinal players, especially Hornsby, have reason to embarrass Wilbert Robinson? Or maybe it was simply one of those days when everything went right for a young first baseman, a future Hall of Famer who had the day of his life, setting a record that has not been surpassed in the 83 years since it was set. ■

Retrosheet Expanded Box Score
Game of Tuesday, September 16, 1924 – St.Louis at Brooklyn (D)

```
St. Louis   410   404   211-17
Brooklyn    010   000   011- 3
```

ST. LOUIS	AB	R	H	RBI	BB	SO	PO	A
Mueller, rf	3	3	2	1	3	0	2	0
Douthit, cf	3	3	1	0	1	1	2	0
Hornsby, 2b	4	2	2	0	1	1	2	2
Blades, pr-2b	0	1	0	0	0	0	0	0
Bottomley, 1b	6	3	6	12	0	0	5	0
Smith, pr-1b	0	0	0	0	0	0	2	0
Hafey, lf	6	1	2	2	0	0	5	1
Gonzalez, c	4	1	1	1	0	0	2	0
Clemons, c	2	0	0	0	0	0	1	0
Toporcer, 3b	1	0	0	0	0	1	0	0
Cooney, 3b	4	0	1	1	0	0	0	0
Thevenow, ss	5	0	0	0	0	0	5	4
Sherdel, p	4	3	3	0	1	0	1	0
Rhem, p	0	0	0	0	0	0	0	0
TOTALS	42	17	18	17	6	3	27	7

BROOKLYN	AB	R	H	RBI	BB	SO	PO	A
High, 2b	4	0	2	0	0	0	4	0
Mitchell, ss	4	0	1	0	0	0	1	4
Wheat, lf	4	0	0	0	0	0	1	0
Fournier, 1b	2	1	0	0	1	0	5	1
Loftus, 1b	1	0	1	0	0	0	3	0
Brown, cf	4	0	1	0	0	1	5	0
Stock, 3b	3	1	1	0	1	0	1	1
Griffith, rf	2	0	0	0	2	0	2	0
DeBerry, c	3	0	1	1	1	0	4	0
Ehrhardt, p	0	0	0	0	0	0	0	0
Hollingsworth, p	1	0	0	0	0	0	0	0
Decatur, p	0	0	0	0	0	0	1	1
J.Johnston, ph	1	0	1	0	0	0	0	0
Wilson, p	0	0	0	0	0	0	0	1
Taylor, ph	1	1	1	0	0	0	0	0
Roberts, p	0	0	0	0	0	0	0	1
Hargreaves, ph	1	0	0	0	0	0	0	0
TOTALS	31	3	9	1	5	1	27	9

BATTING
2B: Bottomley (off Hollingsworth); Sherdel (off Hollingsworth)
3B: Hafey (off Ehrhardt); Gonzalez (off Decatur); Mueller (off Wilson); Hornsby (off Roberts)
HR: Bottomley 2 (4th inning off Decatur, 3 on, 1 out; 6th inning off Decatur, 1 on, 1 out)
2-out RBI: Mueller; Bottomley
RBI, scoring position, less than 2 outs: Douthit 0-1; Hornsby 0-2; Bottomley 8-8; Hafey 2-1; Gonzalez 0-1; Toporcer 0-1; Cooney 1-1; Thevenow 0-1
SH: Douthit 2; Hornsby

BASERUNNING
SB: Douthit (2nd base off Decatur/DeBerry); Cooney (2nd base off Decatur/DeBerry)
Team LOB: 7

FIELDING
PB: Clemons
Outfield assist: Hafey (Mitchell at 2B)
DP: (3). Thevenow-Hornsby; Thevenow-Hornsby-Bottomley; Smith, unassisted

BATTING
2-out RBI: DeBerry
RBI, scoring position, less than 2 outs: Mitchell 0-1; Wheat 0-1; Stock 0-1; Griffith 0-1; DeBerry 0-1
GDP: Mitchell

BASERUNNING
Team LOB: 6

FIELDING
E: Fournier (dropped foul ball)

PITCHING	IP	H	R	ER	BB	SO
ST. LOUIS						
Sherdel W (7-9)	8	8	2	2	2	1
Rhem	1	1	1	0	3	0
BROOKLYN						
Ehrhardt L (5-2) *	0	4	4	4	1	0
Hollingsworth +	3	2	3	3	3	2
Decatur	3	6	6	5	2	0
Wilson	2	4	3	3	0	1
Roberts	1	2	1	1	0	0

* Pitched to 5 batters in 1st
+ Pitched to 2 batters in 4th

Inherited Runners - Scored: Rhem 0-0; Hollingsworth 1-0; Decatur 2-2; Wilson 0-0; Roberts 0-0.

IBB: Hornsby by Decatur.
WP: Decatur; Rhem

GAME DATA T: 1:55; A: 3000.
UMPIRES HP: Bill Klem 1B: Frank Wilson

Retrosheet Play-by-Play Account

CARDINALS 1ST: Mueller walked; Douthit singled to shortstop [Mueller to second]; On a bunt Hornsby singled to second base [Mueller to third, Douthit to second]; Bottomley singled to center field [Mueller scored, Douthit scored, Hornsby to third]; Hafey tripled to center field [Hornsby scored, Bottomley scored]; **Hollingsworth replaced Ehrhardt (pitching);** Gonzalez grounded out (Mitchell to Fournier); Toporcer struck out; Thevenow popped to High; 4 R, 4 H, 0 E, 1 LOB. **Cardinals 4, Robins 0.**

ROBINS 1ST: High grounded out (Bottomley unassisted); **Cooney Replaced Toporcer (playing 3B);** Mitchell grounded out (Thevenow to Bottomley); Wheat lined to Thevenow; 0 R, 0 H, 0 E, 0 LOB.   **Cardinals 4, Robins 0.**

CARDINALS 2ND: Sherdel walked; Mueller walked [Sherdel to second]; On a bunt Douthit popped to DeBerry in foul territory; Hornsby struck out; Bottomley doubled to left field [Sherdel scored, Mueller to third]; Hafey grounded out (Mitchell to Fournier); 1 R, 1 H, 0 E, 2 LOB. **Cardinals 5, Robins 0.**

ROBINS 2ND: Fournier walked; Brown singled to center field [Fournier to second]; Stock flied to Hafey; Griffith popped to Gonzalez in foul territory; DeBerry singled to shortstop (Thevenow to Gonzalez) [Fournier scored, Brown out at home]; 1 R, 2 H, 0 E, 1 LOB. **Cardinals 5, Robins 1.**

CARDINALS 3RD: Gonzalez grounded out (Mitchell to Fournier); Cooney grounded out (Stock to Fournier); Thevenow popped to High; 0 R, 0 H, 0 E, 0 LOB. **Cardinals 5, Robins 1.**

ROBINS 3RD: Hollingsworth popped to Thevenow; High flied to Douthit; Mitchell singled to left field (Hafey to Thevenow) [Mitchell out at second]; 0 R, 1 H, 0 E, 0 LOB. **Cardinals 5, Robins 1.**

CARDINALS 4TH: Sherdel doubled to right field; Mueller walked; **Decatur replaced Hollingsworth (pitching);** Douthit out on a sacrifice bunt (Decatur to High) [Sherdel to third, Mueller to second]; Hornsby was walked intentionally; Bottomley homered to rightfield [Sherdel scored, Mueller scored, Hornsby scored]; Hafey flied to Brown; Gonzalez grounded out (Mitchell to Fournier); 4 R, 2 H, 0 E, 0 LOB. **Cardinals 9, Robins 1.**

ROBINS 4TH: Wheat flied to Hafey; Fournier grounded out (Bottomley unassisted); Brown flied to Hafey; 0 R, 0 H, 0 E, 0 LOB. **Cardinals 9, Robins 1.**

CARDINALS 5TH: Cooney lined to Brown; Thevenow grounded out (Fournier to Decatur); Sherdel singled to center field; Mueller flied to Griffith; 0 R, 1 H, 0 E, 1 LOB. **Cardinals 9, Robins 1.**

ROBINS 5TH: Stock flied to Hafey; Griffith flied to Douthit; DeBerry flied to Hafey; 0 R, 0 H, 0 E, 0 LOB. **Cardinals 9, Robins 1.**

CARDINALS 6TH: Douthit walked; Douthit stole second; Hornsby flied to Brown [Douthit to third]; Bottomley homered to rightfield [Douthit scored]; Fournier dropped a foul fly hit by Hafey; Hafey singled to left field; Gonzalez tripled to left field [Hafey scored (unearned)]; Cooney singled to right field [Gonzalez scored]; Cooney stole second [Cooney to third (on wild pitch by Decatur)]; Thevenow popped to Mitchell; Sherdel flied to Brown; 4 R (3 ER), 4 H, 1 E, 1 LOB. Cardinals 13, Robins 1.

ROBINS 6TH: Clemons Replaced Gonzalez (playing C); J. Johnston batted for Decatur; J.Johnston singled to center field; High singled to center field [J.Johnston to second]; Mitchell popped to Sherdel; Wheat popped to Thevenow; Fournier grounded out (Hornsby to Bottomley); 0 R, 2 H, 0 E, 2 LOB. **Cardinals 13, Robins 1.**

CARDINALS 7TH: Wilson replaced J. Johnston (pitching); Loftus replaced Fournier (playing 1B); Mueller singled to catcher; Douthit reached on a fielder's choice on a sacrifice bunt [Mueller to second]; Hornsby out on a sacrifice bunt (Wilson to Loftus) [Mueller to third, Douthit to second]; Bottomley singled to right field [Mueller scored, Douthit scored]; Hafey popped to High; Clemons flied to Wheat; 2 R, 2 H, 0 E, 1 LOB. **Cardinals 15, Robins 1.**

ROBINS 7TH: Brown struck out; Stock singled to right field; Griffith walked [Stock to second]; DeBerry lined into a double play (Thevenow to Hornsby) [Stock out at second]; 0 R, 1 H, 0 E, 1 LOB. **Cardinals 15, Robins 1.**

CARDINALS 8TH: Cooney popped to Stock; Thevenow flied to Griffith; Sherdel singled to left field; Mueller tripled to right-center [Sherdel scored]; Douthit struck out; 1 R, 2 H, 0 E, 1 LOB. **Cardinals 16, Robins 1.**

ROBINS 8TH: Taylor Batted for Wilson; Taylor singled to center field; High singled to left field [Taylor to third]; Mitchell grounded into a double play (Thevenow to Hornsby to Bottomley) [Taylor scored (no RBI), High out at second]; Wheat flied to Mueller; 1 R, 2 H, 0 E, 0 LOB. **Cardinals 16, Robins 2.**

CARDINALS 9TH: Roberts replaced Taylor (pitching); Hornsby tripled to left field; **Blades ran for Hornsby;** Bottomley singled to right field [Blades scored]; **Smith ran for Bottomley;** Smith was picked off first (Roberts to Loftus); Hafey flied to Brown; Clemons grounded out (Loftus unassisted); 1 R, 2 H, 0 E, 0 LOB. **Cardinals 17, Robins 2.**

ROBINS 9TH: Blades stayed in game (playing 2B); Smith stayed in game (playing 1B); Rhem replaced Sherdel (pitching); Loftus singled to left field; Brown lined into a double play (Smith unassisted) [Loftus out at first]; Stock walked; Clemons allowed a passed ball [Stock to second]; Rhem threw a wild pitch [Stock scored (unearned)]; Griffith walked; DeBerry walked [Griffith to second]; **Hargreaves batted for Roberts;** Hargreaves flied to Mueller; 1 R (0 ER), 1 H, 0 E, 2 LOB. **Cardinals 17, Robins 3.**

FINAL TOTALS	R	H	E	LOB
Cardinals	17	18	0	7
Robins	3	9	1	6

Eddie Brannick

by R. J. Lesch

John Drebinger once wrote of Eddie Brannick, "He has legions of friends, remembers the birthdays of many of then, yet once couldn't recall the date of his own. A gourmet of rare taste, he knows how and where to dine and will order a meal of excellence only to touch scarcely any of it because he is forever hopping up and down, answering phone calls and attending to the difficulties of others. Attired in the height of fashion with a blazing foulard that will knock your eye out at 40 paces, he thinks nothing of also wearing a beard two days old, because his whiskers are very tough, he cannot shave himself and he does not find time to sit long enough in a barber's chair to have them removed. And, though he has seen thousands of ball games, he has never sat through a complete game in his life."

During his 65-year tenure with the Giants, Eddie Brannick went from office boy to club secretary, from Manhattan to San Francisco, from schoolboy shorties to sartorial splendor, from a face in the crowd to coast-to-coast fame.

He was born Edward Thomas Brannick, at 441 West 31st Street, New York City, on July 22, 1892. This was on the edge of the tough Irish neighborhood known as Hell's Kitchen, where, as Brannick put it later, "it was a tossup to see if you became a bad boy or an altar boy." He had the same name as his father, who was of Scottish descent. His mother Elizabeth's family was Irish. Her brother, Tommy Mallon, was a semi-pro ballplayer, and it was Tommy who introduced Brannick to the game.

Brannick attended St. Michael's Parochial School, and would make his way to the Polo Grounds to see the Giants whenever he could scare up a quarter for a bleacher seat. Before long, though, he had the opportunity to see his beloved Giants at close quarters—closer than he ever could have dreamed, and for longer than he could possibly have imagined.

During the heat of the 1904 pennant race, while the Giants were on the road, Giants owner John T. Brush installed a scoreboard in old downtown Madison Square Garden at Madison Avenue and 26th Street, so Giants fans could follow the action. Eddie's cousin Jimmy Mallon was one of the youngsters hired to run the scoreboard. As news of the games came through the wire, boys would post numbers or move figures around the board to show the score, the outs, and who was on which base. Brush put the board up again during the Giants' first Western road trip of 1905, which ran from June 1 through June 22, and Jimmy brought Eddie along to assist.

Brush suffered from locomotor ataxia, a degenerative condition of the nervous system. An invalid, he often hired errand boys. He took a liking to Eddie and, after the western road trip was over, hired Brannick as an office boy on June 27, 1905. Eddie continued to run errands for Brush that summer, and also kept Brush's collection of newspaper clippings about the Giants in a scrapbook. The work paid three dollars a week, excellent pay for a 12-year-old in those days.

In April 1906, when the Giants returned to town for the new baseball season, Giants manager John J. McGraw asked Brush for a boy to work in the clubhouse at the Polo Grounds. Brush sent Brannick, who quit school for good at that point. The gruff McGraw took a liking to the genial lad, and a friendship began which would last until McGraw's death in 1934.

Not that the arrangement was always carefree. Brush, who rarely tampered with McGraw's running of the ball

R. J. LESCH (rjlesch_usa@yahoo.com) lives in Adel, IA, with his lovely wife, Christee. When not doing systems analysis, cheering on the White Sox or researching the Deadball Era, R. J. coaches sabre (naturally) at the Des Moines Fencing Club.

club, drew the line at the Giants' intemperate use of baseballs. In 1908 he made Brannick the custodian of the ball bag. This required Brannick to sit on the bench and to dole out the baseballs as needed. "I want to tell you I kept a sharp eye on them."

One morning Brush sent Brannick to the bank, and Brannick returned late. "If you are the custodian of the baseballs, be here on time or quit!" McGraw thundered.

"I had to go to the bank for Mr. Brush," Eddie stammered.

"I don't care where he sent you," said McGraw. "When I say I want you here at one o'clock, that means one o'clock and not 15 minutes later. And if Brush or anyone else tells you to do something else, tell him you can't do it because you have to be here. Do you understand?"

Years later, Brannick said, "That's when I first knew who was really running the Giants."

It is unclear when Brannick first started to travel with the Giants. Some sources have him making road trips with the Giants during the 1910 season, after club secretary Fred Knowles fell ill with tuberculosis. William M. Gray, a noted theatrical manager and advance agent who knew McGraw and Brush from the prestigious Lambs' Club, was hired as interim secretary, then became secretary when Knowles was unable to return to his duties. Knowles would eventually succumb in 1911. Brannick was a natural choice for the position of assistant secretary. Whether he went on the road with the Giants in 1910, it is certain that he went to Marlin, TX, with the Giants for spring training in 1911. Brannick was 18 years old.

Of the many stories told about Brannick later in life, none perhaps galled him more than the famous "match fields" story. Brannick, so the tale goes, had never been west of New Jersey in his life. As the train sped through the farmlands of Illinois, Eddie was puzzled by winter stubble on the fields.

He asked Sid Mercer, writer for the *New York Globe,* "What's growing in those fields?"

"They're growing matches," replied Mercer.

When Brannick showed skepticism, Damon Runyon chimed in: "Where else do you think matches come from?"

Mercer nodded. "The heads should be coming up soon," he added.

Eddie Brannick

Brannick would never live it down. He would later swear that the story was bunk, but no biography of Brannick, it seems, is without the story of the gullible youngster marveling over the great match fields of Illinois, while reporters stifled chuckles behind him.

Brannick assisted Gray in Marlin, and then got his first chance to fly solo as a road secretary. When the Giants broke camp in Marlin and started back to New York in March, McGraw split up his players into three squads. Each took a different route from Marlin to Richmond, VA, and played exhibition games along the way. Brannick accompanied the third squad, entirely made up of prospects and managed by Otis "Doc" Crandall, himself only 24 and enjoying his first managerial experience. Crandall and Brannick successfully shepherded their charges through two weeks of barnstorming before rejoining the Giants in Richmond.

Brannick served as assistant secretary under Gray through 1911, shouldering road duties and other responsibilities. He stayed on under Joseph O'Brien in 1912, under John Foster from 1913 through 1919, and under James J. Tierney through 1936. Tierney made Brannick the official road secretary in 1922, and for the next 40 years Brannick led the Giants on every road trip.

It seems natural that the young Brannick would have the desire to play ball himself. This is the theme of another famous Brannick story, in which Brannick rushes to the mound to pitch for the Giants in a spring exhibition game. Various dates are given for this feat, all in the mid-1910s, but they seem to agree that the game took place in Columbus, GA. A Fred Lieb account indicates that Brannick's catcher was Bradley Kocher, who was with the Giants in 1915 and 1916, and the injured pitcher was Al Williams, a Fordham hurler who went to spring training with the Giants in 1914 and later earned fame as a Navy aviator. Williams's injury left the Giants' second team without a pitcher that day. Brannick, so the story goes, put a friend in place to watch the turnstiles for him while he jumped into a uniform, warmed up, then pitched seven innings of one-run ball. "Brannick held a 2-1 lead until the eighth inning, when in fielding a ball he turned his ankle. Rube Schauer, whose trade was pitching, then went in and the Giants lost, 3 to 2."

A game between a Giants squad and the Columbus ball club resembling this description (with Kocher catching and Schauer blowing the lead in the ninth) occurred in spring 1916. The newspaper account of the game lists another pitcher and does not mention Brannick, who in any case did not go to spring training with the Giants in 1916. (The Giants went on to win in extra innings, further spoiling the story.) If Brannick actually pitched for the Giants, the box score has yet to be found.

It is true, however, that on June 9, 1912, Brannick pinch-hit in an exhibition game in Long Branch, NJ, which the Giants won, 11-10. The *New York Times* account notes that in his ball playing debut the assistant secretary "ripped a stinging single to right field" in the top of the ninth, then scored. However, his "wabbly" fielding in the bottom half of the frame opened the door to a four-run Long Branch rally, which almost lost the game for the Giants. The *Times* reporter did not note who handled the turnstile duties for the Giants that day.

McGraw, though willing to humor the young man with an occasional exhibition game stint, discouraged Brannick from going further. "You give up the idea of being a big-league ballplayer and stick with the front office," McGraw told Eddie, "and someday you MIGHT amount to something." Brannick agreed. "That was certainly good advice for me."

Brannick was on hand for many of the highlights in Giant history. He was guarding the ball bag on the Giants bench on September 23, 1908, during the infamous "Merkle Game." He was checking the turnstiles at Fenway Park during the last inning of game eight of the 1912 World Series, when Fred Snodgrass dropped Clyde Engle's fly ball. "I knew it before it happened," Brannick said.

"John Heydler was with me and a fan came up and shook my hand in congratulation for the victory of the Giants. I said to John Heydler, 'That jinxes it! We'll lose now.' … By the time I had the turnstile checked Boston had won the series.

"But don't forget," the Giants' goodwill ambassador would say, "we had our good days, too." He considered the 1921 Giants the best team he had ever seen. "They were a collection of star players everybody knew and respected," he said. "They had the psychological edge the great champion has, like a Dempsey or a Louis, of imparting fear to an opponent before a ball was pitched."

Whenever a reporter asked Brannick to name favorite Giants, one name always topped the list: Christy Mathewson. The tall, handsome, gentlemanly Mathewson was everyone's hero, of course. It was with some reluctance, though, that Brannick once had the unpleasant duty of consigning the great Matty to an "upper" on a road trip.

The sleeper cars on trains had upper and lower berths. The upper berths were less desirable because people in them felt the train car's swaying motions more keenly. The curtains sometimes did not block the corridor lights effectively, either. For that reason, sometime early in his tenure, Brannick was nervous when on one trip there weren't enough lower berths in the Pullman sleeper car and six players had to take upper berths.

McGraw told the young Brannick to let the players draw berths out of a hat. Brannick laid aside a lower for Matty, but McGraw said "Nothing doing. Let him draw with the rest. There are no stars on this ball club."

Sure enough, Mathewson drew an upper.

This still took McGraw aback, but as he told Brannick, "That's the way to work for me—always treat all the Giants alike."

To Brannick's relief, Mathewson waved it off. "When I'm on my own," he told the young assistant, "I always buy an upper. It's cheaper."

Brannick usually put Carl Hubbell in the same class as a pitcher, and also listed Mel Ott and Willie Mays as among the top Giants. Few men, of course, had the same opportunity to compare these great ballplayers that Brannick had.

Brannick's personal life began to stabilize after Charles Stoneham took over ownership of the Giants in 1919. Brannick kept his job despite a front-office purge, even becoming good friends with Stoneham's son Horace. In 1920, Brannick "took the pledge." This was around the time when McGraw's drinking began to take its toll; the ugly drunken brawl between McGraw and actor John Slavin was in August of that year. Perhaps his friend's behavior was a factor in Brannick's decision to quit drinking. Brannick became a prodigious coffee drinker instead. In June 1922 he married Kathleen Duggan. Their marriage lasted 53 years.

On February 15, 1936, a month after the death of the elder Stoneham, James J. Tierney resigned as club secretary. New president Horace had to look no further than his good friend Brannick, who by then had already celebrated his 30th anniversary with the Giants. Brannick remained club secretary for the next 35 years.

It was said of the Giants' road secretary that he "never lost a ballplayer or a piece of luggage." He was just as valuable to the reporters and VIPs who traveled with the Giants. Though sticking to his pledge, he always knew where to find alcohol during Prohibition, no matter which city the Giants visited. "Since the passing of McGraw," said one reporter, "the man who can beat Eddie to grabbing the check has yet to be born."

But Brannick's value to the Giants went beyond his logistics skills. "Eddie was a priceless goodwill man for the whole game," wrote Red Smith. "He was naturally gregarious with a genuine liking for people. He didn't drink, but he could stay up all night buying. Wherever he went he made friends for baseball and the Giants. He was at home in the New York of Delmonico's and Rector's and in the New York of Jim Moore's, 21 and Toots Shor's. He was also at home in Chicago and St. Louis and Miami. To a lot of people in those towns, he epitomized New York."

His facility with the press was particularly valuable to a ballclub whose managers—McGraw, Bill Terry, Leo Durocher—had a knack for making enemies. It fell to Brannick to deliver bad news, smooth ruffled feathers, and mend fences. His easy grin, friendly manner, and generous nature made friends for himself and his Giants. Not only did Brannick get along with writers, but also he was voted honorary membership in the Base Ball Writers Association of America and the Press Photographers Association. His gold-mounted honorary BBWAA membership card was one of his most prized possessions.

Outside baseball, Brannick numbered actors, politicians, and business tycoons among his friends. Brannick was even approached to run for New York's Fifth Congressional district, some time during the Roosevelt years, but Brannick declined. "My wife Kathleen was against my going into politics," he said. "Besides, all I ever wanted was to be with the Giants."

His style of dress evolved into something newsworthy as well. Just as rare as a photo of Brannick not smiling is a description of him that does not contain the word "dapper." "He was a dude, from his floppy Panama hat to the two-toned black and white shoes," wrote Jimmy Cannon. "The sports coats are a boisterous plaid, and his neckties are designed to frighten horses." When Brannick went to Italy on vacation following the 1938 season, he returned with several new suits, a rich vocabulary of Italian words, a rosary blessed by the Pope (who had granted an audience), and a mustache. The facial hair gave his reporter friends material for several months. The amusement ended on May 13, 1939, with the Giants in next to last place with a 9-12 record. To kill the jinx, Brannick shaved off his mustache. The Giants won the next day, though not even a clean-shaven secretary could help them finish the season higher than fifth place.

Although Brannick got along with everyone, he inherited McGraw's and Brush's antipathy for the American League and the Brooklyn Dodgers. A fierce National League partisan, he once refused to speak to his good friend Tom Meany for several years after Meany wrote an article titled "The National, the new Minor League" in the late 1930s. Brannick said, "Tommy couldn't have offended me more had he written disparagingly of my brother." As for the Dodgers, he once said, "There is something about Dodgers that I can't stand." Friends would tease him by asking whether it was true that the Dodgers had made him an offer to be their club secretary, just to enjoy Brannick's explosive reaction. Yet upon the occasion of his 50th anniversary with the Giants in 1955, even Walter O'Malley attended the gala in Brannick's honor at the Waldorf-Astoria.

Brannick naturally had a box in the Polo Grounds grandstand, but loaned it to friends. Superstitious, he watched from the bleachers instead, always leaving around the seventh inning to make the rounds and check the gates. When Brannick finally watched a game from beginning to end from his Polo Grounds box, it was

September 29, 1957. The Pirates sank the Giants 9-1, in their last home game in New York. Afterward, Brannick watched sadly as fans tore signs off walls, telephones from booths, and chunks of the pitching rubber and home plate from the field.

Horace Stoneham's decision to move the Giants to San Francisco forced Brannick, the true New Yorker, to make a difficult decision: his city or his ball club? "Eddie would look lost away from Broadway," wrote one reporter. "He's as much a part of the main stem as a Damon Runyon character." In the end, though, when the Giants moved West, Brannick moved with them. One of his first questions, to a San Francisco reporter, was "Will we be able to stir up something against the Dodgers?" When assured that a San Francisco–Los Angeles rivalry was virtually a sure thing, Eddie grinned. "Count me in on the fun." He and his wife embraced San Francisco, though naturally they kept an apartment in New York.

Eventually, even the dynamic Brannick needed to slow down. He developed pneumonia in February 1963 and missed spring training for the first time since 1916. Two years later, he turned over the road secretary duties. At last, on February 23, 1971, he sent a telegraph to Horace Stoneham, announcing his resignation as club secretary. Stoneham informed the press, his voice heavy with emotion. The last link with the Giants of McGraw and Mathewson was gone after 65 years of service. Brannick and his wife retired to West Palm Beach, FL, living quietly until his death on July 18, 1975, at the age of 82. ∎

Acknowledgments

The material in this article comes largely from the Eddie Brannick file in the National Baseball Library, from *Retrosheet* and from the online archives of the *New York Times*. Special thanks goes to Gabriel Schechter for his assistance and encouragement.

Johnny Vander Meer on Pete Rose
(as told to Norman Macht)

I managed the Reds' Tampa farm club in the Class D Florida State League in 1961 and had my first look at Pete Rose in spring training. He was not yet 20, had batted .277 the year before for Geneva in the Class D New York-Penn League. So he came to camp looking for a job. We made up scrubini teams. In his first game he ran down to first base on a base on balls. He popped up a couple times, hit a double, and ran just as hard every time.

There's an old saying in baseball: You show me a guy who will run and I'll show you a pretty good ballplayer. So after the game was over, I said to him, "Do you run that way all the time?"

He said, "Yeah. I'm just hustling for a job."

He wound up hitting .331 and made the All-Star team.

Phil Seghi was in charge of the Reds farm system and he wanted Pete to play second base. I tried him there and decided he wasn't a good second baseman.

He got the average runner going down to first on a double play, but he couldn't get anybody out who could run fast. He was an average pivot guy. Because of his inability to get to second base in time to make the pivot and throw to first, he had to cheat and play close to the base and that opened up the hole at first. And he couldn't go to his right. A good second baseman can go to his right.

I wanted to put Rose on third—he could go to his left okay, and threw well enough—or in the outfield. But Phil Seghi knew all the answers and wanted Pete on second. So that's where he stayed.

Rose really concentrated at the plate. Every ball he took he'd watch right back to the catcher's mitt. We taught him to meet the ball before he hit it. He was good at it and did it his entire career.

Pete could switch-hit and play a couple positions, and that kind of player is valuable. But second base wasn't where he belonged. ∎

Eliot Asinof

A Baseball Life

by Tim Wiles

Every summer thousands of baseball fans flock to Cooperstown to see the annual induction ceremony of new Hall of Famers. In June another draw is the annual Cooperstown Symposium on Baseball and American Culture, where baseball scholars present papers on all aspects of the game and hear a keynote speaker. Those speakers have included a pretty powerful lineup of baseball thinkers and writers, including Marvin Miller, Jules Tygiel, W. P. Kinsella, Leonard Koppett, Andrew Zimbalist, Jonathan Eig, and my favorite, Eliot Asinof.

Best known in baseball circles for writing *Eight Men Out,* the classic nonfiction account of the 1919 World Series and its "Black Sox scandal," Asinof also has a fascinating life story of his own, parts of which he related in his lecture. This columnist sat in the audience thinking that there are no stories better than our true-life stories, at least if we have lived lives as full as Asinof's.

Our speaker began by quoting the oft-cited dictum of Jacques Barzun: "Whoever wants to know the heart and mind of America had better learn baseball." Asinof noted that he once asked Barzun to explain his famous remark, and that Barzun admitted that he didn't know exactly what he had meant. Some of the best writing on cultural matters is impressionistically drawn, as was Barzun's essay. The rest of Asinof's speech wove threads of autobiography with trenchant commentary on the heart and mind of America.

In 1939, he was a self-described "hot shot college ballplayer," who was recruited to play on Doubleday

TIM WILES *has been director of research at the Baseball Hall of Fame since 1995. He is the co-editor of* Line Drives: 100 Contemporary Baseball Poems *(Southern Illinois University Press, 2002) and co-author of the forthcoming* Baseball's Greatest Hit: 100 Years of Take Me Out to the Ball Game.

Field for a U.S. amateur team vs. a group of local all-stars during the summer of '39. Asinof recalled the portable lighting system that had been installed for the night game, and the fact that the local pitcher hit the all-stars' first batter in the mouth, delaying the game while all of his teeth were collected. Asinof batted second, swung at the first two pitches, and made for the dugout. Then the ump called him back for his final cut, which presumably was strike three.

While Asinof's speech was impossibly rich with stories which I would like to relate, I will focus on the following three, which illustrate, to Asinof, how baseball either doesn't reflect the heart and mind of America, or reflects it all too well.

In 1940, Asinof embarked upon a career as a professional ballplayer, signed by the Phillies, who sent him to a low-level farm club at Moultrie, GA. After a long trip from New York, he arrived in Moultrie at about five in the afternoon, the streets busy with people walking home from work. Making his way to the ballpark for his first game as a Moultrie Packer, Asinof saw a black woman approaching him with a baby in one hand and a bag of groceries in the other, and instinctively stepped aside to let her pass. A moment later, the long arm of the South landed on his shoulder from behind, and Asinof was arrested for being courteous to a black woman. A month or so later, Asinof, a good hitter by all the evidence I've seen, hit a triple during a home game. It just happens that the "Colored" seating section was behind third base, and stories of Asinof's chivalry had circulated among the fans in that section. They gave him an ovation for his hit, and he responded by tipping his cap. He was fired the next day.

The next season saw him sent to Wausau, WI, presumably a place where the young ballplayer would not rouse

Eliot Asinof

the rabble with his dangerous racial attitudes. Asinof played well for the Lumberjacks, but the outcome was the same; he was fired. This time his offense was that he was Jewish. In the Midwest in the 1940s, that's one strike against you, but the situation became untenable when the team owner's teenage daughter developed a crush on a Jewish ballplayer. Even if her attention was unrequited, as was the case, there were some things America just couldn't tolerate back then.

World War II interrupted the ballplayer's career, and Private Asinof, who became Lieutenant Asinof with the help of an old buddy named Hank Greenberg, was posted to Adak Island, far out in the Aleutian chain, to defend our interests in the north Pacific. Lieutenant Asinof had plenty of time to write, and a fine critic and mentor in one of his superior officers, Dashiel Hammett. Asinof would write for the base newspaper, raking the muck of Adak, and Hammett would advise him: "You've brought me the what, Eliot, now go back and bring me the why." It would be fine advice for a writer who would later produce not just *Eight Men Out* but also one of the finest baseball novels ever written, *Man on Spikes*. This once-forgotten 1955 classic was reissued in 1998 by Southern Illinois University Press, which also published Asinof's baseball novel *Off Season* in 2000.

After the war, Asinof spent a couple of seasons as a clothing salesman in New York, working on his writing and founding a high-level semi-pro baseball league. When the league folded, mostly due to the advent of television, which was a better entertainment option than sitting outside watching semi-pro ball, Asinof went into writing full-time. Sardonically, Asinof parodied Barzun in his speech, saying, "Whoever wants to know the heart and mind of America had better watch television."

It was television, and movies, in fact where Asinof had much of his early success as a writer. After a while, that too would come to an end, as he found himself blacklisted by the House un-American Activities Committee and Senator Joe McCarthy. In the end, it didn't matter much to Asinof, who found a way to write on, this time in books. Many years later, after the passage of the Freedom of Information Act, Asinof approached the FBI to find out why he had been blacklisted. The thin file on this threat to America contained only one item, though that one piece of evidence was enough to end his career. In the late 1940s or early 1950s, Asinof had signed a petition outside Yankee Stadium urging the Yankees to sign their first black ballplayer.

Did our old friend Jacques Barzun hit the nail on the head when he said, "Whoever wants to know the heart and mind of America had better learn baseball, the rules and realities of the game...?" You decide. ■

"He Never Was Much with the Stick"

The Story of "Silent Bill" Hopke

by Peter Morris

One of baseball's most exciting plays comes when a batter unexpectedly drops a bunt down the third base line. The third baseman charges in frantically and, with no margin for error, usually tries to barehand the ball. The batter is tearing down the first base line as fast as his legs will carry him, and the first baseman and first base umpire are bracing themselves for the expected bang-bang play. Meanwhile the crowd is shrieking with anticipation and all eyes are on the third baseman as he makes his do-or-die effort to pick up the ball cleanly and launches a desperate throw across the diamond.

Such plays are no longer everyday occurrences, but in the late 19th and early 20th centuries they were much more common sights, which placed a great emphasis on a third baseman's ability to execute this most challenging of plays. Jimmy Collins was considered preeminent at foiling bunts among turn-of-the-century third sackers, and his skill in making the play helped him earn a place in the Hall of Fame and led many of his contemporaries to proclaim him the greatest third baseman of all time.

When Collins began to lose a step, there was less of a clear consensus as to who succeeded him as the master of such plays. But many who saw Billy Hopke play believed that nobody was as good at thwarting bunts. Billy who? Billy Hopke spent most of the first two decades of the 20th century traversing minor league circuits without ever getting a shot at the "big show." His story tells us much about the life of minor leaguers of that era and the changing nature of the position he played.

PETER MORRIS *is the author of* Baseball Fever *(2003), the two-volume* A Game of Inches *(2006),* Level Playing Fields *(2007) and the forthcoming* But Didn't We Have Fun?

Hopke's parents, Friedrich Hopke and the former Henriette Fedrau, arrived in America from Prussia on the ship *Hermann* on March 29, 1880, along with a six-year-old son and two infant daughters. The family settled in Cleveland and grew to include four more children. William Friedrich was the first member of the family to be born on U.S. soil, entering the world on November 2, 1881.

After learning the game on the sandlots of Cleveland, in 1902 Billy accepted his first professional engagement as a shortstop with an unnamed team in the Carolina League. His stay there was brief, and he finished that season with Columbus.[1]

Hopke joined Fort Wayne for the 1903 season and immediately made a very positive impression. The team's home field was adjacent to the St. Mary's River, and during one of the club's practices, a young boy named Monroe Gordon toppled into the river and was swept away by the current. Hearing the desperate cries of the boy's companion, Hopke rushed to the outfield fence, squeezed himself through, and plunged into the water.

By the time he reached Gordon, the child had just gone under for the second time. But Hopke, a strong swimmer, arrived in the nick of time and brought the boy back to shore. There, although black in the face, the lad soon revived, at which point Hopke "went at once to his room to change his clothing and to the congratulations of those who were attracted to the scene modestly said that the incidence was of no consequence and that he was only happy that he was providentially present to avert a casualty."[2]

A few days later he showed that he also had the knack of being in the right place at the right time on the diamond. Playing shortstop in an exhibition game, he made a spectacular leaping catch to start a triple play.[3] Hopke's first introduction to the fans of Fort Wayne thus exhibited his modesty and his stellar fielding. This was appropriate, as those were the traits that would continue to be associated with him throughout his stay in Fort Wayne and his entire career.

Manager Bade Myers concluded that shortstop was not Hopke's best position and installed him as the team's everyday third baseman. He spent the next two-and-a-half seasons with Fort Wayne, proving a durable, reliable player and helping the team capture the 1903 and 1904 Central League pennants. In the middle of the 1905 season, the Fort Wayne franchise was transferred to Canton, where Hopke spent another season and a half.

After spending four full years in the Central League, a Class B circuit, Hopke must have been thrilled that off-season to learn that the manager of a Class A team was negotiating for his services. The interested party was William H. Watkins, whose Indianapolis team in the American Association was in need of a third baseman. As rumors spread that Hopke would be his choice, an Indianapolis sportswriter explained that the third baseman had proven to be "a fast man" in the Central League, but that it remained "a question whether he is good enough for the American Association."[4]

The question being alluded to was not how Hopke would perform, as his strengths and weaknesses were well known by this point. Rather, the question was a referendum on the qualifications for playing third base.

Thirty-five years earlier, third base had been viewed as one of the most important defensive positions. The rules of the day specified that a ball was fair or foul based upon where it first touched the ground, enabling batters to master "fair-fouls": balls which struck the turf just inside the third base line but then sped into foul territory. Because he was responsible for covering so much ground, "the third baseman was perhaps the most important man

HOPKE S. S.

Few men have ever played the hot corner as well as Billy Hopke. But batting was another matter...

on the nine, as the position was regarded as the key of the infield."[5]

That changed dramatically when the definition of a fair ball was changed in 1877 in order to eliminate the fair-foul. Gradually, defensive skills became a less prominent feature of the third baseman's job description. But just when managers had been accustomed to regarding the position as a haven for good hitters, it was again revolutionized when the bunt suddenly gained prominence in the late 1880s.

The new tactic put a premium on a third baseman's ability to charge in and field a bunt. At the same time, by forcing him to position himself closer to the batter, it placed a renewed emphasis on quick reflexes. Fittingly, it was at the same time that the bunt became a major part of baseball that third base became known first as the "difficult corner" and then as the "hot corner."[6]

With third base again an important defensive position, managers had to decide whether to station a glove man or a heavy hitter at the "hot corner." While it was easy to see that a defensively challenged third baseman cost a team many runs per season, sacrificing offense was not an easy decision to make. Catchers were already chosen primarily for their glove work, while middle infielders were typically such feeble hitters that one report remarked: "It is desired to get a fast infielder who can hit a .175 clip or better. This would strengthen our team very nicely."[7] Everyone knew that pitchers couldn't hit, so if third base was also reserved for a skilled defender, how was a team suppose to score runs?

This presented a difficult dilemma for turn-of-the-century managers and front offices. Nobody's fate was more directly affected than Billy Hopke's.

Everyone agreed that Hopke was ideally suited to the demands of playing third base. During his stint in Fort Wayne, he had wowed the locals with his defensive prowess. One sportswriter described him as, one of the most graceful players in the game and the way that he can cut up in the infield is a fright. Bad bounders, line drives or bunts look alike to him and with that whip [throwing arm] few have been able to beat out infield taps in his direction. He is a whirlwind on his feet and one of the most pleasing features of his play was the pulling down of high fouls after a long chase to the fence nearest the third base line.[8]

He also brought other valuable assets to a ball club. A Fort Wayne newspaper claimed that he did not miss a single game between 1902 and 1908, and while this is probably inaccurate, he was unquestionably durable.[9] Hopke had also earned a reputation as "one of the most popular players that ever wore a Fort Wayne uniform," and had been regarded with similar esteem during his stay in Canton.[10]

Yet not everyone was convinced that those qualities outweighed his one liability: his bat. At 5' 9", 145 pounds, Hopke didn't have much power. That deficiency wasn't unusual in the early years of the 20th century, but nor did Hopke hit the ball with authority or regularity and that was a problem.

The result was that every glowing description of his fielding skill ended with a disclaimer. The Fort Wayne sportswriter who waxed eloquent about Hopke's fielding and popularity finished up by admitting, "but he never was much with the stick."[11] After offering high praise for Hopke's glove work, Otto Hess added sadly, "If that little fellow could hit he wouldn't be in the minor league today, that's a cinch. It's tough when a great fielder like that can't get his hits."[12]

Fortunately for Hopke, Indianapolis president Bill Watkins was a former third baseman himself and believed that the runs a standout fielder saved at the hot corner could make up for the ones cost by a weak bat. He traded for Hopke, and when player-manager Charley Carr made him his everyday third baseman, the two men got exactly what he expected over the next two years. The little third baseman's defensive skills proved, if anything, better than advertised, and he became "the third base sensation of the American Association."[13]

Teammates and opposing players who had spent time in the major leagues believed that Hopke's glove work compared favorably to that of the game's best third basemen. Del Drake avowed in 1911: "I have not seen a third baseman in the American League this season who has anything on Hopke as an infielder. When it comes to fielding bad bounders he is in a class by himself."[14]

Otto Hess concurred:

This fellow Billy Hopke, the Indianapolis third sacker, is about as keen an infielder as I have ever seen. I don't believe there is a third sacker in the majors who has anything on him as a fielder, unless it's [Bill] Bradley. Bill may have a little on Hopke, but not much.[15]

What especially impressed contemporary observers was that Hopke, like all great fielders, was able to make the most difficult plays look routine. "Hopke is probably the most graceful player in the local outfit," wrote one of the sportswriters who watched him every day. "The apparent ease with which he tosses them to [first baseman-manager Charley] Carr fools many people who think his chances are easy. As a matter of fact, he pulls off some wonderful plays."[16]

This characteristic was reflective of his modest, unassuming personality, which, as on previous stops, quickly made him a favorite. Sportswriter H. G. Copeland of the *Indianapolis Star* described Hopke as "one of the quietest, cleanest and most inobtrusive players" that ever wore an Indianapolis uniform. Local sportswriters dubbed him "Silent Bill," a nickname that Hopke came to dislike.

Eventually, Hopke approached Copeland to complain. "Say, can't you guys cut out this 'silent' stuff?," asked the ballplayer. "It gets me in bad. Lots of people in Indianapolis think I'm a sure enough dummy and they try to talk to me on their fingers." It was the longest speech that the sportswriter ever heard Hopke make.[17] Yet he continued to be plagued by the now-familiar weakness at the plate. After batting a respectable .253 in his first season with Indianapolis, he batted a paltry .201 with only 15 extra-base hits in 1908. As a result, a later summary of his career stated bluntly:

Hopke was as fast as any third baseman in the game when it came to running in and fielding bunts and bounders around third base. When that was said it was all said for Hopke. He couldn't hit a lick and when he got on first base some one had to bat him around.[18]

Hopke's career reached a turning point after the 1908 season. Indianapolis had captured that year's American Association flag behind a standout pitching staff led by Rube Marquard and a stellar defensive infield anchored by Hopke and promising young shortstop Donie Bush. But Marquard and Bush advanced to the major leagues after the season, and Indianapolis acquired Jimmy Burke to play third base over the winter and asked Hopke to move to shortstop.

In one sense the proposed conversion was a logical decision. Managers were growing increasingly reluctant to reserve the hot corner for a slick fielder, so it seemed reasonable to try Hopke at shortstop instead. And he certainly possessed the strong arm and dexterity to play the new position.

Yet there was a critical flaw in this reasoning. Hopke had played shortstop during his first professional season of 1902 but had been exclusively a third baseman since, and with good reason. He possessed lightning quickness—as one of the descriptions cited earlier put it, he was "a whirlwind on his feet." But he did not have great speed, with Copeland describing him as a very slow base runner.[19]

This made him ill-suited to making the switch to a position that placed a much greater emphasis on range. A shortstop also needed speed to be able to cover second base when needed—not to mention the ability to make a pivot. Meanwhile, the new position made far less use of Hopke's most noted skill: his felicity for charging bunts.

"Silent Bill" typically made no public protest about the decision, but his feelings can be surmised from the fact that he held out that spring.[20] He eventually reported but proved no more than adequate in his new position; the glowing descriptions of his defensive work that had been so common when he played third base became conspicuous by their absence. And at season's end, the *Star* pronounced the experiment a failure: "Hopke has proved that he is one of the greatest fielding third basemen in the game, but is not a success at shortstop."[21] Worse, he continued to struggle at the plate as he adjusted to his new position, hitting a mere .207 as the Indians slid back into the middle of the pack.

The result was that the off-season following the 1909 season was even more tumultuous than the one before.

Long a regular on the post-season barnstorming circuit, Hopke's penchant for being in the right place at the right time enabled him to become part of a far more ambitious tour. The American League champion Detroit Tigers had just embarked on a post-season tour of Cuba when shortstop Donie Bush was called home to Indianapolis by his mother's illness. So Bush asked Hopke to take his place, and Billy's glove work earned rave reviews in his first game, playing "a sensational game, accepting 11 of 12 chances" in an 11-inning loss to Cuban power Almendares.[22]

The tour of Cuba was a great professional opportunity for Hopke—and a financial windfall. "They charged as high as two dollars a seat over there right along, and the fans paid it," he explained when he returned to the states flush with cash.

> It looked like a shame to do it, but they finally reduced the general admission to 50 cents. The management was surprised when it found there were less people on hand at the games with the smaller admission than when the higher tariff was in effect. It showed that the Cubans want to see good baseball no matter how much the charge.[23]

According to Hopke, his fielding was subpar during the tour, but that seems to be just his characteristic modesty. In fact, his defensive prowess had impressed the major leaguers enough that there were rumors that he would be traded to the Tigers.[24] Had that happened, Hopke would have been ideally suited to the role of utility infielder for Detroit. But instead the deal did not come to pass, and it soon became clear that "Silent Bill" was more likely to be demoted than promoted.

Indianapolis had acquired Jack Coffey to play shortstop in 1910, leaving Hopke to compete for the third base job with Burke and newcomer Simeon Murch. Murch was a giant of a man by the standards of the day at 6' 2", 220, and the fact that he was being considered for the hot corner said much about changes to the game that would eventually cause another dramatic transformation in the third baseman's job description.

The 1909 season had seen the introduction of a livelier cork-centered baseball. It is hard to tell from the American Association's final statistics, which showed that the league leader batted only .296. But what restrained hitting was the fact that balls were rarely replaced, which meant that the effect of the livelier ball was quickly neutralized.[25]

Over the next few years, however, a new emphasis was placed on replacing used balls, and this in turn caused batters to take fuller cuts. Offense began to soar and bunting started to make less sense as a strategy. Both trends were very bad news for Billy Hopke because they meant that managers were suddenly looking for hitters like Murch to play a position where defense had once been at a premium.

Burke was eventually released, leaving Hopke and Murch to battle it out for the job in spring training. The tussle offered a sneak preview of the future of the position when Murch was named the team's starter. Hopke had given him a stiff fight, but this actually worked to his disadvantage. Other Class A clubs had expressed interest in Hopke earlier in the spring, but by the time the decision to go with Murch was made, they had filled their openings. So Hopke—only a few months after rumors had him finally getting a shot at the major leagues—had his contract loaned to Wilkes-Barre, PA, of the Class B New York State League.[26]

Hopke mostly played shortstop for Wilkes-Barre and contributed greatly to another pennant. In addition to his smooth glove work, as teammate Del Drake recalled, "Hopke surprised himself and everybody else by slugging the ball at .300 and better."[27]

At season's end, however, Billy made it clear that he didn't intend to spend another season in Wilkes-Barre. Watkins had retained an option on the slick-fielding third sacker and reacquired him, but soon again decided he needed more offense at third base. So he sold Hopke's contract outright to Topeka of the Western League in December.[28]

Hopke apparently wasn't excited about the prospect of joining a team that had lost 125 games in 1910 and held out that spring before finally signing a Topeka contract.[29] In July, with Topeka well on its way to another hundred-loss season, Charley Carr, now managing Utica of the New York State League, inquired into the availability of his old teammate.[30] So Hopke finished the 1911 season in Utica. He returned to Utica in 1912—though Carr had departed—and the season produced the fifth pennant of Billy Hopke's career.

He barnstormed in Fort Wayne again after the 1912 season, but his whereabouts at the start of the 1913 season are not clear.[31] In July, he resurfaced in a familiar city—but a new league. A new independent loop called the Federal League had been organized in the Midwest, and Indianapolis fans received the welcome news that "old favorite 'Silent Bill' Hopke is back in town."[32]

It was a bittersweet return. Within days of his debut, word came that he would be sidelined indefinitely with an arm injury—the first serious injury that the durable Hopke had experienced.[33] But by August his arm was well enough for him to man shortstop, and he led Indianapolis to the league title.[34] It was the sixth and final pennant of his career.

After the season, the Federal League decided to declare itself a major league and compete with the two established leagues. It appeared that Hopke might finally get the long-awaited shot at the major leagues, but as so often before, his timing was ever so slightly off. The Federal League was looking for big name players to boost its prestige, and Hopke was not asked to return.

Billy Hopke turned 32 after the season and, between his age and the growing emphasis on third baseman being hard hitters, he must have known that another shot at the major leagues was unlikely to come. But still he soldiered on, although his doings attracted less and less attention and are still difficult to reconstruct.

He signed with York, PA, of the Tri-State League for the 1914 season, a club that struggled badly and moved to Lancaster at midseason.[35] After the year came news that Atlanta manager Billy Smith would sign Hopke to play third base in 1915, but later word had Smith planning to send him to Beaumont of the Texas League.[36] Then in 1916 he was reunited with another old friend when Bade Myers signed him to play third base for Muskegon of the Central League.[37] It showed once again that men who had watched Billy Hopke play appreciated what he brought to a ball club.

Over the next few seasons, Hopke seemed to drop off the baseball map altogether and, with wartime restrictions sharply reducing the number of minor leagues, it surely seemed safe to assume that he had left baseball for good. But then, in the spring of 1920, a Fort Wayne newspaper carried the announcement of Billy Hopke's retirement from baseball. Twenty years of baseball, he explained briefly, was enough for anyone.[38]

"Silent Bill" Hopke's life after baseball was characteristically unostentatious. A bachelor for most of his career, he married a woman named Minerva around 1919 and found work as an auto mechanic. The couple had no children, and Billy died in Cleveland on April 18, 1959, survived by his wife, who lived until 1980.

Billy Hopke was virtually forgotten even before the end of his career and has languished in obscurity ever since. Yet he deserves to be remembered because his career tells us much about what it was like to be a minor league ballplayer during the first two decades of the 20th century.

The fact that he never played in the majors despite well over 2,000 minor league games was, as I have tried to suggest, a combination of bad luck and bad timing. Yet Billy Hopke's timing was not always bad, a fact that many of his contemporaries could attest. One was a young Fort Wayne resident named Monroe Gordon who lived another 83 years after Hopke saved him from the St. Mary's River. He would be joined by all of the fans who were thrilled by the six pennant flags he helped to raise. And the exquisiteness of Billy Hopke's timing could also be vouchsafed by anyone who watched him charge in to pounce on a bunt. ■

Notes

1. *Fort Wayne Journal-Gazette,* February 17, 1903.
2. *Fort Wayne Sentinel,* April 17, 1903; also, *Fort Wayne Journal-Gazette,* April 18, 1903; *Fort Wayne Weekly Sentinel,* April 22, 1903.
3. *Fort Wayne Journal-Gazette,* April 22, 1903.
4. *Indianapolis News,* reprinted in *Fort Wayne News,* December 10, 1906.
5. *Sporting Life,* December 12, 1883.
6. *Sporting Life,* December 30, 1885; *Sporting News,* August 17, 1889.
7. *Newark (OH) Advocate,* March 20, 1907.
8. *Fort Wayne Journal-Gazette,* March 5, 1910.
9. *Fort Wayne Sentinel,* March 11, 1909.
10. *Fort Wayne Journal-Gazette,* March 5, 1910.
11. *Fort Wayne Journal-Gazette,* March 5, 1910.
12. *Fort Wayne Sentinel,* February 5, 1909.
13. *Fort Wayne Sentinel,* September 11, 1907.
14. *Fort Wayne Journal-Gazette,* July 6, 1911.
15. *Fort Wayne Sentinel,* February 5, 1909.
16. *Indianapolis Star,* quoted in *Fort Wayne Journal-Gazette,* June 19, 1908.
17. H. G. Copeland, *Indianapolis Star,* December 17, 1910.
18. *Indianapolis Star,* March 17, 1912.
19. H. G. Copeland, *Indianapolis Star,* December 17, 1910; *Indianapolis Star,* March 17, 1912. The *Fort Wayne Journal-Gazette* of March 5, 1910, contrarily claimed, "On the bases too [Hopke] is a star," but Hopke's very low stolen-base figures belie the assertion.
20. *Fort Wayne Journal-Gazette,* March 6 and 14, 1909.
21. *Indianapolis Star,* December 28, 1909.
22. *Indianapolis Star,* November 19, 1909.
23. *Fort Wayne Daily News,* December 11, 1909.
24. *Fort Wayne News,* December 7, 1909; *Fort Wayne Sentinel,* January 13, 1910.
25. The introduction of the cork-centered ball is usually placed a couple years later, but an advertisement in *The Sporting News* on March 2, 1911, makes clear that it was first used in 1909. See my *A Game of Inches* for a fuller discussion.
26. *Fort Wayne News,* April 18, 1910.
27. *Fort Wayne Journal-Gazette,* July 6, 1911.
28. *Fort Wayne Sentinel,* August 30 and December 17, 1910; H. G. Copeland, *Indianapolis Star,* December 17, 1910; Joe S. Jackson, *Washington Post,* January 12, 1911.
29. *Coshocton Daily Tribune,* March 3, 1911.
30. *Syracuse Herald,* July 16, 1911.
31. *Sandusky Star Journal,* October 19, 1912.
32. *Indianapolis Star,* July 12, 1913.
33. *Indianapolis Star,* July 16, 1913.
34. *Indianapolis Star,* August 2, 1913.
35. *Syracuse Herald,* April 29, 1914.
36. *Syracuse Herald,* December 29, 1914 and February 26, 1915.
37. *Syracuse Herald,* February 17, 1916.
38. *Fort Wayne Journal-Gazette,* April 29, 1920.

Lester Spurgeon Cook

Catcher, Trainer, PCL Legend

by James D. Smith III

When I first became interested in baseball as a little leaguer in 1960-61, my reading and TV experiences eventually led me to San Diego's Westgate Park (opened two years earlier), home of the Pacific Coast League Padres. There I could see Gary Peters, Suitcase Simpson, and the locals in person. When a player got hurt, I watched a short, older man in baggy pants and glasses amble out onto the field, sometimes with his bag. Little did I know that he had played for over 20 years, been a trainer for 20 more, and was a walking archive of baseball knowledge and a Coast League icon.

Lester Spurgeon Cook was born in York, PA, on March 26, 1895, his father a German immigrant. By his mid-teens, Les was living in the Los Angeles area, where he played sandlot baseball and began working as a plumber's apprentice. When opportunity knocked in 1913, he abandoned his dollar-a-day plumbing job to become a professional ballplayer.

While he had contacts with the Vernon (PCL) team, records show his pro debut was with Stockton of the old California League. As chronicled by John E. Spalding in his groundbreaking work, *Always on Sunday,* the league had organizational roots going back to 1886, but was in its last few years of operation. A lifelong catcher, Les appeared in fewer than 10 games for Stockton, as financial losses ended the circuit's season in June. The following 1914 campaign, he played in 29 games as a reserve for San Jose. But in early 1915, the league folded after San Jose had played only six games, washed out by one of the wettest Northern California springs in history.

JIM SMITH *has been a SABR member since 1982, and has contributed to* TNP, BRJ, *and a variety of historical, religious, and sports publications. He teaches at Bethel Seminary San Diego, the University of San Diego, and serves as a pastor at College Avenue Baptist Church.*

Cook's professional career appeared over. The Coast League represented a much higher level of play, and his batting skills (.193 in 1914) were modest. However, as Spalding notes, Les played for 20 more seasons, and had the last appearance in Organized Baseball of any California League alum. To continue his career, the backstop moved to the Texas League.

Playing with San Antonio in 1916, "Cookie" caught in 97 games but batted a microscopic .138. Management liked his defensive skills, however, along with his attitude and ability to work with other players. The following season, in 88 games, he improved to .215 and (at 5' 8" and 150 pounds) was maturing physically. When play ended in Texas, he joined Vernon in the PCL for 11 late-season games. This wasn't enough to secure further local employment, however (residence: 1156 E. Vernon Avenue, in LA), and he toiled in 1918 with St. Paul of the American Association, batting .164 in 20 games. The following year, he was invited back to Vernon, beginning his first full PCL season—and a Coast League involvement that would last for a half-century.

Moving from Vernon to Seattle to Sacramento in 1919, he had over 300 at-bats for the first time (batting .155). Cook also appeared on his first Zeenut baseball card. Most important, he made friends wherever he went. After Les' passing in 1968, Lefty O'Doul remembered:

> We've been pals for 51 years. I'll never forget how we used to shoot rabbits from the train in the old days when we traveled from Salt Lake City to the West Coast. Cookie was good to the players, helpful to the managers and knew how to handle men. He was a grand person and had a sense of humor like no other trainer in the business.

Long before O'Doul had managed the PCL Padres to the 1954 championship, with Cook as his trainer, the wiry catcher's "intangibles" gave him a value far beyond the box scores.

From 1920 to 1922, Cook remained with Sacramento and established a playing pattern: with the PCL schedule approaching 200 games, he annually gathered around 250 at-bats and batted about .210. In his 1923 season, shortened by injury, he managed a heady .333 mark in 27 plate appearances. But his impending transfer to Salt Lake City would bring much more significant developments.

The Salt Lake owner was Bill "Hardrock" Lane, a longtime miner turned club owner who loved both the game and business of baseball. Over the next 15 seasons, as Lane (who died in 1938) would move his franchise from Utah to Hollywood to San Diego, Cook remained a fixture in his organization. In 1924, at altitude, Les posted career highs: 131 games, 345 at-bats, 58 runs, 104 hits, 36 doubles, three home runs, and 57 RBIs while batting .301. The following season, the marks were more familiar: .244 in 105 games.

But once again his contribution went beyond the stats. PCL teammate, later Padres manager (and 1927 Yankee), Cedric Durst called him "one of the most loyal men I ever met in baseball. Les did so much for others."

When Lane located the franchise in Hollywood, from the 1926-35 seasons, Cook, entering his 30s and closer to home, was realistic about his future. One of his nicknames, "Longball," was laden with irony. His playing time was diminishing. For a decade he had been a student of the game, most especially of pitchers' heads and arms. Other players were now soliciting his advice on conditioning or when facing injury. His activity as trainer, initially a sidelight, now was increasingly his vocation. Appearing in only six games in both 1931 and 1932, in 1933-35 he did not play, serving as trainer and, in a newer vein, traveling secretary. Then, in 1936, Bill Lane moved his team yet again, to find a new home in sleepy San Diego.

Witnessing this transition was veteran PCL infielder Eddie Leishman, who 25 years later served as the PCL Padres general manager and Cook's boss:

I've never seen a person more devoted to baseball than Les. He was more than a trainer to the players, managers and club officials. He was an inspiration to all of us in baseball. While his job was to tend the sore arms and bruises of the players, he was also a friend and confidant to the rookie and veteran alike. He has been referred to as 'Mr. San Diego Padre.' Les was just that."

One dimension of Cook's role as friend involved serving (with Vince DiMaggio, et al) as part of the ballplayer quartet that sang at infielder George Myatt's home plate wedding in 1936. The shortstop's best man was second baseman Bobby Doerr.

Doerr remains a unique witness to this era, as an original Padre and HOF member. In my January 2006 interview he recalled Cook's mentorship.

I broke in with Hollywood in June of 1934, just a young kid, and roomed with Les for a while. He did the hotel paying, and I respected him while he held it all together. He had the cash, and carried a pistol, which he hid under his pillow. He was still a pretty good catcher, and we got along well despite the age difference. In '36, with San Diego, he had a picture in the training room of the Rogue River (Oregon) area and said, "Why not come up with Blanche [married 1924, died 1978] and me and spend the winter?" As a youngster, fishing and hunting intrigued me, so I went. He'd been going there since 1918 or '19. Once on site, he said there was a redheaded schoolteacher I might be interested in. I was kinda scared, but that's how I met my wife, Monica. We were married in 1938, and made our home there. Les was an old pro. A spade was a spade. He was rugged and steady. And he was a good trainer—we never had a sore-armed pitcher.

A teenage teammate on those 1936 Padres was native San Diegan and HOFer Ted Williams, who also credited Cook's positive influence.

Cookie was a pro. I thought so from the minute I joined the Padres. Les made a strong impression on me because I knew he came from the old school of baseball...he had played for a good Hollywood team which was crammed with outstanding players. I was young then...but I could see what a fine job he did with the older men, especially the pitchers. They were always going to him for rubdowns to make the old soup bones feel good.

After a 1937 championship year, Williams was off to Minneapolis, then Boston—but the friendship continued.

With his role as trainer and road secretary secure, "The Little Corporal" traveled the Coast League and, after each off-season in the outdoors, looked forward to

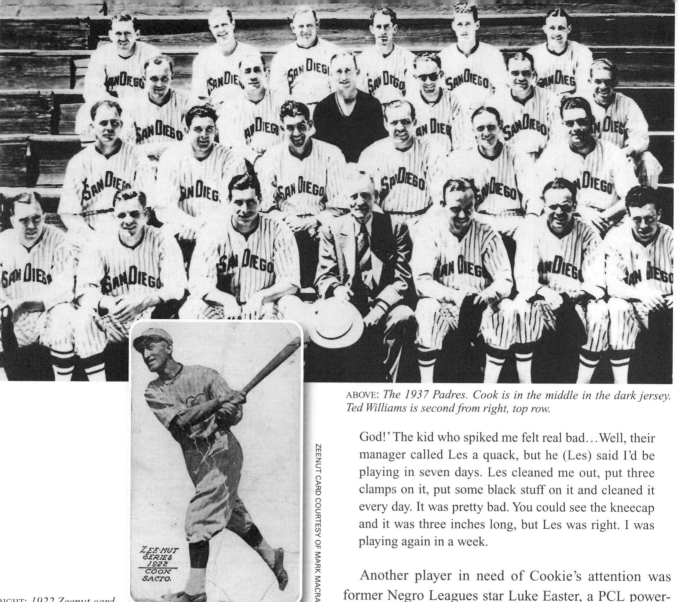

ABOVE: *The 1937 Padres. Cook is in the middle in the dark jersey. Ted Williams is second from right, top row.*

RIGHT: *1922 Zeenut card.*

the rigors of spring training—sharing his knowledge and love of baseball wherever he went. He enjoyed brief appearances in the lineup each season from 1936 to 1939, a total of 10 games, during which he tallied his last two hits in his final game on August 23, 1939. The best statistics available suggest a minor league career of 1,053 games, almost all of them as a catcher, with a .213 lifetime average. While never a star, to those in the game he became a living legend.

There are stories galore. One involves Frank Kerr, an iron man catcher and WWII veteran, who later became a PCL umpire. In Bill Swank's fine book, *Echoes from Lane Field,* Kerr recalls one moment.

There was once this play at home. I blocked the plate and his spikes came right up my shin guard and cut me…Les came out, looked at my knee, and said, 'Oh my

God!' The kid who spiked me felt real bad…Well, their manager called Les a quack, but he (Les) said I'd be playing in seven days. Les cleaned me out, put three clamps on it, put some black stuff on it and cleaned it every day. It was pretty bad. You could see the kneecap and it was three inches long, but Les was right. I was playing again in a week.

Another player in need of Cookie's attention was former Negro Leagues star Luke Easter, a PCL powerhouse on his way to Cleveland. In 1949, he suffered a variety of ailments, most seriously in his knees. He had the right one drained weekly and with care continued in the lineup. Cook devised a new brace for the left one, which enabled him to play through midseason, when he underwent surgery. The previous season, native San Diegan John Ritchey had broken the color barrier in the Pacific Coast League by signing a contract with Padres owner Bill Starr. As he faced with dignity challenges both on and off the field, Johnny's simple statement, "Les Cook was always good to me," remains especially significant. Cook had earlier coached him at San Diego State, filling in for the regular faculty member during wartime, and the relationship of respect and affection was a blessing to each.

Over the years, as the PCL Padres had working agreements successively with the Indians, White Sox, Reds,

ABOVE: *Cook works on slugging Padre outfielder (and Cleveland farmhand) Luke Easter, on May 28, 1949 in the clubhouse at Lane Field.*

RIGHT: *Les doing massage therapy on the right shoulder of Padres pitcher (and Cincinnati farmhand) Sammy Ellis on May 18, 1962 at Westgate Park.*

and Phillies, generations of major league players sought out the grizzled trainer for help in spring training—and he did not disappoint. Longtime *San Diego Union* sportswriter Johnny McDonald has commented on Cook's special talents:

> We can recall many visits by such major leaguers as Frank Robinson, Jim O'Toole, Vada Pinson and Jim Maloney at Cincinnati's minor league complex a few years ago. They preferred his educated fingers on their sore muscles.

Al Hogan began by selling hot dogs at Lane Field in 1947, and eventually became concessions and advertising manager for both minor and major league Padres teams through 1974. His was a unique, behind-the-scenes perspective:

> You'll never know how much Les Cook did to run that club. He'd been with it since Salt Lake City so he knew how things were done under Bill Lane. He was just one helluva guy. He was also the road secretary. He'd get so pie-eyed [anecdotes suggest Early Times masked by Mennen], but let anybody touch that little bag with the

money and he'd get sober right now. He was one of the finest men I ever met…He used to let kids into the ballpark and would say, "There's lots of room."

One of the kids he let into wooden Lane Field would later become a National League outfielder. Bob Skinner managed the PCL Padres in their final 1967 season at homey Westgate Park and begin their sole 1968 season at the 50,000-seat San Diego Stadium (aka Jack Murphy, then Qualcomm). In my November 2006 interview he looked back.

> We'd knock and Les would come to the door. He'd say, "Wait a minute," and when the coast was clear he'd let us into the bleachers. He had a big heart, that guy… When I was a PCL manager the last two seasons, he was past 70 and still trainer and traveling secretary. He had his office and training table in the clubhouse down the right-field line. He was well ahead of his time in his knowledge of muscles and massage anatomy. He was sought out. Les was a real gentleman. He took care of us all. Even at his age, there was still energy. How many hours did he put in that we never saw? He loved Eddie Leishman, the GM. Hey, he loved us all.

The *San Diego Union* and *Evening Tribune* (from which several reflections above are taken) faithfully detailed Les Cook's July 1, 1968, death from a heart attack, while preparing for a PCL road trip to Indianapolis and Denver. As one elected to the San Diego Baseball Hall of Fame in 1966, his life was viewed with affection and respect.

With his Padres granted a National League expansion team for 1969, Les was anticipating a season in the major leagues. Yet in the eyes of his adopted city, and the baseball family, he had seemed a big leaguer forever. As former PCL Padres teammate, roommate, and coach Jimmie Reese observed: "He had more friends in the game than anyone I ever knew." ∎

Acknowledgments

Special thanks to Bill Weiss, Ray Nemec, and Bob Hoie for offering materials on Les Cook's statistics and career, to those providing illustrations, and to Bill Swank for suggestions after reading the first draft.

Cannonball Bill Jackman

Baseball's Great Unknown

by Dick Thompson

"The greatest pitcher I have ever seen," whispered John McGraw as he shoved his way through a jostling home-bound crowd after watching "Cannonball" Jackman strike out eighteen batters in nine innings. That whisper spread from ear to ear and finally developed into a roar, for certainly the famed former New York Giants pilot should know what he's talking about in matters of pitchers and baseball.

– Portsmouth Herald, August 19, 1938

Hank Greenberg and Wes Ferrell were two of the many major leaguers who began their careers playing semi-pro ball in East Douglas, MA, for Walter Schuster, the millionaire owner of a string of textile mills along the Blackstone River on the Massachusetts-Rhode Island border. Schuster hired Lefty Grove of the Philadelphia Athletics for a championship contest in October 1927, paying him $300 with a $10 bonus for each batter struck out. For the 1929 Blackstone Valley League title game he gave Bill Jackman of the Philadelphia Giants $175 and the same strikeout bonus. Greenberg played first base and a pitch-by-pitch account of Jackman's work—he tossed 151 pitches and fanned 14 in winning the 6-1 contest—appeared in the local paper.[1] The victory reportedly brought his season's record to 49 wins against just five losses, and the "ex-major and minor leaguers at the game admitted that Jackman had the goods to be in the big show."[2] Another recap of the game said that "the big pitcher for the Giants is alone worth the price of admission. John McGraw, manager of the New York Giants, is reported to have made the facetious remark that he would pay $50,000 to the man who could make Jackman white."[3]

DICK THOMPSON *lives in Dartmouth, MA. He has been a SABR member since 1979.*

McGraw's statements were not unusual, for many who saw the big right hander in his prime declared him the equal of Walter Johnson and Bob Feller. "Old Will Jackman, the meteor man, could flip 'em faster than Feller can" was the opening stanza for a 1940 *Boston Traveler* article. Today, however, despite being named to the famous 1952 *Pittsburgh Courier* poll of all-time Negro League players and long touted by the mainstream white press of New England, where he barnstormed for nearly 30 years, Jackman has been relegated to the historical-who pile, his name unrecognizable but to the most astute Negro League historians. "I want to live in New England," Bill said while recovering from a broken ankle in 1938, indicating his rejection of the more formal Negro Leagues. "People from all over have treated me great, and don't think I don't appreciate such things."[4] Said the *Philadelphia Tribune* in 1927, "Bill Jackman, who is the premier pitcher of semi-pro circles, and a man who stays out of the big tent only because he desires to remain with the Philadelphia Giants..."[5]

The moniker Philadelphia Giants had been used by many squads over the years. The 1905 Philadelphia Giants—famously led by Sol White, Rube Foster, and Danny McClellan—toured New England, and when McClellan operated his own team of the same name two decades later he used the same northern barnstorming routes. The bookings went so well that he came back every summer, and by the early 1930s, though still calling themselves the Philadelphia Giants, the team was based out of Boston. In the years that followed the squad became the Boston Giants, playing sometimes as the Boston Royal Giants and still occasionally as the Philadelphia Giants, but whatever the designation, Jackman and his battery mate Burlin White remained the headliners.

Undated photo of the Philadelphia Giants, circa 1925-1930. Jackman is standing in the back row, third from the right. None of the other players are identified.

"In an endeavor to pick out the most colorful of his brilliant aggregation," wrote the *Philadelphia Tribune* in 1926, "McClellan chooses his star battery, pitcher Jackman and catcher Burlin White. The populace fell for these two like mice take the count for cheese."

That Jackman was considered a star of the highest caliber cannot be overstated. In announcing his arrival in Palm Beach in January 1927, the *Tribune* wrote, "The Florida sportsmen will get their first opportunity of seeing the great battery of Will Jackman and Burlin White." Smokey Joe Williams, also on the team, was mentioned only as an afterthought. In 1928, the *Chicago Defender* called Jackman "one of the leading Colored pitchers in the east."[6] In 1930, the same publication referred to Jackman and White as "two of the greatest attractions in Eastern baseball" and "the idols of New England baseball fans."[7] For a 1942 preview of Boston's entry in the short-lived Negro Major Baseball League of America, the *Defender* wrote, "First, there's the great battery—the pride of New England—with Bill Jackman on the pitching end and White himself catching. That twosome should account for plenty of victories, in case the boys in the Western end of the circuit didn't know."[8] One of the numerous assessments of the pitcher in the New England papers, this one from 1932, said, "Jackman is the Lefty Grove of the colored baseball realm and has been the envy of every major league baseball manager in the country."[9] Robert Peterson, in his groundbreaking *Only the Ball Was White,* wrote, "Jackman is not often mentioned among the select few, but there are men like Bill Yancey who consider him the best of all." In 1933

and 1934, the Hartford, CT, *Courant* wrote, "Jackman, who really has quite a reputation as being the black Babe Ruth of baseball," and "Jackman, whose fame as a pitcher equals that of the famous Cannonball Redding."

Jackman said that he was unsure of the exact circumstances of his birth, and although he wrote October 7, 1897 in Carta, Texas, on his Hall of Fame questionnaire, his friends in Boston thought that just a baseball age. His father was born in Missouri in 1855 and presumably came to Texas with Sidney Drake Jackman, a noted figure who began the Civil War on the side of the Union but ended it as a Confederate brigadier general. Later a member of the Texas state legislature, S. D. Jackman settled in Hayes County in what later became the village of Kyle. The 1920 U.S. Census lists Charles Jackman, along his wife Bettie and son Bill, living in Kyle. Conflicting census data list both an 1894 and an 1897 birth for the pitcher.

Statistical documentation is unavailable for the early portion of his career, but accounts indicate Jackman played in and around San Antonio—where John McGraw and the New York Giants had their spring training camp—before spending 1920-1922 with the Houston Black Buffaloes, for whom he tossed no-hitters against the San Antonio Black Aces and the Dallas Giants.[10] He drifted up into Oklahoma and then to Maryland, New Jersey, and New York in 1923, where he toured with a squad called the "Lincoln Grout Team." He was with the Boston Monarchs in 1924 and may have joined the Philadelphia Giants later that season, although currently the first documentation of his time with McClellan isn't until 1925.[11] Bill originally threw overhand, and submariner Webster McDonald—who last played in New England in 1924—told John Holway he taught Jackman to throw that way when they were teammates on the Philadelphia Giants.[12] When asked in 1938 if the nickname "Cannonball" indicated his current speed, Bill replied, "Nope, I haven't got any extra speed now. That name was given to me when I used to pitch overhand. And, mister, I did have speed then if I do say so myself. My arms were long and I had plenty of leverage to get the ball away fast. The reason I changed to underhand is because I developed a soreness in my arm. I tried out several ways of pitching and found out that

The 1939 Portsmouth team. **Kneeling, left to right:** *Leo Kennedy, Elliot Pohlhemus, Ed Nelson, "Red" Phinney, Manager Ed Neville, Captain Brud Whalen.* **Standing, left to right:** *Bill Jackman, Bill Lynbourg, Al Plausky, Johnny Reddick, Lee Meserve.*

when I threw them underhand it didn't hurt my arm at all. Then when it became well again I never changed back to the old style because the batters told me it was harder to hit the underhand ball than it was the one I threw overhand."

On May 25, 1949, a crowd of 4,200 watched Jackman open his season by dropping a 3-1 contest to the New England Hobos at Braves Field. The pitcher, who completed his day job as a private chauffer just before game time, struggled over the first two innings, allowing four hits and two runs on 49 pitches. Over the last six frames he threw just 59 more times and allowed but two hits. Jerry Nason, a sportswriter noted for his coverage of the Boston Marathon, penned a lengthy tribute to Jackman in the *Boston Globe,* for the contest was the 1200th of the hurler's career. Nason, who first wrote about Jackman during the 1930s and was still doing so in the 1970s, never completed a column about Bill without declaring him the equal of Satchel Paige.

Early in the 1970s Nason led the Boston writers on a charge calling for the pitcher's induction into the Baseball Hall of Fame. "Kids are not born with prejudice, adults show them the techniques. You remember the school teacher who had a hell of a tough time trying to explain to you why 'Cannonball' couldn't pitch in the big league games in Boston. It was a nice try, but it didn't work."[13] Nason also recalled having to climb a tree as a young boy to watch Jackman "because the adults were

standing three or four deep around the roped-off ball field when he pitched."

Reconstructing Jackman's statistical record is an ongoing project, and to date 340 partial or complete pitching box scores have been retrieved, probably about 25% of his career total. He won 200 of those contests and lost 86. He was 22-3 against opposing pitchers who had major league experience, struck out 10 or more batters in 78 games, and hurled 48 shutouts. None of the sample seasons presented here should be considered complete.

1925 – Jackman was 16-3 in 23 recovered games from Connecticut, Massachusetts and Maine. He was 6-1 in ten contests where he faced pitchers who had or would have big league experience. He won three games in a late-season series against the Pennsylvania Red Caps, including a one-hitter played at Boston's Walpole Street Grounds.

1926 – A 17-6 record in 34 games recovered from Connecticut, Massachusetts, and Rhode Island. His best outings were a no-hitter with 14 strikeouts in Quincy, MA, on July 26, and a 2-0 shutout with 12 strikeouts over Haskell Billings and a Cape Cod League all-star squad in Brockton, MA, on September 16. He pitched in five games over the four-day span of September 9-12, three of them complete, and twice defeated the Lynn squad of the New England League, which had five past or future major leaguers on its roster—Shanty Hogan and King Bader among them.

1927 – A 21-7 record in 32 games recovered from Florida, New York, Massachusetts, Pennsylvania and Rhode Island. Highlights included a three-hit shutout against the Breakers team in the Palm Beach winter league, an 11-inning win over Hilldale in Philadelphia on April 21, a 1-0 victory over former major leaguer Chad See in New York City on April 24 while pitching for Santop's Broncos, a 2-1 loss against Heinie Zimmerman's Jamaica team in New York City on May 8 in which

COURTESY OF DICK THOMPSON/PETER CHICK

he fanned 14, and a 14-strikeout victory over Bill "Buck" Ewing's All-Stars in Amsterdam, NY, on May 19.

His best performance in Massachusetts was a 16-strikeout effort against the Fore River Shipyard team of the Boston Twilight League in Quincy, MA, on June 16 which had four players, including former Princeton ace and New York Yankees pitcher Charlie Caldwell, in the lineup with big league experience. "It is common knowledge that, were Jackman white instead of black, he would be in the big show," reported the *Quincy Patriot Ledger* on game day. "No less an authority than Harold Janvrin, who spent 10 years in the major leagues, admitted as much." The *Boston Traveler* followed up the game with, "If colored ballplayers were allowed in the big leagues, Jackman, who twirls for the Philadelphia Colored Giants, would make the grade with ease."

Over a five-day period in July the Giants drew a cumulative crowd of 49,500 paying fans in southeastern Massachusetts.[14]

1928 – A 13-9 record in 25 recovered games, five of which were played in New York City and the rest in southeastern Massachusetts. He won three and dropped two to Cape Cod League squads, one of the losses being a one-hitter in which bad defense did him in.

The Philly Giants were big favorites in New Bedford on the south coast of Massachusetts. "The reason for their repeated visits is quite obvious," wrote the *New Bedford Standard*. "Every time they play they draw a crowd that hopes to see Willie Jackman stand the batsman on their heads…Willie rarely disappoints his public."

The Frates Dairy team of New Bedford was one of the top semi-pro nines in the area. With the financial backing of Alfred Frates the team was able to induce such major league squads as the Boston Braves, the Chicago White Sox, the Philadelphia Athletics and the St. Louis Browns to the Whaling City for exhibition games. Sensing the popularity of Jackman gave Frates an idea.

"Mr. Frates is anxious to give the Browns the stiffest opposition available and is convinced he will do it," wrote the *New Bedford Morning Mercury* on August 22.

The original intent was to use the Philadelphia Colored Giants against the big fellows. Although there is no rule in major league baseball that forbids a major league club from playing a colored ball team, there is an unwritten agreement between managers that they will not play against such teams, and therefore it looks as if the Giants will be out of luck for Sunday's game.

Though Jackman did not face the St. Louis Browns, he did remain the crowd favorite—several times drawing crowds in excess of 10,000—and he took two duels in New Bedford from Gabby Hartnett's brother Buster, a former Boston Braves farmhand brought in specifically to face the Giants ace. The first of those contests came the day after Bill had tossed a complete game on Cape Cod. "Jackman," noted the local paper, "is forced by contract to do the pitching tonight; otherwise there will be no game, as Mr. Frates has drawn up such an agreement with the management of the visitors."[15] The Giants field manager, Burlin White, was not happy. "There is a limit to human endurance," he complained before the game. "Everywhere the Giants play, it's announced that Jackman will pitch—sometimes without permission or knowledge of the Giants—and I am sure you will excuse the big boy after pitching two innings."[16] Jackman went out and pitched the full nine, allowing just four hits while fanning 10.

Pop Lloyd's Lincoln Giants came to New England at the end of August for a five-game series with the Philadelphia Giants, and McClellan's team—highlighted by a Jackman two-hit shutout—took the first three games. McClellan, to reciprocate, hand-picked an All-Star team which included Jackman, White, Judy Johnson, and Nip Winters to play at the Lincolns' home field, the Catholic Protectory Oval in New York City, at the end of the season. Jackman dropped three games in the series, one due to his teammates' poor defense and then a 3-2 game that ended on a Lloyd base hit in the 11th inning. The *Chicago Defender* called this duel between Jackman and Connie Rector the "best seen at the Bronx oval since the Lincolns inception six years ago."

1929 – A 17-7 record in 26 games recovered from New York, New Jersey, Connecticut, and Massachusetts. This was reportedly one of Jackman's three seasons of at least 50 victories, and two of his losses came at the end of September. Highlights included a three-hit shutout with 15 strikeouts versus Vito Tamulis and the Osterville team of the Cape Cod League at Ridgehill Grove in Norwell, MA—a favorite field of the Giants—and on August 10 a perfect game against the Pennsylvania Red Caps in New Bedford.

Burlin White, after spending the winter as a player-manager in Florida, had pitcher Ted Trent in tow when he rejoined McClellan and Jackman in New England. Trent remained with the Giants for only a short time, leaving to rejoin the St. Louis Stars in June, but while he and Jackman were together, they gave the Giants as formidable a one-two pitching punch as any in baseball.

The 1930s – African American teams that called the Hub home during the 1930s included the Boston Tigers, Boston Royal Giants, Philadelphia Giants, Boston Rangers, Boston Pullman Porters, Colored House of David and the Boston ABC's. The Providence, RI, Giants were also prominent in that period, fielding a team of veteran Negro Leaguers who copped the second-half pennant in the 1931 Boston Twilight League. Favorite playing fields for these teams, among many others, included Boston's Carter Playground and Lincoln Park, built specifically for African American teams in the Roxbury section of the city by Danny McClellan's business partner John H. Prioleau in 1931.[17] The major dilemma, and one that potentially kept Boston from being a franchise city for the formal Negro Leagues, was that while white fans turned out in large numbers to watch black teams face white teams, the fan base for black versus black contests—despite the efforts of promoters like Arthur "Fats" Johnson, Bob Russell, McClellan, and Burlin White—was insufficient. The other detriment, it was felt, was that the talent was dispersed on too many teams. One or two strong black teams would have been a better draw.

None of that mattered to Jackman. He just pitched. "Will Jackman, hailed as the greatest colored pitcher in the country today, gave a practical demonstration of his wizardry…to register his fourth consecutive shutout within a period of ten days," noted one suburban Boston paper in May 1930.[18]

On consecutive October 1931 weekends in Togus, ME, the Philly Giants faced a team which included major leaguers Del Bissonette, Milt Gaston, Don Brennan, Jack Russell, and Danny MacFayden. Crowds of 8,000 and 6,500 watched the teams split, Bissonette fanning to end the first contest and then hitting a game-winning, walk-off single in the second. The four big league pitchers,[19] who divided the innings fanned eight batters over the two contests. Jackman, who pitched all of the Giants' innings, fanned 20 and called his punch-out of Bissonette one of his most satisfying accomplishments. Striking out Wally Berger four times in a game is what he listed as his biggest thrill on his Hall of Fame questionnaire.

Jackman had been the center of controversy in the Cape Cod League in August 1931 when a sportswriter noticed him sitting on the Orleans bench with a rolled-up uniform under his arm. When asked why he was there, Bill replied that he was going to pitch. The game was rained out before it started, but Jackman "came close to causing the biggest eruption of Cape league history."[20] The Cape circuit, at that particular time, fell under the auspices of Organized Baseball, for each team was allowed four professional players on their roster. Freddy Moncewicz, a Boston College graduate who played briefly for the Boston Red Sox in 1928, played in the Cape Cod League every year from 1926 through 1934.

Though some sources claim Danny McClellan died in 1931, the New York and Boston newspapers reported him alive and well, and he and Burlin White—who toured with Syd Pollack's Cuban Stars in 1933—had parted ways. By the middle of the decade McClellan was residing in Boston and operating the Philly Giants while White was running his own club, the Boston Royal Giants. Jackman jumped back and forth between both. Additionally in 1933 and 1934 he played for the Waltham Town Team in the Boston Twilight League, a circuit that fielded some teams with as many as five players with big league experience. The Waltham paper referred to Jackman as "the greatest colored pitcher in the universe and a certain major league star but for his racial handicap."[21] His agreement with Waltham allowed him time for barnstorming trips to northern New England and the Canadian Maritime Provinces with White and McClellan. White's Giants ranged as far as Ohio in 1934—where they showed up with "a splendid record, having defeated the Homestead Grays, the Pittsburgh Crawfords and several other clubs of the

This photo is believed to be the 1929 Douglas, MA, team of the Blackstone Valley League. Jackman is standing in the back, fourth uniformed player from the left. The player to the right of Jackman is believed to be Hank Greenberg.

National Colored league,"[22]—and Winnipeg, Manitoba, Canada in 1936.

Jackman started off 1935 with White's Giants, but in May he joined the Brooklyn Eagles for his only full season in the Negro Leagues, and though not named to the East-West All-Star game, he did very well in the fan-based voting. "Big Bill Jackman," wrote the *New York Amsterdam News* on July 6,

> …who has figured so prominently in past Eagle successes, was pretty much the hero of the series. On Saturday Jack put down the Giants 6-3, with six hits. He was idle Sunday; but on Monday returned to save the occasion with a splendid relief performance.

Only four Jackman games have been recovered from 1937, and all were played in Hartford, CT, where he dropped three games to Schoolboy Johnny Taylor before shutting out the New York Black Yankees on three hits.

The first duel with Taylor on May 9 was a corker, a 5-4 contest that went 20 innings. Jackman later recalled that he just joined the Philly Giants after wintering in Texas and pitched the entire contest sans spring training. He allowed 15 hits and fanned 10 while Taylor struck out 22. Taylor told the *Boston Chronicle* in 1938 that he considered this his greatest game, more satisfying

than the no-hitter he tossed against Satchel Paige in the Polo Grounds.

"Burlin White, with Big Bill Jackman, form some sort of a legendary greatness in New England baseball history,"[23] wrote Boston's leading African American sportswriter Mabe Kountze early in 1938. White had worked all that season with Boston Braves president Bob Quinn, planning to bring the Homestead Grays to play the Boston Royal Giants in Braves Field. The Grays never made it, so the Jackman-White battery had to settle for a 4-3 victory over the House of David on July 6 in what was the first incidence of an African American team performing in a then current Boston major league stadium. "I've never seen a ball jump away from a batter as Jackman's pitches were that historic afternoon here in Boston's senior major league park…," recalled Kountze a few years after the fact, "…for this was the same Jackman that…Cuban Johnny Taylor…acclaimed as being smarter than Paige."[24]

1939 saw Jackman compile a 14-1 record while pitching on Sundays for the Portsmouth City team in New Hampshire. Ten times he reached double-digit strikeout totals, including a two-hit shutout with 15 strikeouts and then a 16-K performance against a Cape Cod League all-star squad comprised of players from

Villanova, Boston University, Boston College, and Holy Cross. In September, Jackman faced the Lynn Frasers, a team that claimed two national amateur titles.[25] "The visitors were powerless before the offerings of the sensational 'Cannonball' Jackman," wrote the *Portsmouth Herald*. "Thirteen batters went down swinging before his tricky underhand pitches." Following the Frasers were the champions of the Boston Park League. "It was the veteran Jackman who personally accounted for the deflation of Dick Casey's New England title aspirations. His sweeping underhand curves completely checked whatever batting prowess the Caseys had." Finally it was a 2-1, 10-inning, 13-strikeout performance against the Cordage Park team of Plymouth, MA, on October 7 that gave Portsmouth the bragging rights for the New England semi-pro title. "I'd like to have seen him pitch when he was 29," said the *Herald*'s baseball writer of Jackman, comparing him to the National League champs. "He probably had more oomph on the ball than the whole Cincinnati pitching staff."

The 1940s and Beyond – With baseball's color line a frequent topic of both the white and black New England presses at the turn of the decade, the Lynn Frasers—who drew impressive crowds as soon as they began booking top Negro League teams in Massachusetts in the 1930s— dropped a 10-3 contest on July 16, 1940, to the Homestead Grays in front of 8,000 fans in their new stadium—Fraser Field.[26]

Bad weather and poor publicity were blamed for the small crowd that attended the Philadelphia Stars' defeat of the Baltimore Elite Giants on September 8, 1942, in the first game played between Negro League teams at Fenway Park. The Boston black media praised the Red Sox management, especially Eddie Collins, for "cooperating 100%" with promoter Fats Johnson.

Former American League first baseman Jack Burns—who first faced Jackman in the 1920s—used his influence to arrange four games between his Fore River Shipyard nine and visiting Negro League teams at Fenway Park in 1943. Fore River defeated the New York Black Yankees and the Cuban All-Stars, played the Birmingham Black Barons to a draw, and lost to the Kansas City Monarchs. The *New York Amsterdam News,* opining that the Negro League teams had to play their best at every opportunity versus white teams to further the desegregation cause, referred to this series as embarrassing and chastised the players for letting a team of "old, broken-down and refused material of the majors" beat them. The Fore River team, which had at least five former big leaguers on its roster, was exactly the type of aggregation of players that Bill Jackman had been dominating in New England for 20 years.

Reporting on Jackman's first recovered game of the decade—a one-hitter with 16 strikeouts while pitching for White's Philly Giants in New Bedford on June 4, 1940—the local paper said,

Jackman and White are the greatest Negro battery in baseball history. You can talk about your big time heroes but if Jackman and White ever were able to get into the majors, there is little question but what we'd have another pair of nationally famous diamond greats."

Early in 1940 the Plymouth, MA, *Old Colony Memorial* wrote,

The return of the Philadelphia Colored Giants to New England baseball circuits this year, after a lapse of three years, has got baseball managers all over the states quite a bit anxious for a booking because they have heard that Will Jackman and Burlin White have kissed and made up…the Jackman & White combination is still powerful enough to pack baseball diamonds in New England.

The rift between the pair was not serious. It was just that Jackman had a better payday in Portsmouth, NH, where he went 16-0 pitching on Sundays in 1940 (18-1 recovered overall), and his victory over the Lynn Frasers on October 6 gave Portsmouth a second consecutive New England semi-pro title. Bill's center fielder in that game was Eddie Waitkus, and the Frasers had former Red Sox player Skinny Graham in their outfield and Stan Andrews of the Boston Braves behind the plate.

Jackman and White were together on the Boston Night Hawks in 1941 when Bill recorded an 18-strikeout performance. "There are two great baseball attractions for colored baseball in New England," wrote the *Boston Chronicle* that summer. "The Boston Night Hawks, who are burning up the diamond with their sensational playing, and the greatest pitcher in Negro baseball, Dixie Jackman."[27]

Bill's recovered record for 1942 currently stands at 10-1, and he averaged 16.5 strikeouts per game in the eight contests he and White worked as the Sunday battery for a team near Taunton, MA. Former SABR member and Taunton native Hank Martyniak, who pitched in the Boston Braves chain in 1946 and 1947, opposed Jackman in one of those games. As a youngster Martyniak had idolized Bill, and pitching against him—Jackman won with a one-hitter—was one of his "proudest moments."

Retired US Air Force colonel John Corbisiero, now 79 years old and living in San Antonio, TX, was a catcher in the Pony League in 1950. His professional experience came following his graduation from Middlebury College and before the Korean War, when he embarked on his military career. In 1944 he had the opportunity to play briefly, and catch Jackman, for the Watertown Arsenal team, a nearly all-black squad in the Boston Park League. "He was easy to catch because he had such great control," John emailed in the summer of 2006.

> I was amazed at how tall, lean, and very muscular this man was in his late forties. It makes me feel good that at one time during the life of two of the greatest baseball players of our time, I was chosen to step in for Burlie White as a catcher for the great Cannonball Jackman.

Pitcher Allyn Stout won 160 professional baseball games in his career, including 20 in the major leagues, where he last appeared for the Boston Braves in 1943. The *Lynn Item,* after Jackman and the Boston Giants defeated Stout and the Lynn Frasers on July 9, 1944, wrote, "Old Pa Time has been reaching for Jackman for a long time, but the 46-year old pitcher with the underhand magic is not yet ready to enter the portals of Hasbeenville from which there is no return."

On July 17, 1944, Jackman, White, and the visiting Boston Giants defeated the Brooklyn Bushwicks by a 3-1 score in front of 10,000 fans. Yet in Boston on August 24 only a small crowd was on hand to watch Boston's Mayor Maurice Tobin make the presentations on "Will Jackman Day" at Fenway Park. Following the game, which Bill dropped to Pat Scantlebury and the Cuban All-Stars, William "Sheep" Jackson, the *Chronicle*'s sports editor, wrote, "It was a sad gathering….it was to be Will Jackman day…a player whose hurling has thrilled thousands in this section for the past 20 years. It was to be a tribute to Will and the colored fans were to honor this great pitcher—one of their own. But alas, Ole Joe and his friends stayed at home." Jackson went on to argue that this lack of support by Boston's black fans for black players was noticed by the "few baseball men" who had been trying to do something about it.

Jackman finished up 1944 with six late-season victories for the Windsor, VT, Conomatics. He fanned 15 in a two-hit shutout on October 1 for the "Twin-State Semi-Pro championship," and in a 2-1 loss to Jeff Tesreau's Dartmouth Indians struck out 18.

After winning in front of 11,500 fans in Yankee Stadium in August 1945—allowing just an infield single over the first seven innings—the *Chicago Defender* wrote "Bill Jackman, a white-haired submarine ball specialist, turned in a three-hit shutout versus Miami. He struck out ten batters and aided his own cause by accounting for five runs, with four hits in five trips to the plate."[28]

Jackman always displayed long-ball ability, and nearly 40 of his home runs have been recovered. Fore River field in Quincy, MA—built in 1916—was the site of one of Bill's longest home runs, reputed to be the first ball ever hit over the left-field fence. "What big leaguers during the war period failed to do," wrote the *Quincy Patriot Ledger* in 1926, "the mighty Jackman did with the admirable air of one who is utterly at ease in his chosen element."[29] In 1927, he hit a walk-off grand slam against the Town Talk team of Worcester. A late-season 1928 blast in Brockton earned him "one of the greatest ovations given a ballplayer in this city." His July 1929 home run at Ridge Hill Grove was described as "one of the longest hits seen at the field in many a day." When he beat the Reading team of the Boston Twilight League at the end of the same month, "Jackman put the ball over the bushes in center for a home run, a very long hit." His two 1929 Labor Day blasts in Plymouth were called "two of the longest home runs seen on the local field for some time." Though still unsubstantiated, old-timers claim that in 1946 when the Giants used both Fenway Park and Braves Field for their home games, Bill hit a ball off the wall above the Fenway triangle seats in center field. In 1950, the *Portsmouth Herald* wrote of Jackman, "In an appearance here last summer he wasn't

Jackman with a Boston police officer, circa 1945-1950.

Sunset Stars on weekends in 1946. In mid-week he commuted to New York, where he pitched for the Brooklyn Bushwicks, and his specialty was facing Negro League teams. Having already claimed victories over the Homestead Grays and the New York Black Yankees that season, Nahem—despite fanning 22 batters—dropped a 3-2 contest to the Boston Giants in extra innings on June 12. Jackman, working five shutout relief innings, was the winner. The Newport players were stunned by Jackman, who had perfected an underhand knuckleball, and the game was talked about in Newport for decades. "The fans demanded a rematch," went a 1971 *Newport Daily News* recollection. "They figured that it was an accident for a pitcher with 22 strikeouts to lose a game. The game was arranged with a guarantee that the aged Jackman pitch the distance if he were able to last."[32] The rematch came on July 17, and Nahem fanned 13 but lost to Jackman's three-hit shutout. The *Newport News* described their batters as "baffled" and "toyed with" by Jackman.

Though little documentation has yet been recovered for the last few years of his career, Jackman stated that he continued to tour through the 1953 season. In 1947 over 5,000 fans turned out in Taunton for "Jackman and White Night." The pair were presented with inscribed silver trays by Mayor John Parker, who in 1971 as the Massachusetts senate minority leader was the driving force behind the Commonwealth's presentation of a Golden Dome Citation to "Will 'Cannonball' Jackman—One of America's Greatest Baseball Players."

The Portland, ME, *Press Herald,* in 1947, after the breaking of baseball's color line, opined that they would not be surprised to see Jackman pop up in a big league uniform. "Jackman, fans will recall has been pitching for more than 30 years, part of the time in the Negro National League but generally for touring teams. He is a big rangy ageless underhand flinger regarded by big leaguers who have faced him and scouts who saw him

too decrepit to hobble to the plate and smash a long home run just to show the youngsters a thing or two." In describing a 450-foot home run hit by a New Hampshire high school lad in 1957, the same paper commented that the distance was "as far as many of the blasts spanked by Cannonball Jackman."[30]

"Despite their great age," commented the *Taunton Gazette* on Jackman and White in 1948, "these two timeless baseball stars are still the greatest drawing cards in New England." Following a 1946 Boston Giants game in Taunton, the *Gazette*'s headline was "106-Year-Old Battery Stops Twi League All-Stars." Bill wasn't due to pitch but the fans demanded it, and Jackman responded with, "Taunton has always been good to us, and today we'll give them all we've got." The crowd wasn't disappointed, for "Jackman certainly lived up to his reputation. The 54-year-old pitching marvel struck out 12 hitters, including the last batter, after he had called in his outfielders."[31]

Newport, RI—where Jackman first performed in 1926—also saw some dazzling work from the hurler in the post-war era. Sam Nahem, in between major league stops, had played for a military team in Newport, where his pitching had turned him into such a favorite that he declined professional offers to pitch for the Newport

Jackman with Boston's mayor Kevin White, July 1971.

work in his prime, as one of the greatest pitchers of all time."[33]

Just prior to a 1951 complete-game effort in Taunton, the *Gazette* said, "Jackman and White are two of the finest athletes and gentlemen baseball fans have ever known," and opined that had there not been a color line, "Jackman would no doubt have become one of the greatest pitchers in the history of baseball."[34]

Shortly after the end of the Second World War, Jackman took a job as a chauffeur for the Chick family of Dedham, MA, and remained in their employ for nearly 20 years. His name appeared frequently in the Boston sports pages. In March 1967 the *Boston Globe* began a column on Jackman with "One of the greatest pitchers of all time…"[35] and in September of the same year the *Globe*—with an intriguing placement under a photo of Bob Gibson—announced that Bill would be pitching in an old-timers game.[36]

In failing health by the early 1970s, Jackman lost both his wife of 40 years and his friend Burlin White in 1971. Sensing the decline, his many friends, former teammates and fans rallied around him. The Friends of Will Jackman Committee, in close coordination with the office of Boston's Mayor Kevin White, the Boston Red Sox, and his former employer and greatest booster,

Eleanor Chick, announced that Will Jackman Day would be held on July 14, 1971, at the Carter Playground.

The accolades quickly followed.

"Will Jackman was one of baseball's great pitchers; also, a powerful hitter…" wrote Roy Mumpton, the sports editor of the *Worcester Evening Telegram*, about the hurler and his teams.

> They played in practically every city and town in New England which had a ball park—out at the New England Fair Grounds, in Prospect Park at Auburn, and against the Nortons, the American Steel & Wire and Town Talk, the powerhouses of the once fast Worcester Industrial League.[37]

The *Dedham Transcript* said, "The very sound of the name…brings immediate recollection of Jackman's achievements on the mound for the touring Philadelphia Colored Giants."[38]

Bob Finnigan of the *Quincy Patriot Ledger,* begrudging baseball's color line, wrote, "The legacy that William Jackman left baseball is held now only in the memories of those that saw him play the game."[39]

The *Wakefield Daily Item* noted, "It's a long-time in coming—an all-out public honoring of one of the all-time greats in baseball…"[40]

Art Ballou of the *Boston Globe* said,

> Some experts rate Jackman with Satchel Paige, which is saying a lot, but in his heyday it was accepted by all and sundry that Jackman was far superior to his white counterparts on the sandlots. And, he was eminently successful in barnstorming games against major leaguers."[41]

Joe Fitzgerald of the *Boston Herald* interviewed Jackman. "I didn't care who came to bat," Bill told him. "I had no fear. I beat every man I pitched against at least once. I went against Paige twice, and we split. I had good stuff, but when I could have helped a major league team, none wanted me."[42]

Three-thousand fans showed up for Bill's night. Old friend Judy Johnson, accompanied by his wife and Mrs. Bill Yancey, made the trip from Philadelphia. Among the former major league players and Boston Red Sox officials in attendance were Neil Mahoney, Jack Burns, Sam Mele, Frank Malzone, Dick Donovan, Ted Lepcio, and Tom Dowd. Tom Yawkey's publicity director, Bill Crowley, presented Jackman with a lifetime pass to

Fenway Park. Several Boston Celtics players were also on hand, and additional photos from the period provided by the Chick family show Jackman with Dom DiMaggio, longtime Red Sox radio announcer Ken Coleman, and Red Sox manager Eddie Kasko.

Jackman died suddenly in Marion, MA, on September 8, 1972 while visiting friends. In addition to the Boston and local New England papers, his passing received notice in *The Sporting News* and the *Washington Post*.

"Jackman was a black man, and was born too soon to enjoy the break in the 'color line' brought about by Jackie Robinson and the late Branch Rickey," read the posthumous tribute to Bill on the editorial page of the Portsmouth, NH, paper.

However, there are many Portsmouth sports fans who will argue that Jackman at his best was even better than the legendary 'Satch' Paige.

Folks in Portsmouth swear Jackman would have been a great major league pitcher and they were probably right. His only problem was that he was born too soon.[43] ∎

Notes

1. *Milford Daily News*, September 16, 1929.
2. *Worcester Daily Telegram*, September 16, 1929.
3. *Woonsocket Call*, September 25, 1929.
4. *Portsmouth Herald*, August 19, 1938
5. *Philadelphia Tribune*, June 16, 1927.
6. *Chicago Defender*, October 20, 1928.
7. Ibid, May 3, 1930.
8. Ibid, May 17, 1942.
9. *Lowell Sun*, July 22, 1932.
10. *Philadelphia Tribune*, January 29, 1927.
11. *The Chicago Defender*, on February 28, 1925, lists "Jackman" on the Lincoln Giants' spring roster. This project has not found any documentation that he actually pitched for them.
12. John Holway. *Voices from the Great Black Baseball Leagues*. New York: Dodd, Mead, 1975.
13. *Boston Evening Globe*, July 6, 1971.
14. *Philadelphia Tribune*, July 14, 1927.
15. *New Bedford Mercury*, August 9, 1928.
16. *New Bedford Standard*, August 10, 1928.
17. *Philadelphia Tribune*, March 19, 1931.
18. *Waltham News-Tribune*, May 15, 1930.
19. Brennan did not debut in the majors until 1933. In 1931 and 1932 he won 15 and 26 games for the New York Yankees' Newark farm club.
20. *New Bedford Evening Standard*, August 13, 1931.
21. *Waltham News-Tribune*, July 17, 1933.
22. *Mansfield News-Journal*, July 14, 1934.
23. *Boston Chronicle*, March 12, 1938.
24. Ibid, August 17, 1940.
25. Based on 1934 and 1937 tournaments in Springfield, MA and Louisville, KY.
26. Alan E. Foulds. *Boston's Ballparks & Arenas*. Boston: Northeastern University Press, 2005.
27. *Boston Chronicle*, July 26, 1941.
28. *Chicago Defender*, August 11, 1945.
29. *Quincy Patriot Ledger*, June 1, 1926.
30. *Portsmouth Herald*, June 17, 1957.
31. *Taunton Gazette*, July 29, 1946.
32. *Newport Daily News*, July 14, 1971.
33. *Portland Press Herald*, July 18, 1947.
34. *Taunton Gazette*, June 2, 1951.
35. *Boston Globe*, March 5, 1967.
36. Ibid, September 8, 1967.
37. *Worcester Evening Telegram*, July 14, 1971.
38. *Dedham Transcript*, June 24, 1971.
39. *Quincy Patriot Ledger*, July 2, 1971.
40. *Wakefield Daily Item*, July 13, 1971.
41. *Boston Globe*, July 13, 1971.
42. *Boston Herald*, July 11, 1971.
43. *Portsmouth Herald*, September 15, 1972.

Acknowledgments

Dick Thompson would like to thank the following individuals for assistance with this article. Gary Ashwill, Bijan Bayne, Charlie Bevis, Rich Bozzone, Peter Chick, Dick Clark, Jim Collyer, Robert Cvornyek, Rick Durkee, Alan Foulds, Frank Geishecker, Rick Harris, John Holway, Kerry Keene, Ted Knorr, Neil Lanctot, Doug Malan, Ray Nemec, Bob Richardson, John Russell, Glenn Stout, Dixie Tourangeau, Brian Walsh of the Dartmouth Public Library and Barbara Rhoad of the Windsor, VT, Historical Society.

Emmett Ashford

Entertainer and Pioneer

by Mark Armour

He spent 20 years as a professional umpire, baseball's loneliest profession, passing judgment on the performances of the game's great athletes and egos. Many people have pursued this particular job, but Emmett Ashford had the added burden of breaking racial barriers throughout his career, as a black man whose job required maintaining authority over white men. Doing his work with disarming charm, quick wit, and irreproachable dignity, he won over fans, players, and even his fellow umpires, leaving the game with countless friends and admirers.

Emmett Littleton Ashford was born on November 23, 1914, in Los Angeles. His father Littleton, a policeman, soon abandoned the family, and Emmett and brother Wilbur were raised by their mother. Adele was a highly motivated and ambitious woman who worked as a secretary for the *California Eagle,* a black newspaper. Ashford himself earned money selling *Liberty* magazine, building his route up to 300 customers, and later was a cashier in a supermarket.

Ashford excelled at Jefferson High School, rising to co-editor of the school paper, the *Jeffersonian,* and becoming a teen journalist for the *California Eagle.* He also played baseball and ran sprints for the track team. When he graduated in 1933, he was the senior class president, the first black student so honored, and a member of the scholarship club. Ashford then attended Los Angeles Junior College and Chapman College, where he played baseball.

About 1936, Ashford scored well on a civil service exam and landed a coveted job as a clerk with the post office, a position he held for 15 years. In the late 1930s he had a brief career as a semi-pro baseball player before turning to officiating. According to Ashford, he played on a white team called the Mystery Nine, who wore uniforms with question marks on the fronts. One day the umpire didn't show up, and Emmett (who rarely played) was called into emergency service. He was soon busy officiating recreational baseball and softball in Southern California.

In 1937, Ashford married Willa Gene Fort, and the couple had two daughters, Adrienne and Antoinette. The next several years were taken up with family, post office work, and umpiring. Soon after he finished a three-year stint in the United States Navy during World War II, Emmett and Willa divorced. He continued to umpire, moving up to major college baseball, working regularly. He often officiated with Bill Stewart, who had umped in the American League in the 1940s. Ashford credited Stewart for teaching him the major league strike zone.

In 1951, Ashford took a leave of absence from his post office job for a two-month trial in the Southwestern International League, becoming the first black umpire in Organized Baseball. Les Powers, the league president, claimed, "Ashford has the making of a big league umpire." After the season, Ashford was offered a full-season job, so he resigned from the postal service, leaving behind 15 years of pension. "For some people, it might have been a hard decision—giving up assured future security for the uncertainty of umpiring," he later related. "But not for me."

The following offseason, the Southwestern International League announced plans to field an "all-Negro" club, to play only road games. Ashford was named general manager and asked to put together a team. Two days later Chet Brewer, former Negro League star, was

MARK ARMOUR *should be busy researching the life of Joe Cronin, but he keeps getting sidetracked by all of the fascinating people that came into Cronin's life during his 50 years in the game. Emmett Ashford was one.*

hired as the club's manager. Ultimately the team had a series of "homes" during the season, including Ensenada, Mexico; Riverside, CA; and Porterville, CA. The team did not remain all-black, though many former Negro Leaguers did play for them (including Brewer), as did two future major leaguers (Tom Alston and Dave Roberts).

As for Ashford, he relinquished his role with the club before the season began, and returned to umpiring. By midsummer the league folded, and he hooked on with the Arizona-Texas League. In December 1952, *The Sporting News* first suggested that Ashford might be destined for the major leagues. Ashford responded to the story, pledging to "do all in my power to justify your faith." He moved up to the Western International League in 1953 before a promotion to the Pacific Coast League in 1954.

During his 12 years in the PCL, Ashford became the best-known umpire in the minor leagues. Ashford was a showman, a loud, and energetic presence to whom the crowd paid close attention. Between innings he often sprinted down the right-field line to keep his legs loose. He constantly interacted with the crowd, doffing his cap and giving little speeches.

Ashford spent most of his time during the season alone, not hanging out with his fellow umpires. As he later related to Larry Gerlach,

> I didn't come to town and have to go to the ghetto to enjoy myself. I stayed downtown and went to the theater and the opera. I just love some opera—know the librettos of a few. I made a host of friends; many of them were attorneys and doctors who invited me to their homes and nice functions. I'd meet with the lawyers for lunch in Spokane, and, shoot, in Vancouver, I think I could have run for office.

In the offseasons, Ashford refereed Pac-8 basketball and small college football. As early as the fall of 1958 he umpired in the Carribean winter leagues. He was also a constant after-dinner speaker on the West Coast, and ran several umpiring clinics.

In 1963, PCL president Dewey Soriano named Ashford the league's umpire-in-chief, making him responsible for the organization and training of the crews, and for advising the league on disputed games or rules. In June 1963, the league hired its second black umpire, Osibee Jelks, from the Northwest League. On July 4, a game in San Diego was officiated by Ashford and Jelks (the third crew member was ill), the first all-black umpiring crew in a minor league game.

By the early 1960s, writers on the West Coast began clamoring for Ashford's promotion to the majors. A.S. Young also took up the cause in the *Chicago Defender* (March 28, 1963), suggesting of major league presidents Joe Cronin and Warren Giles, "Whereas they hire, and approve the hiring of Caucasian umpires solely on the basis of qualifications, they refuse to act on the Ashford case—and probably won't until the Ashford campaign, which should be unnecessary, becomes embarrassing." In 1965 Cronin was considered the leading contender to replace the retiring Ford Frick as baseball's commissioner, but Jim Murray, writing in the *Los Angeles Times* (July 2, 1965), supported Bill Veeck for the top job, with Ashford as his umpire-in-chief. Both endorsements were due to Cronin's foot dragging on Ashford.

Ashford's most famous on-field incident took place during the 1964 playoffs in the Dominican Republic. After

Ashford at the pinnacle of his sport, umpiring at Yankee Stadium.

a strike call on Julian Javier met with prolonged disapproval, Ashford motioned the pitcher to continue, and rung up strike three. Javier reacted by slugging Ashford in the mouth, cutting the umpire's lip open and swelling his jaw. Ashford retaliated by hitting the Cardinal infielder with his mask, temporarily forgetting that Javier was a local hero. Ashford finished the game, applying ice packs to his mouth between innings. Javier received a three-game suspension, and Ashford had to be talked out of resigning from the league after the weak penalty.

Despite whatever frustrations he must have felt in the minor leagues for 15 years, he remained a cheerful and optimistic man his entire life, a disposition which stood out in his profession. He charmed his critics and admirers alike, relying on his quick wit and intelligence to get him through a crisis. In one Southwest city early in his career Ashford needed to find a place a black man could sleep. He went to the best hotel in town and approached the desk. "Sir," he explained, "I am that barefoot, uncultured Negro man you have been reading about, and I wish to seek lodging in your excellent establishment." He got the room, and his charm would get him many other rooms and many meals in restaurants.

In mid-September 1965, he got a long-awaited phone call. The voice on the telephone was Dewey Soriano, telling Ashford that he had sold his contract to the American League. "It was the last thing I remember for several days," recalled Emmett. He always spoke fondly of Soriano's support throughout his years in the PCL, and for helping him get to the majors.

The nation's press was thrilled, though not willing to give baseball too much credit for its tardy step. Melvin Durslag, writing in the *Los Angeles Herald-Examiner* (October 2, 1965), figured that Emmett was "bound to raise the game to his refined level." Bill Slocum, in the *New York Journal-American* (April 14, 1966) wondered, "If corporate Baseball has joined the 20th Century, can Mississippi be far behind?"

After his protégé's promotion, Soriano claimed, "The only reason Emmett hasn't made the major leagues before this is that he is a Negro." Soriano later elaborated: "Emmett was very popular wherever he went, with the players and the fans. I've known him since 1953 and it is an all-out total effort—not showboating. With more Emmett Ashfords, baseball games would be better run and a lot more fun for the fans. I didn't make him umpire-in-chief his last three years out here for comedy."

Ashford had a high-pitched voice that he utilized like a megaphone, keeping the fans aware of where he was and what he was doing. During his first spring training in the majors he interrupted an Angels-Indians game in Tucson to explain to the crowd a recent discussion with the Indians manager. Removing his cap, he bowed to the throng behind home, loudly intoning, "Ladies and gentleman...Mr. Tebbetts was merely questioning the strategy of the opposing manager...I thank you." Putting his mask back on, he resumed the game. His fellow umpires soon realized what they were up against. The next day, Bill Valentine turned to the crowd himself: "Ladies and gentlemen, I'm sorry to inform you that the eminent Emmett Ashford will be at third base and not behind the plate today."

Prior to his first season, Ashford reflected, "I feel proud being an umpire in the big leagues. Not because I am the first Negro, but because umpires in the major leagues are very select people. Right now, I just want to vindicate Mr. Cronin's faith in me.... But first, I've got to buy me a pair of eye glasses," he added, his sense of humor ever present, ready to strike.

Emmett Ashford's regular season debut took place on April 9, 1966, in Washington's D.C. Stadium, the traditional American League opener. His first major league hurdle was getting into the ballpark.

Ashford umpiring in the PCL, 1955.

Vice President Hubert Humphrey was in attendance to throw out the ceremonial first ball, and the Secret Service needed to be convinced that a black man was there to umpire the game. Humphrey later kidded Ashford, who had worked at third base, that he hadn't had any plays to call. "No plays, no boots," responded Ashford, "but it was the greatest day of my life." Joe Cronin told his new employee, "Emmett, you made history today. I'm proud of you."

Ashford was a sensation right away, but not principally because of his race. His style, well-known on the West Coast, took the conservative major leagues by storm. The stocky (5' 7", 185 pounds) Ashford sprinted to his position between innings, stepping on the bases or leaping the pitcher's mound, and raced around the field after foul balls or plays on the bases. *The Sporting News* was impressed enough to claim, "For the first time in the history of the grand old American game, baseball fans may buy a ticket to watch an umpire perform." The fans did not always need to watch Ashford; they could just listen to his high-pitched cannon of a voice as he called out a batter or runner.

On a strike call, Ashford jerked his right arm first to the side, then up, then down like a karate chop. That completed, he would then reach either up as if twice yanking a train whistle, or to the right as if opening a car door. Even while dusting the plate he knew every eye in the house was on him, and he behaved accordingly, pirouetting on one foot and hopping back to his position. Emmett would say, "I didn't go to umpiring school because they weren't taking blacks in those days, so I evolved my own style." Ashford was also known for his natty attire on and off the field. While umpiring he wore polished shoes, a freshly pressed uniform, cuff links, and a handkerchief in his suit pocket.

In his first game behind the plate, Andy Etchebarren, the Orioles catcher, recalled diving into the stands after a foul ball:

> I knew I couldn't reach the ball, but I dove into the seats thinking a fan would put the ball in my glove or I could grab it off the floor. But while I was reaching I looked around, and who was in the seats with me but Emmett. I couldn't believe it.

In a later Baltimore game, Frank Robinson quipped, "That Ashford gets a better jump on the ball than Paul Blair [the Orioles' fleet-footed center fielder]."

Though he was generally well-liked and admired by the people in the game, the open question was always whether he was a good umpire—whether his style came at the expense of substance. His flamboyance certainly left him open for abuse, as he was generally the center of attention even when everyone agreed with his calls. Red Sox manager Dick Williams, after a controversial Ashford call in 1969, called the arbiter "a little clown." Joe Pepitone and Pete Ward, in separate incidents, had to be restrained from going after Ashford. "When he calls you out on a third strike," complained one player after a typically emotive Ashford punch-out, "you feel like he's sending you to the electric chair."

Ashford toned down some of his mannerisms as his big league career progressed. "Sure, I was a showboat," he told the *Boston Globe*'s Ray Fitzgerald (August 16, 1970). "For 12 years, that was my routine in the Coast League. I couldn't change overnight, but I'm different now. I've toned myself way down." But still, "I'm not exactly without color," he said, using a favorite double entendre.

In 1967, Ashford was named to work the All-Star game in Anaheim, though he saw little action working the left-field foul line. Ashford realized another dream in 1970 when he umpired the World Series. Unfortunately for Ashford, and for baseball fans, he was slated to work the plate in the sixth game, but his turn never came: the Orioles beat the Reds in five. "Maybe it's best," he said later, "The World Series would never be the same."

When Ashford turned 55 in December 1969, he had reached the American League's retirement age for its umpires, a rule occasionally bent. He was given one additional year, but after the 1970 season Ashford announced his retirement. "I'm afraid that by continuing I would only dilute the thrills of the last five years and especially those I received by umpiring in the 1970 World Series," Ashford said.

An unwritten baseball credo suggests that a well-officiated game is one in which the umpire is unnoticed. By that standard Emmett Ashford was not a good umpire. Not surprisingly, his fellow umpires were the hardest people to win over.

Bill Kinnamon worked on the same crew with Ashford in 1969, and later recalled to Larry Gerlach,

> I think he was a good umpire. On the bases and behind the plate he was no better or worse than the rest of us, but it is no secret that his eyes weren't too good when it came to balls hit into the outfield at night. The man was about 50 years old when he came into the league, and I think Emmett would be the first to say that he came up after the peak of his career. If he had come up 10, 15, 20 years earlier, he would have been one hell of an umpire.

Speaking of Ashford's impact on the game, Kinnamon said,

> He was good for baseball. I never saw him do anything detrimental to baseball. No one ever found any fault with his deportment off the field. He was a gentleman. And the people absolutely dearly loved him. One night, as we were leaving Yankee Stadium together, some kid all of a sudden yelled, "Emmett!" The next next thing I knew, he was standing there talking and signing autographs for a couple of hundred kids. Nobody recognized me; I just sat there on a railing and waited. He signed an autograph for every last kid. That's the kind of man he was, and that's the kind of feeling there was for him.

As Ashford often said, he did not go through the traditional umpire training, and therefore that particular doctrine was not instilled. Kinnamon further explains some of the tension:

> There was resentment toward him among the umpires. Everybody knows there was. Emmett knew it, but he shrugged it off. Many guys simply didn't accept Emmett. Politics or pull had nothing to do with it. Some questioned his umpiring ability. And Emmett had his idiosyncrasies—the cuff links, jumping over the mound on his way to second base, his showmanship, things like that. But mostly I think it was the publicity Emmett got. It's natural for there to be resentment when there were five reporters around Emmett's cubicle and none around anybody else's. Everywhere Emmett went he was news, good copy. Emmett got more ink in one year than the top five umpires in our league got in their whole career.

It probably didn't help when teams would ask the league for Ashford to umpire their games. In 1968, Athletics owner Charlie Finley wanted Ashford to umpire his home opener—the inaugural game at the new Oakland Coliseum. Umpire crews generally rotate their roles from game to game—from third base, to second, first, and home. For this game Ashford was due to ump second base, but at Finley's urging he got the more visible home plate assignment.

In early 1971, Ashford was hired by Commissioner Bowie Kuhn as a public relations adviser, a role which allowed him to speak and hold clinics on the West Coast, and as far away as Korea. He also umpired the occasional minor league or college game, old-timers games in Dodger Stadium, pleasing the crowd as always. He was umpire-in-chief for the Alaskan summer league for three years. Ashford earned money doing TV commercials (he played a cashier in an ad for the A&P grocery chain), film (as an umpire in *The Bingo Long Traveling All-Stars & Motor Kings*) and television (episodes of *Ironside* and *The Jacksons*). He was also on *What's My Line* during his first year in the major leagues.

Ashford died at Marina Mercy Hospital in Marina Del Ray, CA, on March 1, 1980, of a heart attack. At his funeral, he was eulogized by Commissioner Kuhn and Rod Dedeaux, longtime USC baseball coach. He was cremated, and his ashes are interred in Cooperstown, NY.

In looking back on his career, the ever positive Ashford focused on his good fortune: "Think of all the people who live an entire life and do not accomplish one thing they really wanted to do. I have done something I wanted to do. I have that satisfaction." This is only fitting, as Ashford's class and style provided so much satisfaction to others. ∎

Sources

In researching this article, I made use of Ashford's extensive clipping file at the National Baseball Library and articles published in the *The Sporting News* throughout his career. (Detailed citations are available upon request.) Larry Gerlach's *The Men In Blue* (Viking, 1980) includes interviews with Ashford and several of his contemporaries. Robert C. Hoie's article in the 1979 *Baseball Research Journal* ("Riverside-Ensenada-Porterville, An All-Negro Minor League Team") outlines Ashford's affiliation with the 1952 club. Ashford's daughter, Adrienne Cherie Ashford wrote a short book *Strrr-ike!!,* which outlines his early life. Bob Sudyk's article in *The Sporting News* ("Emmett Ashford: Only His Suit Is Blue", April 23, 1966) provided the backdrop to Ashford's debut in the major leagues and his first game. *Retrosheet*'s ridiculously essential website includes detailed game logs for umpires.

An Unusual Record

Ted Wingfield's One Strikeout in 75 Innings in 1927

by Bob Bionaz

Pitching in relief in the final innings of a 12-2 loss to the Philadelphia Athletics on August 10, 1927, sore-armed Boston right hander "Ted" Wingfield notched the final strikeout of his major league career and the only strikeout he recorded in 74⅔ innings of pitching that season. Wingfield's one strikeout in 74⅔ innings, or .12 strikeouts per nine innings pitched, endures as the worst single-season strikeout per nine innings figure ever recorded in major league history (over 31 innings). In addition, Wingfield's career mark of 1.106 strikeouts per nine innings pitched stands as the worst career mark for any pitcher with more than 500 innings pitched. Although Wingfield had been the bellwether of the Boston staff for two seasons, an arm injury suffered before the 1927 season reduced his effectiveness. Unequaled in baseball history, Wingfield's single strikeout in nearly 75 innings is a mark that will likely stand forever and deserves to be ranked with baseball's "unbreakable" records.

Because records and numbers occupy such a prominent place in baseball lore, even casual fans are likely familiar with Henry Aaron's 755 home runs, Joe DiMaggio's 56-game hitting streak, the single-season home run records of Babe Ruth, Roger Maris, Mark McGwire, and Barry Bonds. Periodically, writers and fans muse about what baseball records might be "unbreakable." For example, in September 1995, *The Sporting News* published the top twenty "unbreakable" records chosen by fans. They included offensive records like Pete Rose's 4,256 hits, Hack Wilson's 190 RBIs in 1930, Babe Ruth's 457 total bases in 1921, Owen Wilson's 36 triples in 1912, and pitching milestones like Cy Young's 511 career victories and 751 complete games, Jack Chesbro's 41 victories in 1904, and Walter Johnson's 110 career shutouts.[1] The reason for *The Sporting News* survey? The pending eradication by Baltimore's Cal Ripken of one heretofore untouchable record, Lou Gehrig's 2,130 consecutive games, described by one *Sporting News* reader in 1978 as "incredible . . . it may well stand for all time."[2] In the 11 years since the fans chose their 20 top "unbreakable" records, one record on the list, George Sisler's 257 hits in 1920, has been eclipsed, by Seattle's Ichiro Suzuki in 2004.

The fall of two of baseball's most enduring offensive records in the last few years suggests that baseball fans should exercise caution when declaring a particular mark impervious to assault by modern players. Nevertheless, changes in the game since the modern era began in 1901 make some records—particularly pitching records—truly unapproachable. For example, Cy Young's career marks for victories, losses, innings pitched, games started, and complete games will never be threatened. Similarly, Jack Chesbro's 41 victories in 1904, Ed Walsh's 464 innings pitched in 1908, and Grover Cleveland Alexander's single-season shutout record of 16 in 1916 will likewise stand unless the major leagues return to the style of play prevalent between 1901 and 1919. To illustrate, in the past 20 seasons only one starter, Roger Clemens with 18 in 1987, has recorded more than 15 complete games, and no major league pitcher has pitched even 300 innings in a season since Steve Carlton in 1980. While Chesbro, Walsh, and Alexander enjoyed seasons unimaginable by today's standards, some of their contemporaries nearly matched them. Three other pitchers from the first decade of the 20th century exceeded 400

ROBERT BIONAZ *has been a SABR member since 1992. He grew up in the San Francisco Bay Area and is a long-suffering fan of the San Francisco Giants. He is an Associate Professor of History at Chicago State University.*

innings pitched in a season, with Joe McGinnity and Walsh turning in two separate years of 400-plus innings. Jack Coombs of the Philadelphia Athletics notched 13 shutouts in 1910 and Walter Johnson recorded 12 in 1913, while Ed Walsh won 40 games for the 1908 White Sox. Compared to the mediocre numbers posted by many of today's league-leading pitchers, these amazing pitching records from baseball's Deadball Era seem almost otherworldly.

The dawn of the 1920s ushered in an era of potent offense and few strikeouts. The 1920-29 seasons featured a .285 major league batting average, and 9.62 runs per game compared to the .254 mark and 7.89 runs per game posted by hitters between 1901 and 1919. Home runs increased to nearly 9,900 between 1920 and 1929, a better than 33 percent increase over the 7,381 home runs clouted by major league hitters between 1901 and 1919. Earned-run averages soared from 2.88 in the 1901-19 period to 4.03 in the 1920s. Along with increased scoring, batting, and earned-run averages came a drop in strike-outs: from 3.67 per nine innings in 1901-1919 to 2.91 per nine innings in 1920-29. In fact, batters in the 1920s struck out less frequently than hitters in any other modern decade. Not surprisingly, some of the lowest strikeout per nine-inning ratios were posted by pitchers during the era. Several 1920s hurlers who pitched more than 200 innings in a season finished with marks just above one strikeout per nine innings, and one, Ernie Wingard of the St. Louis Browns, actually fell below one strikeout per inning in two seasons, 1924 and 1925. Wingard's ratio of .950 strikeouts per nine innings in 1924 stands just above Slim Sallee's 1919 record of 24 strikeouts in 228 innings, or .949 strikeouts per nine innings. 1920s pitchers with more than 200 innings in a season who posted fewer than 1.5 strikeouts per nine innings were Cleveland's Sherry Smith with 1.24 in 1924 and 1.14 in 1925; Jack Russell of the Red Sox with 1.21 in 1928, Hal Carlson, pitching for the Phillies and Cubs in 1927, with 1.45 and Russell again with 1.47, in 1929. Between 1920 and 1929, no American League hurler fanned more than 194 hitters, and other than Dazzy Vance, who won seven consecutive strikeout crowns from 1922 to 1928, no National League pitcher recorded more than 173 strikeouts in a season. However, the anemic strikeout totals posted by pitchers in

Ted Wingfield

the 1920s hardly reflect ineffective pitching. Wingard won 13 games with a 3.51 ERA in 1924, Smith won 34 games for the Indians from 1924-26, Russell won 17 games combined for two last-place Red Sox teams in 1928-29, and Carlson copped 16 wins in 1927. Most notably, Slim Sallee, the single-season leader in strikeout futility, won 21 games for the world champion Cincinnati Reds in 1919, posting a 2.06 ERA.

In common with his contemporaries, Wingfield's below-average strikeout totals do not reflect his pitching prowess. In fact, his major league record stamps him as an average major league pitcher. His earned-run average of 4.18 compares favorably to the American League's mark of 4.15 from 1923 to 1927. Similarly, his marks for hits per nine innings and batting average allowed are both within three percent of league averages for his five-year career. Even more important, in his two years of regular pitching for the Boston Red Sox, he led the staff in victories both seasons with 12 in 1925 and 11 in 1926, representing nearly 25 percent of the 93 victories the Red Sox won in those two campaigns. In

1925, he posted a 3.96 ERA, a full run lower than the team mark of 4.97, and in 1926, Wingfield's 4.44 performance again bettered the team ERA of 4.72.

Born August 7, 1899, in Bedford, VA, Wingfield grew up in the Roanoke area. He joined the United States Army at age 17 after a fight with his brother and served 14 months in Europe during World War I. In 1918, during the Argonne offensive, Wingfield was exposed to mustard gas and hospitalized for two months. Following his discharge in June 1919, Wingfield played semi-pro baseball for teams in Roanoke, and Elizabethton, TN. While playing for the N & W Athletic Club in Roanoke, Fred Wingfield became known as Ted Wingfield, the name that appears in baseball compendiums. According to his daughter, Charlotte Robinson of Greeneville, TN, her father played on a team with several Freds, and the manager gave each one of them a nickname. Wingfield's happened to be Ted. His play eventually attracted the attention of Chattanooga Lookout manager Sammy Strang Nicklin, and Wingfield ultimately signed a professional contract with the Lookouts of the Southern League in 1921. One account of Wingfield's early career opined that he cemented his position with the Chattanooga team by impressing the musically inclined Nicklin with his singing voice, causing the manager to take "such an interest in him he became a regular member of the team." When I mentioned this story to Robinson, she laughed and exclaimed, "What nonsense, Daddy couldn't carry a tune!"[3]

In his first season with Chattanooga, Wingfield served as the club's regular shortstop, although he hit an anemic .226. At short, he committed 70 errors in 116 games for a fielding percentage of .892, helping the Lookouts to a league-leading 345 errors and a league-low .943 fielding percentage. He began the transition from everyday player to pitcher during the 1921 season as he made a handful of appearances on the mound, posting a 2-2 won-lost mark. Although sportswriter Les Stout claimed that Nicklin switched Wingfield to the mound because his fielding was so "ragged," Wingfield recalled that his "clowning around" in 1921 began his transition to pitching. Warming up for the first game of a doubleheader against New Orleans, Wingfield began throwing curves to a teammate. Nicklin, apparently impressed with the quality of Wingfield's curveball, decided to start him

on the mound in the second game. Wingfield won the game, 5-3, "and from that time on he was a pitcher." In his next two seasons with Chattanooga in 1922 and 1923, Wingfield won 14 and lost 24 with an ERA of 3.46. He also continued to play in the field, making 59 appearances at shortstop and playing 25 games in the outfield, and improved his hitting, raising his average to .246 in 1922 and increasing it again to .265 in 1923.[4]

Although Wingfield later claimed, "I never should have switched to pitching," it was as a pitcher that he made it to the majors, being called up in 1923 by the Washington Senators. He debuted with them on September 23, pitching a scoreless inning in relief of Walter Johnson and, ironically, recording a strikeout. In spring 1924, *Washington Post* and *New York Times* sportswriters described the young right hander as a pitcher of "promise." He pitched effectively during spring training, including a long relief stint against the Boston Braves on April 9, and impressed Washington manager Bucky Harris enough to make the club's opening day roster.[5] Although Wingfield pitched well in four early season games with the eventual world champions, Washington returned him to Chattanooga on May 12, where he posted an 11-6 record and hit .272, playing both shortstop and second base along with his mound duties. In early September, the Boston Red Sox purchased his contract from the Lookouts and brought him back to the American League. After one relief appearance against the St. Louis Browns on September 12, Wingfield made three late season starts for Boston and pitched well, although he went 0-2, losing complete games 4-3 to the Browns on September 14, and 3-2 to the Tigers on September 23. Wingfield finished the 1924 season with an 0-2 record and a 2.45 ERA in 32⅔ innings.[6]

In 1925, Wingfield became the "ace" of the Boston staff. He made his first start on April 27 and won his first major league game on May 2, a complete-game 5-4 victory over the New York Yankees, playing that day without Babe Ruth in the lineup. On August 8, Wingfield notched his first major league shutout, a 3-0 blanking of the Chicago White Sox.[7] At this point of the season, the Red Sox had won 31 games, Wingfield 6. During the remaining 47 games, Wingfield notched 6 of Boston's 16 wins. Even more impressive, after September 8, while the Red Sox won only 8 times, Winfield won 5, beating the Yankees twice, followed those wins with victories over the Browns and the Indians, then ended his season with a five-hit 3-1 victory over the world champion Washington Senators, who rested some of their regulars. During this 23-day stretch, Wingfield pitched perhaps the two most impressive games of his major league career. On September 13, he beat the Yankees and Waite Hoyt, 2-1, surrendering only five hits, with Bob Meusel, Babe Ruth, and Lou Gehrig going 0-for-9. Four days later, he held the hard-hitting St. Louis Browns, a club that finished the season with a .298 average and scored nearly six runs per game, to only four singles in a 2-0 victory. Wingfield ended the 1925 season as the leading winner on a pitching staff that included veteran stars like Howard Ehmke and Jack Quinn and future Hall of Famer "Red"Ruffing.[8] He also finished second on the staff with 18 complete games and 254⅓ innings pitched. As a team, the Red Sox finished the season with the worst record in baseball, 47-105, a .309 winning percentage. Boston was 49½ games behind the pennant-winning Senators and 21 games behind the seventh-place Yankees.

The 1926 season saw the Red Sox continue their woeful play as their winning percentage actually declined to .301. Although the club won 46 and lost 107, Wingfield recorded an 11-16 mark to again lead the staff in victories. He was not as effective as he had been in 1925, however. Wingfield won only two games after August 3, and only one after a 1-0 win over the White Sox on August 19, as the Red Sox closed their forgettable season by going 4-28. His last win of the 1926 season came in a gritty 3-2 victory in 10 innings over the second-place Indians on September 20. Entering the day trailing the eventual pennant-winning Yankees by 3½ games, the Tribe had to win the game. However, Wingfield held the Indians to only seven hits, costing the Cleveland club "a royal opportunity to cut the leaders' margin," since the Yankees lost a doubleheader that day to the White Sox. He finished the season with a 4.44 ERA in 190⅔ innings, again second on the staff, and his nine complete games tied for the staff lead. Although Wingfield's 1925-26 record of 23 wins and 35 losses seems unimpressive, during one 154-game stretch between July 31, 1925, and July 30, 1926, Wingfield won 16 games, almost one-third of the 49 wins the Red Sox garnered during this period. Wingfield also pitched effectively against the league's good teams during 1925 and 1926, as 13 of his 23 victories came against first-division ball clubs, with three coming against eventual pennant winners Washington and New York. In fact, Wingfield beat the Yankees more frequently than any other opponent, notching six wins against them in 1925-26, causing one sportswriter to describe him as a "Yankee Killer."[9]

After two successive 100-loss seasons, the Red Sox hired as manager Bill Carrigan, who had led the club to two world championships in 1915 and 1916. Carrigan's return caused American League umpire Billy Evans and league president Ban Johnson to predict better things for the team in 1927. Evans found "a half dozen reasons" during spring training to think the Red Sox would be better, and Johnson considered Boston not only a potential first-division team, declaring the team "will be in a pennant fight…there is not a club in the league that should be counted out of a first division chance," but a potential pennant winner, mainly because manager Carrigan "unquestionably has the courage and character that mean new spirit and better results in Boston."[10] Other observers were not quite so sanguine about Boston's chances. Although Frank Getty of the *Atlanta Constitution* and Shirley Povich of the *Washington Post* disagreed about which team would win the American League pennant, they both predicted a last-place finish for the Red Sox. Getty and Povich proved prescient as the club lost its first six games and settled into eighth place, a spot in which it remained the entire season. By the end of May, the club had posted a .289 winning percentage and trailed the fabled 1927 Yankee team by 15 games, en route to a final mark of 51-103, 59 games behind New York.

After two years as Boston's biggest winner, Wingfield proved a major disappointment in 1927, mainly because of a "sore arm" he began suffering in spring training. Some 40 years later, Wingfield remembered, "I hurt my arm that spring, the first ball I threw I could feel it in my shoulder. Then I began to throw underhanded." His daughter confirmed her father's physical problems, maintaining, "The Red Sox knew he had a sore arm but they kept pitching him."[11] After a two-inning relief stint on opening day, Wingfield made three successive starts, pitching effectively in only one of them. By May 3, his record stood at 0-2, his ERA at 5.82. Carrigan used Wingfield out of the bullpen for nearly a month, and he continued to struggle, allowing four earned runs in four and one-third innings of work. On May 31, Wingfield started against the Senators and won his last major league victory, a 4-1 decision over Senator right hander Hod Lisenbee. Wingfield made three more starts in June, pitching well. He worked seven innings and allowed seven hits and two runs to the Tigers in a 5-3 loss on June 8, then followed that performance with an eight-inning effort against the St. Louis Browns on June 13, allowing nine hits and two runs in a 2-0 loss to Elam VanGilder. Eight days later, Wingfield pitched his final complete game in the majors, a 7-3 loss to the powerful Yankees. At this point, Wingfield had pitched 52⅓ innings with a 1-6 mark and an improving 4.47 ERA. He had allowed 16 walks and struck out no one, shattering all previous records for strikeout futility.

Since 1900 only three major league pitchers have pitched more than 20 innings in a season without recording a strikeout: Left hander Leo Townsend of the 1920 Boston Braves led the group with 24⅓ innings and no strikeouts, followed by left hander Stan Baumgartner of the 1926 Philadelphia Athletics and right hander Aloysius "Wish" Egan of the 1902 Detroit Tigers, both of whom worked 22⅓ innings without recording a strikeout. Since 1900 the worst strikeout ratio in major league history among pitchers with at least one strikeout belonged to right hander Dick Braggins of the Cleveland Blues, who recorded one strikeout in 32 innings in 1901, a strikeout per nine innings ratio of .281. Wingfield had passed Townsend's mark in his May 31 victory over the Senators, finishing that game with 28⅓ innings and no strikeouts.[12] In his next five appearances, Wingfield extended his strikeout-less streak to 66⅔ innings. On August 10, he struck out Athletics infielder Chick Galloway with two outs in the sixth inning, finally ending his strikeout drought at 67⅓ innings. With this strikeout Wingfield eradicated Braggins' single-strikeout record as his strikeout per nine innings ratio stood at .129.[13]

Wingfield pitched only two more games in the majors after August 10, ineffective appearances against the Detroit Tigers and Cleveland Indians. In early September,

the Red Sox sent him to Portland of the New England League after a stretch in which the right hander allowed 17 hits and 10 earned runs in eight innings, raising his season ERA from 4.32 to his final mark of 5.06.[14] Although Wingfield clearly pitched poorly in August, his demotion might have been the result of questions about his arm injury. In early August, *Sporting News* beat writer Burt Whitman blamed Wingfield and "Red" Ruffing for most of the team's pitching problems, writing that Wingfield "has been bothered by hypothetical sore arms all season….He has been told by specialists that it is all in his head—that sore arm—but nevertheless he has been of very little use to Carrigan this year."[15] Whether the demotion stemmed from just poor pitching, the club deciding Wingfield lacked the requisite commitment to perform for Carrigan, or a combination of both, his release marked the end of a major league career that saw him post a 24-44 record in 553⅓ innings of pitching.

During the next two years, Wingfield saw limited duty with Nashville of the Southern Association and Minneapolis of the American Association. He continued to suffer the effects of the sore arm he developed in 1927, pitching 81 innings for Nashville in 1928 and only 14 for Minneapolis in 1929. He also went 0-6 for Hartford of the Eastern League in 1929. After his organized baseball playing days ended, Wingfield continued to play ball on the weekends for semi-pro teams in Virginia and Tennessee, began a 35-year career as a rural letter carrier for the U.S. Post Office, and demonstrated considerable talent as a baseball executive. In 1936, he helped organize the Class D Appalachian League, resurrecting an association of Tennessee and Virginia ball clubs that had disbanded in 1925. When the league began play in 1937 with four teams, Elizabethton, Johnson City, and Newport in Tennessee, along with Pennington Gap, VA, Wingfield served as president of the Elizabethton Red Sox. The league then expanded to six teams in 1938, adding clubs in Kingsport and Greeneville, TN. Wingfield's Elizabethton team enjoyed consistent success during his tenure as president, winning regular season championships in 1937 and 1938. Although the club lost in the playoffs both years, it won the league championship in 1939, after finishing second during the regular season. The club not only succeeded on the field, Wingfield made it a financial success as well; the club finished the 1939 season "in good financial condition," and Wingfield was reelected by the stockholders for another term as the club's president.[16] The league Wingfield helped build still operates today as a 10-team short-season Class A "rookie" organization. Elizabethton remains a member along with Johnson City from the reconstituted 1937 league, and two additions from 1938, Kingsport and Greeneville, continue to field teams. In 2005, the Elizabethton entry won the league championship and in 2006 posted the loop's best record, continuing a tradition begun by the 1937-39 clubs. Finally, the Bluefield Orioles, a member of Baltimore's farm system since 1958, enjoy the longest affiliation with a major league club of any minor league franchise.[17]

In the 1950s, Wingfield became involved in youth baseball, coaching little league in Elizabethton. In 1969, the Postal Service forced Wingfield to retire because he had reached the age of 70. He continued to follow major league baseball, although the amount of time it took to play a ball game disturbed him. In 1971, he compared the brisk pace of baseball in the 1920s with the early 1970s version that saw "pitchers take too long between deliveries and batters get out of the box too often." The advent of the designated hitter in 1973 disgusted him, a predictable reaction for an old pitcher who took pride in his own hitting ability, including a .234 lifetime major league average and only 14 strikeouts in 192 at-bats. After retiring from the post office, he spent his time playing golf and fishing. Wingfield's nephew Buddy described him as a "great fly fisherman," and fondly remembered many enjoyable hours spent with his uncle fishing for trout in the rivers around Elizabethton. Wingfield suffered a pulmonary embolism in July 1975 and died July 18 at the age of 75.[18]

As he reminisced about his career in 1971, Wingfield clearly understood his good fortune, telling Henry Jenkins: "I look back on pitching in the majors as the best part of my life. We rode the best trains [there were no airplane trips then] and had the best of everything." Wingfield might have added that he played during one of the game's greatest eras, with and against some of its most fabled stars. As did the majority of major leaguers prior to free agency, Wingfield never made much money

playing ball; his daughter claimed his highest salary as a big leaguer was $750 a month, or around $4,000 a year. Along with many of his contemporaries, he spent years in the minors, then continued to play semi-pro baseball after his retirement because he loved the game. Considering the quality of the team with which he performed, Wingfield made a creditable record in major league baseball. To be sure, his is not a well-known name, and his record-setting performance in 1927 languishes in obscurity. In fact, Wingfield's 1927 record deserves to be ranked along with the record-setting pitching performances of Jack Chesbro, Grover Cleveland Alexander, Cy Young, and Ed Walsh, as one of baseball's "unbreakable" marks.[19] ■

Notes

1. *The Sporting News,* September 11, 1995, p. S-12. Several records have been modified due to additional research. See *SABR Encyclopedia of Baseball* at www.sabr.org. Except where otherwise noted, all statistical data is from *Retrosheet,* www.retrosheet.org

2. *The Sporting News,* September 9, 1978, "Voice of the Fan," p. 4.

3. Biographical data obtained from an articled titled "Boston Baseball Hopes" by Les Stout, ca. 1925, and article titled "Harmony Saved Wingfield's Job" by John Drohan, ca. 1925, in Wingfield File, Hall of Fame Library, Cooperstown. Interview with Charlotte Robinson, December 10, 2006. Although known now primarily by the nickname, contemporary reports almost always referred to him as Fred Wingfield.

4. The different accounts of Wingfield's transition are from *Stout,* ca. 1925; and article titled "Betsy's Ted Wingfield Was Once Star Pitcher for Boston Red Sox" by Henry Jenkins, Elizabethton Star, March 15 1953, p. A-9; and "Sideline Review" by Henry Jenkins, Elizabethton Star, ca. 1971. Both articles provided courtesy of Elmer "Buddy" Wingfield.

5. *Washington Post,* April 1, 1924; p. S3, *New York Times,* April 13, 1924, p. S1; *Washington Post,* April 10, 1924, p. S1.

6. *New York Times,* September 13, 1924, p. S2; September 16, 1924, p. 18; September 24, 1924, p. 26; *Washington Post,* September 20, 1924; p. S1. Wingfield's Chattanooga figures are from *The Sporting News,* December 15, 1921, p. 8; December 28, 1922, p. 8; November 29, 1923, page 7; December 11, 1924, p. 7. The account of Winfield's conversion from regular player to pitcher comes from an anonymous article titled "Wingfield, Red Sox Pitcher, a 'Convert',"ca. 1925, in the Wingfield file, Hall of Fame Library, Cooperstown.

7. *New York Times,* May 3, 1925, p. S1; *Atlanta Constitution,* August 9, 1925, p. B3.

8. *New York Times,* October 2, 1925, p. 18; September 18, 1925, p. 19.

9. For an account of the August 19 shutout see *Chicago Tribune,* August 20, 1926, p. 17. For accounts of the September 20 game see *New York Times,* September 21, 1926, p. 23; *Washington Post,* September 21, 1926, p. 17; quote is from *New York Times,* September 21, 1926, p. 23. The "Yankee Killer" reference is taken from "Betsy's Ted Wingfield," in the *Elizabethton Star,* March 15, 1953, p. 9-A.

10. *The Sporting News,* April 14, 1927, p. 7; *Washington Post,* April 10, 1927, p. 21.

11. From "Sideline Review" *Elizabethton Star,* ca. 1971; Robinson interview, December 10, 2006.

12. Statistics on Townsend, Baumgartner and Egan are from David S. Neft, Richard M. Cohen and Michael L. Neft, *The Sports Encyclopedia: Baseball* (New York: St. Martin's Griffin, 2001), 17, 127, 148. All information regarding Wingfield's daily pitching record for 1927 supplied courtesy of Hall of Fame Library, Cooperstown.

13. The account of Winfield's strikeout is taken from www.Baseball Library.com.

14. *New York Times,* September 2, 1927, p. 11.

15. *The Sporting News,* August 18, 1927, p. 1.

16. For Wingfield's obituary see *The Sporting News,* August 9, 1975, p. 40. For season and playoff results for the Elizabethton team see *The Sporting News,* September 16, 1937, p. 7; September 8, 1938, p. 10; September 14, 1939, p. 13. The club's financial success was reported in *The Sporting News,* November 23, 1939, p. 3.

17. Elizabethton is now an affiliate of the Minnesota Twins. For a brief history of the Appalachian league, see www.minorleaguebaseball.com. For Wingfield's post-1929 career see, "Sideline Review," ca. 1971. Robinson interview, December 10, 2006. For his 1928 and 1929 statistics, see *The Sporting News,* December 27, 1928, p. 8; December 19, 1929, p. 9.

18. Details of Wingfield's personal life provided by "Buddy" Wingfield and Charlotte Robinson in conversations on December 9-10, 2006. See also, "Sideline Review," ca. 1971.

19. "Sideline Review," ca. 1971; Robinson interview, December 10, 2006.

Bibliography

Interviews

Charlotte Robinson, daughter of "Ted" Wingfield, December 10, 2006.
Elmer "Buddy" Wingfield, nephew of "Ted" Wingfield, December 9-10, 2006.

Internet Sources

Baseball Library – www.Baseball Library.com
Minor League Baseball – www.minorleaguebaseball.com
Retrosheet – www.retrosheet.org
SABR Baseball Encyclopedia – www.sabr.org

Newspapers and Periodicals

Atlanta Constitution
Chicago Tribune
Elizabethton Star, Elizabethton, Tennessee, Courtesy of "Buddy" Wingfield
New York Times
The Sporting News, St. Louis
Washington Post

Wingfield's File National Baseball Hall of Fame Library, Cooperstown

Drohan, John, "Harmony Saved Wingfield's Job," ca. 1925.

Stout, Les, "Boston Baseball Hopes," ca. 1925

"Wingfield, Red Sox Pitcher, A Convert," ca. 1925.

Encyclopedias

Neft, David S., Richard M. Cohen, and Michael L. Neft. *The Sports Encyclopedia: Baseball.* New York: St. Martin's Griffin, 2001.

Don Who???

by Keith Carlson

Consider the following list: Nap Lajoie, Rogers Hornsby, George Sisler, Ty Cobb, Joe Jackson, Ted Williams, Harry Heilmann, Bill Terry, Don Padgett. The first eight names are familiar, and all except Jackson are enshrined in the Hall of Fame. Who, though, is the ninth player, and why is he on the list? Answer: The list is all the major league players since 1901 who batted .399 or better in a season, with at least 150 at-bats.

Admittedly, the list is contrived, but the question is why is Don Padgett is on the list at all. He had his big year in 1939 with the St. Louis Cardinals and had one at-bat too many to have a .400 average, finishing with .39914.

He is obviously overlooked in the annals of baseball history because he had only 233 at-bats. All the others on the list had at least 456 at-bats (that was Williams in 1941, with 147 walks) in their .400 seasons.

The question of course is why did an "almost .400 hitter" have only 233 at-bats and play in only 92 games? Was he injured? Was he feuding with the manager? Was there some other explanation? Was it just a fluke?

An Unimpressive Start (April 18 - May 25)

The accompanying table shows Padgett's batting average during the 1939 season. (An Excel chart with his cumulative batting average is available on request.) Obviously, small samples introduce considerable volatility in batting average, but four periods might shed light on the mysteries underlying his performance.

Of the team's first 29 games, Padgett played in only eight and did not start in any one of them and did not play in 21. He was considered a pinch-hitter or a backup first baseman, although he appeared as a late-inning sub in only one game during this first period. With Johnny Mize firmly entrenched at first base, Padgett saw little action at that position.

Padgett came up to the Cardinals in 1937 as a corner outfielder after hitting .329 for Columbus (Triple A) in 1936. He played mostly right field, with stalwarts Joe Medwick and Terry Moore the regulars in left and center. He hit .314 in 123 games in his rookie year. This performance would seem to guarantee regular status in 1938.

Enos Slaughter, however, had a monster season for Columbus in 1937 (.382 and 122 RBIs) and was brought up to the majors in 1938. Both Slaughter and Padgett saw considerable action in 1938 and had very similar years offensively. Slaughter hit .276 in 112 games; Padgett hit .271 in 110.

Slaughter could play all outfield positions, but Padgett was limited, apparently because he was "big and slow." (He was 6', 190 pounds, did not steal a base in 1938, and grounded into 12 double plays in 388 at-bats.) As a result, he was tried at first base and catcher, both new positions to him.

Going into the 1939 season, it was clear manager Ray Blades preferred to go with Slaughter in the outfield, Mize at first, and an experienced Mickey Owen established as the starting catcher, Padgett was left out.

Because there was really no regular position for a defensively challenged player like Padgett, he was relegated to pinch-hitting duties and occasional late-inning substitutions at first or catcher. Another factor working against him early in the season was a dislocated shoulder suffered in spring training, setting him back almost a month.

Furthermore, the team was doing well with Owen catching, winning 20 of 29 games. With limited appearances, Padgett was unimpressive in the first month-plus of the season.

KEITH CARLSON *is retired and lives in Bridgeton, MO. A member of SABR since 1984, he is a lifelong Cardinal fan.*

The Surge (May 26 - June 22)

In the first 16 games of this period, Padgett went 3-for-8 as a pinch-hitter. He had a couple of RBIs.

On June 10 and 11, the team played doubleheaders both days. After losing both games to Philadelphia on June 10, Padgett got a start at catcher in the first game on June 11. He went 2-for-4 in that game, with two RBIs, and, as a substitute for Mize late in the second game, hit a triple with the bases loaded, winning the game.

Although he did not start the next two games, he was 1-for-2, either pinch-hitting or subbing. He then was started at catcher the next three games, going 7-for-10, with five RBIs and two home runs.

As a result, during this 25-game period Padgett went 15-for-26, batting .577 and boosting his average from .125 to .471. Unfortunately, this hot streak did not translate into a winning record for the team—11 wins and 14 losses.

Continued Excellence (June 24 - August 26)

After this remarkable performance, it appears manager Blades began a partial platoon of Padgett with Owen at catcher, because Padgett batted left and Owen right. From June 24 to July 30 (36 games), Padgett started 20 games, and all were against right-handed pitchers (in fact, of his 56 starts all season, only one was against a left-handed pitcher).

He continued his strong hitting with a .434 average during this two-month period, although his average dropped slightly from .471 to .446. On July 30, in a home game against Brooklyn, he twisted his ankle rounding first on a single, but hit a home run later. This put him out of action as a starter for the next 13 games, but he did pinch-hit three times.

Returning as a starter at catcher on August 15, he started somewhat slowly, going 6-for-24, but on August 21, he got hot again. In the next six games, he got 14 hits in 24 at-bats. For this full period of 33 starts and nine other appearances, Padgett's average "cooled" from .471 to .438, but team performance improved to 36-25.

Back to "Ordinary" (August 27 - October 1)

For the final month-plus of the season Padgett hit a more pedestrian .315. After the August 28 game, an unspecified illness sapped his strength, limiting him to

Don Padgett with the Phillies.

occasional pinch-hitting duties, without any hits, through September 8.

After returning to action as starting catcher on September 9, he warmed up with 21 hits in his next 50 at-bats. This takes us to September 24, after which he got only two hits in 13 at-bats during the last eight games of the season.

He was hitting .414 as of September 23, but slipped to .399 by September 28, the day the Reds clinched the pennant by beating the Cardinals, 5-3. Padgett did not play in either game of the doubleheader in Chicago on September 30 (Larry French, a left hander, started the first game, and Bill Lee, a 19-game-winning right hander started the second).

In the last game of the season on October 1, however, he was sent in as a pinch-hitter with the score tied in the eighth inning. According to John Snyder, *Cardinals Journal* (Emmis Books, 2006):

> …Padgett lined a clean single up the middle, but upon reaching first base learned that the first-base umpire had called time a split second before the pitch because a ball rolled loose in the bullpen. Padgett returned to the plate and drew a walk in what proved to be his last plate appearance to finish the season with an average of .39914. Had the hit stood, his season batting average would have been .402.

The year 1939 was a remarkable one for Don Padgett, and quite a successful one for the Cardinals, as they finished second behind the Reds in the pennant race. We don't know all of the thinking about whether or not to play him.

Clearly, the manager was often confronted with the dilemma of when and where to play him, because the positions he could possibly play were filled with capable players, in particular, Slaughter, Medwick, Mize, and Owen. His catching numbers did not appear to be unusually bad. He had a fielding average of .978, while Owen fielded .983 (and batted .259). It was hard to keep Padgett's bat out of the lineup, but obviously, the manager liked having the experienced Owen behind the plate.

Padgett's playing time was affected by a pinch-hitting role during the first 45 games of the season, as well as 13 games during the summer because of an ankle injury and an illness in late August and early September. It isn't clear whether anyone was aware of his flirtation with .400 during the last three games of the season, after the Reds had clinched the pennant—or even cared. Mize's big year seemed to attract most of the attention.

The rest of Padgett's career—all of which was spent in the National League—was less than stellar, however, suggesting .399 was a bit of a "fluke," and was achieved mainly by facing right-handed pitching. ∎

Acknowledgments

This essay originated from conversations with David Stephan, a specialist in the analysis of lost playing time among major leaguers, and also benefited from his comments. Matt Rickard also provided editorial comments. All the contents, however, including any errors, are solely my responsibility.

Almost all of the information assembled here came from Retrosheet.org and ProQuest at Sabr.org (*New York Times* and *Washington Post*). Some additional information was gathered from the *St. Louis Globe Democrat*, and Dave Martin checked selected issues of *The Sporting News*. Padgett's daily log (an Excel spreadsheet) is available on request from the author.

SUMMARY – PADGETT, 1939

Period	Team G	W-L-T	GS	PH or Sub	DNP	AB	H	AVG
4/18-5/25	29	20-9-0	0	8	21	8	1	.125
5/26-6/22	25	11-14-0	5	13	7	26	15	.577
6/23-8/26	62	36-25-1	33	9	20	126	54	.429
8/27-10/1	39	25-13-1	18	6	15	73	23	.315
TOTAL	**155**	**92-61-2**	**56**	**36**	**63**	**233**	**93**	**.399**

PADGETT CAREER TOTALS

Year	TM	G	AB	H	HR	R	RBI	AVG	SLG
1937	STL	123	446	140	10	62	74	.314	.457
1938	STL	110	388	105	8	59	65	.271	.425
1939	STL	92	233	93	5	38	53	.399	.554
1940	STL	93	240	58	6	24	41	.242	.387
1941	STL	107	324	80	5	39	44	.247	.349
(Military service)	–	–	–	–	–	–	–	–	–
1946	BRO-BOS	63	128	30	3	8	9	.234	.336
1947	PHI	75	158	50	0	14	16	.316	.380
1948	PHI	36	74	17	0	3	3	.230	.270
CAREER		**699**	**1,991**	**573**	**37**	**247**	**338**	**.288**	**.415**

SOURCE: *Total Baseball (Fifth Edition)*

Smoky Joe Wood's Last Interview

by Franz Douskey

I met Joe Wood in the early 1980s after I called and said I'd like to interview him. His daughter invited me over. Joe and I spent a lot of time together, often watching Red Sox games on television and comparing players from different eras. All this was before a taped interview, which took place on May 11,1984. When he was up to it, I saw Joe a few times after that. He died in July 1985.

FD: *How did you first break into Organized Baseball?*

SJW: It was an all-girls team. The National Bloomer Girls were out of Kansas City run by Logan Galbraith. We had moved to Kansas, where my brother was born, in 1887, two years before me. My father was an attorney, and I was playing on the town team when the National Bloomer Girls came through. They had three more weeks of their season and they needed a shortstop. I wasn't the only male on their team. They offered me 20 dollars to play with them, and I thought, "My God, that's a lot of bucks." I told my folks and they said I could go. The season ended in Wichita, and they gave me my fare home. That was my first baseball experience. Soon after my brother ran into Ducky Holmes, a former major leaguer. He told Ducky that he had a kid brother who's a pretty good ballplayer. How about getting him a job in professional ball? Ducky contacted the owner of the Cedar Rapids Club, of the Three I League, owned by Belden Hill. I signed as an infielder, for 90 dollars a month. But I never reported to Cedar Rapids, because Belden Hill wrote me and said he had too many infielders. He used

FRANZ DOUSKEY *has published in* The New Yorker, The Nation, Rolling Stone, Yankee, Down East, SCD, Baseball Diamonds *(Doubleday & Company), and dozens of other publications. He has taught at Yale University, lectured at the Harvard Graduate School and is President Emeritus of IMPAC University.*

to visit me during 1912, the year I won 34 games, and he used to curse his bad luck for not letting me report to him in the first place, but transferring my contract to Jay Andrews, who was managing the Hutchinson club in the Western Association. Hutchinson, Kansas, was only 116 miles from where I lived, by way of the Santa Fe railroad, so I was tickled to death. My dad took me down and introduced me to Jay Andrews and some of the players like Skinny Horton, Flea Hardy, Turk Dunnum, and they all had sore arms. Jay Andrews came up to me and asked, "Joe, can you go in and pitch a little." I said I'd go in, and then they never let me out. Then I was sold to Kansas City. We played against several major league clubs as they were coming up from the South from spring training. In August 1907, I was sold to the Boston Red Sox. Fred Lake came down to look at me, and John R. Taylor, who was the president of the Red Sox at that time, sent me a contract for $2,400. That was 400 dollars a month for six months. Instead of going to Boston, I went back home and told Mr. Taylor he'd have to come up with more money before I'd report to Boston. When I got to Boston, I was single, and you know how women chase after ballplayers. I used to tear around quite a little, but I still pitched good ball for them. I asked for more money. Taylor, the president of the club, said, "Whenever you decide to get your feet on the ground and pitch good baseball, we'll give you the money." So I went right along, from 1908 on. In 1911, I had a pretty good year. 23-17.

FD: *In 1908, when you came up from Kansas City at age 18 to pitch for the Red Sox, did you room with Tris Speaker right from the start?*

SJW: That was a coincidence that happened, and run into a friendship that lasted forever. When I went to the Red Sox, that was August 1908. Speaker had joined the

Red Sox in 1907. They sent him to the Southern League and he led the league in hitting. He came back to the Red Sox about a week or two after I did, and it just so happened our secretary, Eddie Reilly, put Speaker and me as roommates. And we were roommates for 15 years. Even in Cleveland, where he was instrumental in bringing me there.

FD: *You had a remarkable year in 1912. Thirty-four wins, five losses. Three wins in the World Series. You were 21, at the start of a spectacular career, Then in the spring of 1913, you slipped fielding a grounder ball and broke your thumb.*

SJW: That was the last time I ever pitched a good ball game. At the same time something happened to my shoulder. Was it because I changed my motion? I'll never know. The same thing happened to Dizzy Dean. You do some damn thing to protect what the trouble is and that way something else develops, and that's it. We never know.

FD: *You did come back to a degree. You were 10-3 one year, then 15-5.*

SJW: Well, Christ, I only pitched half a season. I couldn't throw a ball. Couldn't raise my arm for three weeks. We had to keep playing ball to keep our contracts. I only pitched two full seasons in the big leagues, 1911 and 1912. The rest are all half seasons. One year I had appendicitis. The next year I had a busted artery in my leg, my ankle. Had it cut out, then I had a broken toe. And that's how it went. The last year I pitched, in 1915, I led the league in earned run average, but it was only a partial year. And that's why it's a problem for the Hall of Fame. I'm not interested in the Hall of Fame. I tried to get my son to not bring it up, but he wanted to do it. I told him I had no interest in it.

FD: *You may not want it. But when I speak with players from your era, and with baseball historians, your name does come up.*

SJW: I know that, but I just didn't have enough consecutive full-year time. I don't give a damn about it. I have no interest whatsoever in being in the Hall of Fame. It's all political. There are players in there that weren't even considered good ballplayers in my day. If there were any

players who played in my heyday on the committee, I'd be in there. I know that. They talk about fastball pitchers. Walter Johnson said there was nobody faster than me, and that's true. If anybody could throw faster than me, it was Walter Johnson, so he'd know. In those days we didn't have any ways of measuring. I talked to Larry Lajoie and Honus Wagner. I pitched against them in exhibition games, because they trained in Hot Springs, same as the Red Sox. They stayed at the Easton Hotel; we stayed at the Majestic. I pitched against Lajoie, Wagner, and Cobb, and they'd give you their honest opinion. Nobody was faster than me. I keep appearing in books like *The Glory of Their Times, The Ultimate Baseball Book,* and *The Greatest One Hundred Players of All Time.* I appreciate it, but I pitched with a bad arm. Come the 1915 World Series against the Phillies, Bill Carrigan came to me and asked, "How's your arm, Joe?" "Terrible," I told him, "but if these fellows can't carry you through, I'll go in there." That's why I was in the corner, in the bullpen, every day. It was Foster, Leonard, Shore, and Mays who pitched us through. My arm was terrible. That's why I laid out the 1916 season, I couldn't even raise my damned arm. Just like today, you get my left hand when we shake hands. The X-rays show there's nothing in my right shoulder joint whatsoever. It's bone against bone. I haven't slept on my right side since back then,1913. Almost 70 years ago. But that's what happened. Nowadays, they'd probably give a shot of cortisone in there or take a rest. Whitey Ford said when he'd get a little kink in his arm, he'd take a little rest for two or three weeks. Not only that. They pitch you once every five days now. When I played, it was every fourth day. All those things go into the thoughts of what happened. I'll never know except I pitched hard when my arm was sore. I even pitched when I was in so much pain, I had to use my left arm to get my right arm into the sleeve of my coat.

FD: *You once rigged a trapeze in an attempt to rehabilitate your arm.*

SJW: That's right. I hung one in my attic, in Pennsylvania, in the home I built in 1913, the year I got married. I couldn't throw a ball 10 feet. I thought it might stretch my arm out. I hung from it all winter long, but it didn't do any good. Even now, when I threw out the first ball at Fenway this spring, I threw it left-handed. Why did I hang from a trapeze all winter? The whole reason is that people who played baseball when I played baseball loved the game. They would have played for nothing. The boys who play now are just there for what they can get out of it. You take Fred Lynn. A whale of a ballplayer. Get a sore throat and he'd want to come out of the ball game. I've thought about him a lot. He could have been another Ty Cobb, but he didn't have the temperament. Every damn little thing and he'd want to get out of a ball game. Not giving to his capabilities. I've often thought about that. Players seemed to get results from a chiropractor, in New York, named Crusius, so I went to him. I went to him all during the winter of 1915 and the spring of 1916. I worked out in the Columbia University gym all winter, and I got to the spot where I thought it was all right. I got a call from (Tris) Speaker. He had moved from Boston to Cleveland. He asked how my arm was and I told him it was all right. I thought it was. I never lied to anyone in my life. I joined the Cleveland club and it was the same damn thing. The only way I knew how to play outfield was that this was the start of the war, and all the eligible men were going into the Army. Well, a lot of former major leaguers were in the minors and they were calling them back up in order to fill out the team. One day, Eddie Miller, was playing left field, and he got hit in the chest with the ball. (Laughs.) So, they put me out there and I started hitting. I knew damn well if I was going to play the outfield I'd have to hit more that I did when I pitched. I choked up on the bat and got a lot of hits and hit pretty well. Hit about .380. But I was always a family man. I'd go on a trip for three weeks, and when I'd get home, my boys didn't know who I was. For that reason I left baseball and eventually got to be the baseball coach at Yale, in 1922. I grabbed that job in a minute because I wanted to be with my family more than I wanted to be just playing baseball. I coached baseball at Yale for 20 years. And I bought this house right here, and my wife was always crazy about this house. She passed away three years ago this month. My daughter and her husband were nice enough to move in with me so I wouldn't be alone.

Smoky Joe Wood

FD: *How has the game changed over the years?*

SJW: They think winning 20 games is a hell of a stunt. When I came up in Boston and you only won 20 games, it was a bad year. Absolutely. In my day a pitcher could no more catch a ball in one hand, with the glove on, than he could fly. You very seldom saw a backhand play. You see them every day now. Gloves are huge. The ball gets lost in them. You can't miss. They have a hard time getting the ball out of the glove. I can remember when I first broke into the league, when Stuffy McInnis came in with the Athletics with his big glove, the first baseman's trapper mitt. He led the league in fielding five years in a row [Ed. note: six times but only three in a row,

1920-22]. That was the first big glove I ever saw. Stuffy McInnis was one of the fellows who came up to you at the tail end of a season, when it didn't matter, and say, "Look, it doesn't matter to you, let me get a hit or two and I'll get picked off or caught stealing, or some damn thing." It wasn't wrong; it meant a little bit more to him to have a hit or two on his batting average. He'd get picked off or slow down on his way to second base. But he never used it to his advantage, betting or anything like that. The gloves are bigger and the ball is much livelier because they want to get the crowds in, and so on. The catcher catches the ball with one hand. If they caught the ball with one hand and dropped it years ago, they would've been fined. Now they all catch one-handed. We never caught the ball above our heads like the fielders do now. We caught it down low, what we called the basket catch, because you caught it near your bread basket, your stomach, and that way you were ready to throw. Another way the game has changed is they have a coach for the catcher, a coach for the pitcher, a coach for hitters, and bullpen coach, a running coach, seven or eight coaches. In my day we learned from each other. We talked about the various things that happened in the games we played in. If you didn't learn, you didn't stay around for very long. But now, my God, the pitching coach goes out first, then if they're going to take the pitcher out, the manager goes to the mound. The age of specialization. Sometimes I hardly recognize it as baseball.

FD: *Often, one ball lasted the entire game, and it wasn't necessarily round at the end of nine innings. Pitchers occasionally doctored the ball. Did you ever throw a shine ball, mud ball, or coffee ball?*

SJW: Didn't need to. A coffee ball was the same as a mud ball, getting the mud to stick on. Some of the fellows used paraffin and hid it in their trousers. Eddie Cicotte used it. We called him "Knuckles." We called it a shine ball. Rub the ball on the paraffin on his pants. He was on the Red Sox when I come up. He got caught up in the Black Sox thing, which ended his career. I don't know too much about that. Of course some used slippery elm to throw a spitball, Stanley Coveleski used it, which was perfectly legit. You were allowed to have one or two pitchers on the club who threw it. Al Sothoron was not

supposed to throw it on Cleveland, but he did use it. Every once in a while an umpire would ask to see the ball. Instead of throwing the ball, Al Sothoron would roll the ball on the ground so it would pick up dirt. Ed Reulbach had the mud ball. Buck O'Brien on our club, he had a razor blade inside of his glove.

FD: *Let's talk about players who should be in the Hall of Fame but aren't. For example, Carl Mays had an outstanding career, but then there was the Ray Chapman incident, the only player to be killed playing major league baseball.*

SJW: Carl Mays should never be in anyone's book. I don't know how true it was, but we heard that Mays threw at Ray Chapman intentionally. I was one of the ones that carried him off the field. Chapman was a grand person. Mays went and got the ball and threw to first base, claiming Chapman was out. We heard right after the game that Mays said he was going to get Chapman. A grand person.

FD: *Which players have been overlooked by the Hall of Fame?*

SJW: We had a third baseman on the Red Sox. A clutch hitter all through his career, and you never hear his name mentioned. I wouldn't trade him for ten Frank "Home Run" Bakers. His name was Larry Gardner. A hell of a ballplayer. Loved the game. Graduated from University of Vermont with Ray Collins. He was more valuable to the team than Harry Hooper, but you won't see that anywhere. Pepper Martin was the same way. He'd tell the catcher he was going to steal, but they seldom got him out. And Pete Reiser was a great ball player. Ran into too many walls, but he loved to play.

I can name you a lot that should've been forgotten and weren't. I'll give you one and he'll admit to himself. Eppa Rixey. Do you know that name? He said that when they picked him, they must've gone to the bottom of the barrel. That's right. He was never a top-notch pitcher. Tom Seaton and George Chalmers and Grover Cleveland Alexander were on his team, and they were better pitchers. Eppa was a hell of a fine guy, but nowhere close to Seaton and Chalmers, both forgotten. Rabbit Maranville has no business in the Hall of Fame. Neither does Ray Schalk or Frank Baker. Nine or ten home runs a year and they call him "Home Run" Baker. I know Frank Baker very well. The only time I went through the Hall of Fame, I went with Frank Baker. Had my picture taken with him. My God, so many players in there that weren't even considered good when they played. You never know how good a player is until you're on the same club together. You take Sam Rice. A fine fellow and a good player with Washington. When he got into the Hall of Fame, he said, "If you want to know who should be in the Hall of Fame, I can name them for you. Honus Wagner, Larry Lajoie, Tris Speaker, and Ty Cobb." He said there are six or eight of those and that's it. The rest of us, it's a different thing. That's the way he described it. Sam Rice said, "Other fellows got in there that shouldn't be in there. And I question whether I should be in." And Sam Rice was right.

FD: *Do you think Shoeless Joe Jackson should be in the Hall of Fame?*

SJW: Well, I don't think he'll get in unless they exonerate him of all liability in that scandal. He had the reputation and all, and this is only hearsay, that he could not read or write. I know this. Another thing that was told to me that Joe and his roommate would go out for meals. Whatever his roommate ordered, Joe would say, "Bring me the same," because he couldn't read the menu. But I don't think Joe Jackson would honestly throw anything. No, no. The ringleader was Chick Gandil. Abe Attell, the prizefighter, was the middleman, so they say. Joe Jackson hit .375 in that series, and he hit the only home run. And

he didn't make any errors, so I don't know. You know, we ballplayers used to talk together, and I remember those who played with him considered him the greatest natural hitter there ever was. And that was amongst the players who knew him! About him teaching Babe Ruth how to hold a bat and swing, I don't think there's a bit of truth to that. And remember, I played against both of them, and Ruth was a teammate of mine with the Boston Red Sox when he came up. Babe Ruth was an absolute natural, like Joe Jackson. Eddie Cicotte, Charlie Hall, Ruth, Eddie Carter, and I used to go out at noon to pitch batting practice to each other, because, in those days we had to hit. And we had some damn good-hitting pitchers. I think Walter Johnson hit better than .250 for his career, and could hit home runs, even with that dead ball. And you know about Babe Ruth.

FD: *Who was the toughest hitter you faced?*

SJW: Oh, hell, most all of them. One fellow from St. Louis was as good as I ever pitched to. Some days I can remember his name, some days I can't. Pete somebody, I think it was. Sam Crawford of the Detroit club hit me a hell of a lot harder…. Eddie Collins used to hit me hard. What the hell was his name. Pete somebody. St. Louis Browns. I know you never heard of him (Pete Compton). He could hit me. Jesus. I couldn't get a ball by him.

FD: *What about your own career?*

SJW: I was 115 (now credited with 117 wins), wins and 57 losses, better than two out of three games. And my lifetime ERA was 2.03, just behind Ed Walsh and Addie Joss, third on the all-time list. And one year I hit .366 with Cleveland, a lifetime batting average of .298 [Ed. note: .283]. Not too bad for a man who couldn't lift his arm. And they list me as the Red Sox's greatest pitcher, and that includes Cy Young, who had some great years in Boston. And that's the gospel truth. Just like I used to tell my kids when they were growing up. "Always tell the truth and you don't have to remember what you said." I can go over my career till my dying day and come up with the same figures. All I know is that there was no one faster than me. But I don't care about it. I had my day and it's over, and that's it. ■

The Best-Pitched Game in Baseball History

Warren Spahn and Juan Marichal

by Jim Kaplan

Like raging dinosaurs in some prehistoric swamp, the Milwaukee Braves' Warren Spahn and the San Francisco Giants' Juan Marichal slugged it out for four hours, 10 minutes, and 16 innings, all through the night of July 2 and into the early minutes of July 3, 1963. Spahn, 42, personified an aging Tyrannosaurus rex defending his grip on the animal kingdom with wits, tenacity, and memory. Marichal, 25, embodied an emerging Mapusaurus roseae: young, strong, fast, and confident. By the time their epic standoff ended with a single run at 12:31 a.m, they had completed a battle of the ages for any species. It was arguably the greatest pitching duel in baseball history.

Never have two Hall of Famers pitched as well over such an extended game in which each faced a lineup of fellow Cooperstownians and other fine players. In addition to Spahn and Marichal, Willie Mays, Willie McCovey, and Orlando Cepeda of the Giants and Hank Aaron and Eddie Mathews of the Braves were bound for induction. Other substantial hitters included Braves left fielder Lee Maye, who had sizzled all June, and Giants third baseman Harvey Kuenn, catcher Ed Bailey, and right fielder Felipe Alou. For that matter, Spahn, who would lead all National League pitchers with 35 career homers, and Marichal, who batted over .500 with men on base one season, wielded mean bats themselves.

So how did Spahn and Marichal repel these fearsome hitters past midnight? The stars and their stars had to be properly aligned. Entering the season, the strike zone had been expanded from "knees to armpits" all the way to "knees to top of shoulder level." The Giants and Braves were playing night ball at San Francisco's typically breezy, chilly Candlestick Park, a pitcher's paradise because balls don't carry as far in cold weather as they do when it's humid.

July 2 was cool, with the usual west-to-east wind rippling across from left-center to right-center that presented a major obstacle for right-handed batters and helped left handers but sometimes sent shots by lefties into foul territory. So it was a pitcher's night at a pitcher's park. And the game began with Spahn and Marichal, two of the hottest pitchers in baseball. Spahn won four times in April and was 11-3 with five straight victories by July 2. He had just shut out the Dodgers and hadn't allowed a walk in 18⅓ innings. Moreover, he was facing precisely the same eight position players he had no-hit in April 1961. Marichal, who had won 13 games as a rookie and 18 in his second year, was already 12-3, with eight straight wins. He had no-hit Houston, 1-0, just 17 days earlier, getting 23 infield outs and throwing only 89 pitches despite two walks.

Warming Up on a Cold Night

Marichal took his warm-up pitches from the bullpen mound rather than on the sideline, because it was closer in height to the one on the diamond. In competition, he toed the inside of the rubber closest to first base to improve the angle for pitching away from left-handed hitters and to give his slider more room to break away from right handers. "When we had a meeting before the game, it was only Mays, Bailey, and myself," Marichal says. "Willie would direct the left fielder and right fielder where to play. Having Willie behind me

JIM KAPLAN *is former editor of* The Baseball Research Journal *and author of* Lefty Grove: American Original *(SABR, 2000). He wishes to thank the following SABR members for assistance on this story: Peter C. Bjarkman, Jim Charlton, Bill Deane, Dennis Degenhardt, Roland Hemond, John Holway, Rod Nelson, Crash and Sheila Parr, Jay Roberts, John Zajc, Phil Sienko, Dave Smith, Bob Sproule, Saul Wisnia, and Rich Westcott.*

made my position easier." He had no idea at the time how prophetic those words would be on July 2, 1963.

Spahn's warm-ups, this day as every day, seemed perfunctory. "He used to drive me crazy," says Spahn's son Greg, a real estate executive. Greg was born on the eve of the 1948 World Series and hit .524 as a high school senior but had to give up baseball when shoulder problems sidelined him at the University of Oklahoma. "He'd throw five pitches on the sideline, then talk to someone, throw another five and then talk." But there was method to Spahn's pre-start madness. The joking kept him loose: "The more pressure I feel, the more I kid around." The pitches had purpose. "He'd throw five fastballs, five screwballs, five curves, five changeups," Greg continues, "and see what was working.…If he had trouble, it was usually in the first or second inning. Then he'd figure out what to do."

Spahn and Marichal weren't overpowering but shared excellent control, a fine repertoire of pitches, and a high leg kick that obscured a batter's sightlines. As catcher Del Crandall explained, Spahn showed the batter three things: the sole of his right shoe, the back of his glove, and finally the ball. Spahn leaned forward in an almost courtly bow to the hitters, then rocked back, his right leg raised above his head in what *The Sporting News*'s Dave Kindred called a five minutes to six position, followed by an overhand delivery that was as smooth and regular as a dipping oil-field pumping jack back home in Oklahoma. Since every pitch was thrown with the same motion, the batter had no idea what to expect.

And there was something else. Because of an old separated shoulder from high school football, Spahn couldn't raise his right hand higher than his shoulder. As he moved toward the plate, his glove rose slowly, then descended quickly through the hitter's line of vision. "People kept telling me that the motion of the glove really bothered hitters," Spahn told Kindred. "So I kept doing it. Whatever bothered hitters, I was for."

No one was sure what they'd seen from Marichal. Richie Allen thought he threw five pitches, Joe Torre said seven, Billy Williams 12, and Lou Brock 16. "People were intrigued by his motion, but he was as much ball as motion," Bailey says. "Juan was not a pattern-type pitcher. He was unorthodox." What amazed fellow Giant pitcher Bobby Bolin was his control: "With that kick, I don't think anyone else could keep his body pretty straight and get the ball over."

In the Beginning

Marichal and Spahn sailed through the first three innings, Marichal yielding one hit, Spahn one, Marichal getting the most mileage out of his fastball, Spahn learning quickly that his screwball was getting right-handed hitters while his curve curbed lefties. More than anything, acquiring the screwball after he was supposedly washed up 10 years earlier had crossed up righties and extended Spahn's career.

Orlando Cepeda's stolen base in the second inning must have infuriated Spahn. He had one of the best pick-off moves in baseball, one so sure and sudden that he picked off Jackie Robinson twice in one game. Even Lou Brock was cautious about running on him. Cepeda, who stole eight bases that season and 142 in his career, probably ran on catcher Crandall rather than pitcher Spahn.

Sailing Through the Sixth

Hank Aaron led off the fourth by flying out deep to left field, the wind holding up his drive. Marichal got Eddie Mathews on strikes, but Norm Larker walked and Mack Jones singled him to second, bringing up Crandall. Frequently Spahn's personal catcher, Crandall knew Spahn so well he was rarely shaken off. Crandall would bat only .201 in 1963. But there would be no easy outs, no pit stops that July night. With two out and two on, Crandall hit a sinking liner to center. Willie Mays elected to one-hop it rather than dive, and he nailed Larker at the plate in "one amazing motion," according to the *Chronicle*'s Stevens, and on a "100 percent perfect peg," according to his colleague Bill Leister.

Menke replaced the sore-legged Mathews in the fourth and got two hits and a stolen base before the game played out. No easy outs, no pit stops. Through six scoreless innings, Marichal had a four-hitter and Spahn a two-hitter.

Cruising Through Nine

Marichal was throwing plenty of fastballs now. The Braves blew a chance to go ahead in the seventh when Crandall singled and was thrown out at second after shortstop Roy McMillan swung and missed on a hit-and-run. If he'd stayed put, Crandall might have scored when Spahn himself doubled off the fence in right field. Marichal got out of the inning and breathed easily. "Did you see [Spahn] hit that ball?" Marichal asked after the game. "It was going out of the park, and then that wind caught it. What a break that was!"

Marichal was being a good sport, because the wind probably helped Spahn's drive. In the eighth, Ernie Bowman replaced Jim Davenport (who had earlier replaced José Pagan) at shortstop; after Aaron walked, Bowman made a great stop in the hole to throw out Menke. Aaron moved to second on the play but was left there when Larker flied to Willie McCovey. With the game still scoreless in the ninth, it was Spahn's turn to breathe a sigh of relief. When McCovey launched one of his patented moon shots, the ball flew somewhere over the right-field foul pole. It was called foul by first base umpire Chris Pelekoudas, fair by the Giants, the fans, and most of the swells on press row. "The ball was foul when it left the bleachers, but fair when it passed over the fair pole," Marichal says.

The Giants protested bitterly but futilely and went down 1-2-3.

Extra Innings

So on to extra innings with these worthies. It was not unusual at the time for pitchers to work overtime, and downright commonplace for Spahn and Marichal. Between 1947 and 1961, Spahn started 531 games (including the World Series). Fifty-two of those games went into extra innings; Spahn completed 23 of them and pitched into the 10th inning without getting a decision three other times. He also had pitched in what might be called extra-extra innings, losing a 15-inning game in 1952 and a 16-inning game in 1951. For his part, Marichal had lost a 17-inning game while pitching for Springfield, MA, in 1959.

There was not just stamina at work but incentive. Both men had been denied moments of greatness they must have coveted. Granted, Marichal had his no-hitter. Still, he bruised the index finger of his pitching hand and lost a fingernail while bunting in the 1962 World Series and had to leave a game he was winning in the fourth inning,

never to reappear in a fall classic. Spahn had plenty of thrills, but not the one schoolboys dream of. Sure, he and Johnny Sain had been immortalized by the "Spahn and Sain and pray for rain" poetry during the 1948 pennant drive. Yes, in the World Series Spahn lost his only start, in game two, and won game five with 5⅔ innings of one-hit, seven-strikeout relief. Granted, he was Pitcher of the Year in 1957 and won a 10-inning game while losing another, 3-1, in the Series, but he fell sick with the flu and watched from his hotel room when Lew Burdette took Spahnie's scheduled start on two days' rest and beat the Yankees in game seven. Spahn was 2-1 in the 1958 Series, losing only in extra innings, but the Yankees won in seven games. Even the extraordinary no-hitters Spahn pitched at ages 39 and 40, throwing tantalizing sliders and screwballs the batters couldn't wait to hit but missed or grounded to short, hadn't moved him inordinately. "No-hitters aren't that much fun," he told Jim Thielman, who writes cooloftheevening.com. "Every pitch you make can blow it, and you go out there in the ninth inning and look around and all the infielders are scared because they're going to screw it up."

After nine innings, Spahn had allowed five hits and Marichal six. While Greg Spahn and 15,920 other fans sat shivering in the stands, the pitchers heated up. Spahn walked his duck walk slowly to the mound, "head down, taking his good old time," in the words of another Braves pitcher, Bob Sadowski. Marichal had always run to the mound and raced through his warm-ups to combat the Candlestick cold, and this night was no exception. "You were supposed to take seven warm-up pitches, but I'd run to the mound and sometimes take eight, nine, or 10," Marichal said on the phone from Santo Domingo. "Then I'd run from the mound to rest longer."

The Braves appreciated Marichal's hurry-up style, which was never intended to show up his plodding opponent. When the Giants were batting, Marichal sat with a warm-up jacket, a towel over his pitching hand to keep his fingers loose, chewing Bazooka gum. "I chewed it so hard, people thought I'd get tired, but it helped me concentrate," he says. He retired nine straight batters in innings 10-12. Spahn yielded a single bunt hit. Neither pitcher wanted to be taken out. Every inning after the ninth, Marichal said he told manager Alvin Dark, "Alvin,

Juan Marichal of the Giants.

do you see that man pitching on the other side? He's 42 and I'm 25 and you can't take me out until that man is not pitching."

Memory is a cruel mistress. Looking back over the years from his South Carolina retirement, Dark remembers a different conversation. "Larry Jansen, who won 23 games for the Giants in 1951 and then hurt his arm, was our pitching coach, so we were very conscious about pitchers working too long and injuring themselves. We had just started keeping pitch counts. 'I don't want this kid to get hurt,' I was thinking. I kept going to the mound the last three or four innings asking Juan, 'Are you all right?' And he always said he was."

Dark admits that Marichal passed any conceivable pitch count, but he wasn't worried. "If a guy gets wild or starts getting his pitches up, you know his arm might be tired, but that wasn't the case with Juan." Dark never asked a reliever to warm up.

Milwaukee manager Bobby Bragan insists he never even went to the mound. "I was a member of the Phillies [1940-42], and I can remember hearing that Connie Mack of the Philadelphia A's would take three pitchers to Detroit for a weekend series," says Bragan, who still runs a youth foundation in his 90th year. Not only could Spahn and Marichal pitch any length of a complete game, Spahn's old manager insists, they could throw a fastball, curve, or changeup on any count. Just watching Spahn and marveling, Bragan can still see his absolute concentration: "When he was pitching, he would walk by his brother."

Denouement

People have always wondered what it was like on the bench as the game moved from memorable to historical. Did players turn to teammates and say, "I'm going to tell my grandchildren about this one?" In truth, they were just trying to get through the night. "I'm completely blank about the game," says Frank Bolling, who played all 16 innings at second for the Braves, going 2-for-7 at the plate and handling seven chances without an error. "When you're in a game like that, you don't think of anything until it's over. You just want someone to score."

As the game progressed, Spahn was drinking very little water, because it gave him a stomach ache. But what Spahn did touch was unusual, to say the least. When he and Burdette were teammates, the guy pitching would come off the field and find his friend waiting in the runway behind the dugout holding a lit cigarette for him. "There was no rule against smoking when people can't see you," Burdette says. On July 2, 1963, Burdette was a Cardinal, so Spahn probably lit up an unfiltered Camel on his own. He smoked while chewing Beechnut gum. Spahn kept adding sticks during a game, leaving him with a large chunk in his mouth that gave the erroneous impression he was chewing tobacco.

In the Giants' 13th, Bowman singled, then wandered too far off first. Spahn threw behind him, and Bowman was retired in the ensuing rundown: pitcher to first to shortstop. But the old man appeared to be weakening. In the 14th, Kuenn doubled to lead off, and Spahn intentionally passed the dangerous Mays, ending his consecutive walkless streak at 31⅓ innings. McCovey fouled to the catcher and Alou flied to center, but Cepeda loaded the bases when Menke made an error. Bases loaded, two outs: the game's most dramatic moment. Bailey lined to Mack Jones in center. Whew! With a second chance, Spahn retired the side in order in the 15th.

Meanwhile, Marichal was cruising. He gave up a harmless single in the 13th, a walk in the 14th, nothing in the 15th. The 16th inning started around 12:20. Under the curfew in effect, no inning could start after 12:50. Hardly anyone had left the park. The wind had died down. Marichal got through the top half, surrendering only a two-out single to Menke.

Marichal had thought each of the last three innings would be his last. "After I pitched the 16th inning, I walked off slow, waiting for some of the players coming in from the outfield," he told the *Oakland Tribune*. "I was waiting for Willie Mays. I said, 'Willie, this is going to be the last inning for me 'He said, 'Don't worry, Chico, I'm going to win this game for you.'"

In the bottom of the 16th, Spahn threw one screwball after another to the right-handed Kuenn, getting him at last on a fly to center. The pitch that extended his career was extending the game.

As Mays stood in the on-deck circle, Marichal called to him, "Hit one now." His teammates chuckled. Mays stepped in. He had been limited to two outfield flies, two infield grounders, a strikeout, and an intentional walk. Swelling now, Spahn threw another scroogie to Mays. And suddenly it was all over.

The screwball hung. Mays swung. "You never knew for sure in Candlestick Park when the ball was hit anywhere between left-center and right-center because the wind could hold it up, but this one was hit hard and down the line, about 30 feet fair," Dark says. In *Sports Illustrated*, Ron Fimrite described "a high arc to left field, where, after hanging in the night sky for what seemed like an eternity, it landed beyond the fence."

Giants 1, Braves 0, an eight-hitter for Marichal, with four walks and 10 strikeouts, a nine-hitter for Spahn, with one intentional walk and two strikeouts. Marichal allowed just two singles in the last eight innings, while retiring 21 of 24 batters. Spahn threw 201 pitches, Marichal 227. Pro-rated over Spahn's 15⅓ innings and Marichal's 16 full, Spahn had been throwing on a 147-pitch nine-inning rate to Marichal's 152.

While Mays rounded the bases and disappeared quickly into the night, the crowd stood and cheered both pitchers and, for that matter, themselves for sticking it out. Each spectator was given the "Croix de Candlestick," a round orange badge for anyone surviving an extra-inning night game at The Stick. "We were riveted," says Fimrite. "It was the best game I ever saw."

"It was the greatest game I've ever seen by two pitchers," Dark said. And maybe the last of its kind. Since 1960 only Gaylord Perry, on September 1, 1967, pitched 16 innings, and he was taken out for the last five innings of a 21-inning game, the sissy. "If they had that today, they'd fire the manager and general manager—everyone but the players!" Marichal says.

Spahn patiently remained on the field for a broadcast interview. His teammates were silently waiting for him in the clubhouse. When he arrived, everyone stood, applauded, and lined up to shake his hand. "If you didn't have tears in your eyes, you weren't nothing," Sadowski says.

Then the writers converged. "It didn't break at all," Spahn said of the last pitch, which left him slumping off the mound. "What made me mad is that I had just gotten through throwing some real good ones to Kuenn."

It may be that the weather had helped keep Spahn in the game—as Sadowski observes, better to have pitched in 55 degrees than 85. Spahn said he was a little tired. "Look, I made 10 or 12 mistakes in the game," he added. "I was inside on a lot of right-handed hitters, when I usually pitch them outside, and I got away with it. That gives me a certain amount of satisfaction.

"I had a good curve tonight, too, and I'm pretty proud of that. It gave me a weapon against the left handers."

That wasn't all, an admiring Hall of Famer Carl Hubbell, who attended the game as director of player development for the Giants, said. "Here is a guy 42 years old who still has a fastball," he marveled. "He just kept busting them in on the hands of our guys and kept getting them out." Hubbell added: "He ought to will his body to medical science."

Of Marichal, who retired 16 straight late in the game, Dark said, "He didn't throw many breaking pitches, thus tiring his arm, but just kept slipping across the fastball with a loose and fluid motion. He got stronger."

"Oh, my back," Marichal said. "But tonight was beautiful."

After answering reporters' questions, Spahn spent several hours in the clubhouse drinking beer, with his son and several teammates in attendance, everyone telling him what a splendid job he did in a gallant defeat.

After his no-hitter, Marichal had gone to a Spanish-language movie house and watched a lousy western. Following the 16-inning win, he held himself upright long enough to let hot water pound his arm in the shower—not everyone used ice in those days—then went home and collapsed into bed. "But I didn't feel so bad

Willie Mays of the Giants.

pitching in San Francisco, because of the weather. You don't lose so much salt. It wasn't like the night in Philadelphia when I lost 8½ pounds, or the afternoon game in Atlanta when I lost nine."

The *San Francisco Chronicle* carried a front-page headline JUAN BEATS SPAHN. "There were lesser page one stories that day—something about a nuclear test ban and the FBI 'smashing a Soviet spy ring,'" Fimrite reported in *SI*. "But for one day at least, an epic pitching duel dominated the news. It was, I told the guys in the office, a rare exercise of sound editorial judgment."

Despite the banner headline, the game was little more—at least at the time—than a one-day story. "There wasn't the hype then that there is today," says Crandall, who like some other players in the game can't remember a single detail. They were not to be blamed. Exhausted from the long game, thinking of the next one, they had no luxury to sit back and look into history.

Warren Spahn of the Braves.

Pitching In, Pitched Out

The next day Spahn took Marichal aside in the visitors clubhouse. Oh, to have been a fly on the wall when the winningest pitcher of the 50s (202) passed on his ineffable wisdom to the winningest pitcher of the 60s (191). "He said to be careful in your next start," Marichal says. "He said, 'I know you pitch every fourth day, but try to take an extra day.' I only got one. It was almost mandatory to pitch every four days."

Marichal was thrilled to have beaten "one of the best" and honored to be approached by him. "I learned a lot from that man. When I wasn't pitching, I would watch him, how he approached batters, how he went in and out, up and down. You learn every day watching a pitcher similar to you." Marichal not only learned to pitch like Spahn

but think like him: "Sometimes you'll start with one or two pitches and then switch to another in the later innings."

"[Marichal] worked so easily and smoothly, he should be able to take his next turn or, at most, require one extra day of rest," Dark said. Indeed, Marichal got that one extra day of rest, pitched on July 7, and gave up five hits and two runs over seven innings in a 5-0 loss to the Cardinals. He hadn't lost much stuff, and he hadn't lost much spirit either, because he was fined $50 for buzzing Bob Gibson. "A few weeks later, I pitched 14 innings in New York," Marichal says. "I struck out Tommie Agee four times. Then he hit a ball that I think is still going." [Ed. note: Marichal's memory is highly faulty. This game actually took place six years later, on August 19, 1969.]

His confidence boosted, his knowledge of hitters and pitching expanded, Marichal pitched 10 of his 18 complete games and got 12 of his 25 wins after July 2. Marichal finished at 25-8, with a 2.41 ERA, his first under 3.00. Equally telling, he broke into the top 10 control artists, finishing seventh with 61 walks in 321 innings, or 1.71 per game. And he didn't let up for the rest of the decade:

	IP	K	BB	BB/G	ERA
1962	263	153	90	3.08	3.32
1963	321	248	61	1.71	2.41
1964	269	206	52	1.74	2.48
1965	295	240	46	1.40	2.14
1966	307	222	36	1.06	2.23
1967	202	166	42	1.87	2.76
1968	326	218	46	1.27	2.43
1969	299	205	54	1.62	2.10

Fractional IP not included.

In a career lasting from 1960 to 1975, Marichal was one of eight right handers since 1900 to win at least 100 more than he lost. Extending his career with, yes, a screwball he used effectively against left-handed hitters, he went 243-142, with a sterling .631 winning percentage and equally an eye-catching 2.89 ERA. In eight All-Star games he had an 0.50 ERA. He won 25 games twice and 26 once. He was 37-18 against the arch-rival Dodgers, 24-1 at Candlestick Park. Though he won more than anyone in the 1960s, someone else was always chosen for the Cy Young Award. Marichal never got a single vote during the 1960s, when only one first-place vote was allowed per ballot.

Spahn's post-7/2/63 life was more complicated. He said that his career went downhill after the game. Well, yes and no. Five days later—yes, he got an extra day off, too—he strained a tendon in his arm throwing a slider to John Bateman but finished the game and beat Houston, 5-0, on five singles. Then he missed the next 18 days before returning on July 25 and losing to Burdette and the Cardinals, 3-1. Nonetheless, Spahn won six times in 23 days, won 10 of his last 12 decisions, threw three shutouts in September, finished at a jaw-dropping 23-7, and become the oldest pitcher to win 20. His career-low walk total of 49 in 259⅔ innings decreased for the fourth year in a row, and his 17th consecutive 200-inning season was a modern record. A bargain-basement beauty, Spahn finally pushed his career salary over $1 million. As of this writing, only one player in the last quarter century—Seattle's Jamie (The Ancient Mariner) Moyer in 2003—has had a 20-win season past the age of 40.

That said, Spahn declined quickly after 1963. While suffering through a 6-13, 5.69 ERA season in 1964, he said his timing was off and he was pitching defensively. Catcher Bailey believes Spahn's knees—he would endure seven operations on them, his cartilage torn and ground from high kicks and hard landings—finally got to him. But Spahn wasn't through playing. After the season he was sold to the Mets, who wanted to use him as both pitcher and pitching coach. Oh, did his presence produce quotes for the writers. "With Berra and him, we are conducting a university this spring," said Casey Stengel, who had managed Spahn with the Braves and would now oversee him as a Met. And good old Yogi Berra, recruited to warm up Spahn, said, "I don't know if we're the oldest battery, but we're certainly the ugliest."

Spahn spent the '65 season with the Mets and Giants—"I pitched for Casey Stengel before and after he was a genius," he said after departing—before being released with a combined record of 7-16. His final season concluded a 363-245 career and dropped his winning percentage below .600 (.597) while raising his ERA above 3.00 (3.09).

After the 1965 season, no one bid on his services. "I didn't retire from baseball," Spahn said. "Baseball retired me." When Spahn pitched three games for the Mexico City Tigers in 1966 and three games for the Tulsa Oilers

in 1967, people got the mistaken impression that he was staging a comeback. Actually, he was demonstrating technique to a Mexican team he was coaching, then trying to improve attendance for an American team he was managing.

Spahn would hold court at the Hall of Fame, thrilling contemporaries like Hank Aaron, Stan Musial, and Willie Mays as well as younger immortals like Johnny Bench and Fergie Jenkins, all the while sucking on a long-necked beer. In August 2003, the Braves unveiled a nine-foot bronze statue of Spahn kicking high outside Turner Stadium in Atlanta. Ailing with a broken leg, four broken ribs, a punctured lung, internal bleeding, and fluid buildup in his lungs, Spahn, 82, was wheeled in to see the work. "I took great pride in mooning people," he said. "That's the reason I developed that leg kick."

It was one of the last and best memories of Spahn: kicking and joking. After outliving his wife LoRene by 25 years, Spahn died on November 24, 2003.

Of his father, who came of age during the Depression, Greg Spahn says, "He didn't buy lavish shoes or clothes. My dad threw away nothing—he was even a string saver. He kept all plumbing fixtures; you never know when you can use one. He kept all 363 balls from his wins, each with the opponent and score on it. I got a friend to crawl through a space in his house, and he found 31 bats."

One piece of memorabilia remains poignantly missing from the Spahn estate: the last screwball to Willie Mays 31 minutes into July 3, 1963. "That pitch probably bothered him more than any other he ever threw," Greg says. "For years he said that if he had one pitch he'd like to take back, that was it." ∎

Merle Harmon

by Maxwell Kates

He was a sports broadcaster and former college football player from the Midwest. Tall and gray-haired, he sported a crooked nose as a football injury badge. Answering to the name Harmon, he called gridiron action working for ABC telecasts. It would be understandable to many if he were often mistaken for the great Tom Harmon of Michigan, particularly if his broadcasting partner were former Wolverine footballer Forest Evashevski. Would you believe this misunderstanding actually occurred at a banquet prior to an Alabama-Mississippi game in Birmingham? The emcee even misintroduced the mike man as Tom Harmon. After assuming the podium, the broadcaster handled the scenario with class and professionalism. Even his posture and his diction were dead ringers for Tom Harmon. "But I ask you," he proclaimed, "who is this guy standing before you? Is he Tom Harmon, the great Michigan All-America and Heisman Trophy winner? If you're saying yes, then the gag's on you. I'm the other guy."

Just who was "the other guy?" He was the elder Merle Reid Harmon, and he was in the ninth grade when Tom Harmon won the Heisman Trophy in 1940. Merle played college football, but never reached the professional ranks. He served his country during the Second World War, but not as an Air Force pilot. Although he worked in movies, "not one soul has ever mentioned seeing me in one." And, no, his children were never married to Pam Dawber or Rick Nelson. The preceding anecdote summarizes Merle's executive summary well—a knowledge of sports, a love of people, an acumen for broadcasting, and a sense of humor, allowing him to laugh at himself when necessary.

Merle was born on June 21, 1926, in Salem, IL, the son of a greengrocer. During his childhood, his impoverished economic situation was far from unique among Americans. Raised as a member of the Community of Christ, Merle retained his values of family and faith throughout his career and during his subsequent retirement. Growing up 60 miles from St. Louis, the Cardinals naturally became his favorite team. Although he loved to listen to the antics of Dizzy, Daffy, Leo the Lip, the Arkansas Hummingbird, and the Wild Hoss of the Osage, his childhood hero was the broadcaster France Laux.

As a high school student, Harmon sold magazines door-to-door to help his family during the summer. He kept $2 for himself, enabling him to budget a trip to St. Louis to see the Cardinals play at Sportsman's Park. Round-trip train fare cost $1, streetcar tickets cost a dime each way, a bleacher seat was worth a quarter, and a hot dog, a soft drink, and a bag of peanuts set him back an additional 30 cents. At the end of the day, Merle was left with a quarter, just enough to purchase a team pennant and a Cardinals pencil. Returning to school in September, he remarked, "I protected that pencil with my life, making sure my friends saw it and asked me where I got it. As a poor kid in the Depression years, that pencil was my status symbol. It was proof that I had been to St. Louis to see a big league baseball game."

Young Merle enlisted in the United States Navy in 1944, serving on a troop-landing craft in the South Pacific. Following the Allied victory, he registered as a student at Graceland College in Iowa. It was there as a

---

MAXWELL KATES, *at age 12, purchased a Chicago White Sox cap from Merle Harmon's Fan Fair in Plantation, FL. When he asked who Merle Harmon was, his mother replied that "the name probably sounds made up." Years later, Kates worked with Harmon on a radio broadcasting project, and told him this story. A SABR member since 2001, Kates now works as a staff accountant in Toronto.*

A REVIEW OF BASEBALL HISTORY

sophomore in 1946 that he met a freshman co-ed named Jeanette Kinner. Merle immediately confided in his cousin, "Glen, you see that girl over there? I'm going to marry her!" Although Jeanette was unofficially engaged to another man, it was Merle who ultimately won her heart. Merle and Jeanette were married on December 31, 1946. They raised five children, Merle Reid Jr., Keith, Kyle, Bruce, and Kara, and presently have grandchildren living across the country.

After graduating from the University of Denver with a bachelor's degree in radio in 1949, Merle began his career in Kansas as the voice of the Class C Topeka Owls. Although the Great Depression was long over, the Owls continued to live and travel frugally. Meal money was $1 per day and the lodging allowance was $3— a sum which could not buy an air-conditioned room on the road. The team bus would have fit perfectly on the set of *Little Miss Sunshine*. Carrying 17 players, the bus traveled at a maximum speed of 40 miles per hour— downhill—and often had to be pushed to a service station for refueling. Money was so tight that the players even resorted to brawling to determine who got to drive the bus for a stipend of $50 per month.

Needless to say, conditions on the road were enough to make basic needs such as sleep seem luxurious. Harmon's baptismal in minor league broadcasting occurred in late July as the Owls were in St. Joseph to play the baby Cardinals—led by a fiery second baseman named Earl Weaver. Merle worked nearly eight hours of a doubleheader as a broadcaster and technician in triple-digit heat despite a splitting headache. Amid a comedy of errors, hits, runs, passed balls, and wild pitches in the second game, Merle pleaded with the radio audience for forgiveness for "not being able to go all out on the broadcast tonight. You know how it is with a bad headache." As he told Nick Purdon of the Canadian Broadcasting Corporation in 2004, the fans were not sympathetic. One woman even sent Merle a postcard—"Don't tell us your troubles. Broadcast the game!" It was the most important piece of professional advice that he ever received.

Merle remained in Topeka through the 1952 season, and recalled his highlight in the Kansas state capital— the opportunity to see a young shortstop for Joplin in 1950 who "at 18…already hit balls out of sight." The Oklahoma Kid in question was none other than Mickey Mantle. Merle also began broadcasting football, basketball, and track and field for the University of Kansas. By 1954, he earned a promotion to the Kansas City Blues of the American Association. That November, Chicago banker Arnold Johnson bought the Philadelphia Athletics from the debt-ridden Mack family. To Merle's surprise, Johnson intended to retain him as the Kansas City broadcaster in 1955 after moving the Athletics from Philadelphia. Merle credited the tireless campaigning of Ernie Mehl for successfully bringing an American League team to Kansas City. After Johnson died in 1960, Chicago insurance magnate Charlie O. Finley purchased 52 percent of the team from his estate. The following year, Finley organized "Poison Pen Day" to admonish Mehl, sports editor of the *Kansas City Star*. Outraged, Merle boycotted the event. "Ernie got baseball here in '55—and Finley's trashing him!" By valuing loyalty to his convictions ahead of his employer, Merle was fired from the Athletics in 1961.

Merle would not be looking for work for long. In August 1961, the Athletics were visiting the Yankees in New York. After broadcasting the baseball exploits of Roger Maris the night before—along with several other Athletics alumni now uniformed in pinstripes—he received a phone call early one morning. Half-asleep, he heard the voice on the other end ask, "Would you be interested in doing a national sports show for ABC television?" Disbelieving the sincerity of the other gentleman, Merle assumed it was a player making a crank call. Merle responded by directing him to contact his agent. The other man responded with "…we'd be glad to contact him, but we'd like to see you because we're leaving for Chicago today to do the [football] All-Star Game." This was no player. Rather, it was Chet Simmons of Sports Programs, a department of ABC Television. Thus began a 12-year working relationship with ABC for Merle. Each weekend the network would import him to New York from his home in Kansas City to broadcast programs such as *Saturday Night Sports Final* and *College Football Scoreboard*.

In 1965, Merle's duties with ABC were expanded to include *Game of the Week* baseball contests. He opened the season in Boston, where he proudly witnessed his color commentator break the color bar for broadcasting. Who called the game with Merle? Jackie Robinson, that's who. Ironically, the game was played at Fenway Park, the very ballpark where he was denied the opportunity to play for the Red Sox two decades earlier. From 1963 to 1972, Merle also broadcast football play-by-play on radio, first for the Kansas City Chiefs and then for the New York Jets.

Although Merle's broadcasting career took him to dozens of outposts, he is perhaps most associated with the city of Milwaukee. He worked for the Marquette University basketball team as well as the Braves and Brewers. Cream City had been baseball's veritable hotbed when the Braves moved from Boston in spring training 1953. The Braves drew better than two million fans in each of the four years that followed, shattering their own National League attendance record in 1957—the year "Bushville" upset the Bronx Bombers for the world championship. Ultimately, the Braves fell from contention, Milwaukee County Stadium barred fans from bringing their own beer, and by 1963 attendance fell below one million. To the radio audience at home, broadcaster Earl Gillespie had been as integral to the Milwaukee Braves as Warren Spahn, Eddie Mathews, or Hank Aaron, but even he could read the writing on the wall. When Braves president Louis Perini sold the club to a syndicate led by William Bartholomay, Gillespie submitted his resignation.

Merle accepted the post, but it was a thankless position. Although the Braves contended in 1964, the season was clouded by rumors surrounding the team's future in Milwaukee. Only a court order in 1965 prevented them from jettisoning the Dairy State for greener pastures in Georgia. Broadcasting Braves games during a lame duck season became a veritable Catch-22 for Merle. "They had to play…in a city which knew it was losing them. If I praised the Braves, people said 'Don't root for traitors.' If I didn't, diehards said, 'Don't mess up another club.'" Despite once again contending well into September, the Braves attracted only 555,584 spectators to Milwaukee County Stadium before departing for Atlanta. On the other hand, calling Braves games allowed Merle the opportunity to work alongside Mel Allen during the 1965 season. How about that!

That final weekend of the 1965 season marked one of the most tumultuous of Merle's career. The Braves were visiting the first-place Dodgers in Los Angeles. Meanwhile, the second-place Giants, hosting Cincinnati, had not yet been eliminated. After calling the Dodgers game on Friday night, Merle would air the final *Game of the Week* for ABC on Saturday. The trouble was that as Friday dawned, he still did not know where he would be working the following day. If the Dodgers won and clinched a tie, he would fly to Cleveland to broadcast the Indians. If the Dodgers lost, he would travel to San Francisco. Merle had an outside chance of flying to Chicago to catch a connecting flight to Minneapolis, where he would broadcast the Twins, champions of the American League. The only place he was certain of not working was Los Angeles, as it would pose a conflict of interest for the Milwaukee announcer to call a Braves game on network television.

Merle had reserved flights for San Francisco, Chicago, and Cleveland, but he could not board any until the Dodgers game had concluded. As it happened, the game was scoreless entering the 10th inning. Hurriedly catching a cab, he asked the driver to turn on the game. He arrived at the airport during the 12th inning—the game was still scoreless. The driver asked, "Which terminal you going to?" Merle replied, "I don't know." In a scene reminiscent of Howard Jarvis as a taxi passenger in the movie *Airplane,* Merle asked the driver to pull over and listen to the game. The meter was still running. Finally, the Dodgers won—Merle was boarding a United flight to Cleveland. The plane was ready to taxi as he arrived at the terminal. In an era less constrained by security restrictions, Merle hurdled over the conveyor belt and ran through the baggage room before finally reaching the plane as the doors were set to close. Only then did he realize he was going to the wrong city—"I'm supposed to be in San Francisco!" He panicked. Arriving in Cleveland hours later, Merle's fears were eased by ABC executives when they told him he had indeed flown to the correct destination.

Following a one-year hiatus from baseball, he returned in 1967 to work for the Minnesota Twins. Slugging infielder Harmon Killebrew propelled the team to an Opening Day victory with one of his 573 career home

Merle Harmon interviews Herb Score. The 1955 American League Rookie of the Year winner later joined the baseball broadcasting fraternity after his career ended prematurely.

runs. Following the game, a fan exclaimed, "Nice game, Harmon" while passing Merle. In another case of mistaken nomenclature, the broadcaster had no idea that Killebrew was walking immediately behind him.

Working in the Twin Cities allowed Merle the opportunity to broadcast games alongside Halsey Hall. A Minnesota baseball legend since the 1930s, Halsey adopted "Holy cow!" as his signature call while Harry Caray and Phil Rizzuto were still children. Where Halsey and his trademark cigars traveled, humor was certain to follow, as was the case during a Sunday doubleheader at Comiskey Park. Excited by a fifth-inning rally, Halsey accidentally knocked his lit cigar off his desk, igniting a fire in the broadcast booth. As Merle described the situation years later, Halsey proceeded to stomp the fire with his feet, creating a unique dance step, albeit not quite ready for *American Bandstand*. Later in the game, Merle noticed that Halsey's sports coat had caught fire. A consummate professional, Halsey continued to call the game despite a considerable hole charred into his sleeve. As Arno Goethel wrote the following day in the *St. Paul Pioneer Press*, "Halsey Hall is the only man I know who can take an ordinary sports coat and make a blazer out of it."

For the second time in three years, Merle broadcast a sudden-death pennant race as the season drew to a close. The Twins were in Boston playing the Red Sox during their "Impossible Dream" summer campaign. In a race also involving the Tigers and the White Sox, Boston proved triumphant. Though privately disappointed, Merle received a reprimanding letter from a Minnesota fan for sounding "...as excited when the Red Sox made big plays as [he] did when the Twins made big plays." Merle appreciated the disapproval, knowing he had conducted himself properly.

Merle was set to begin his fourth season with the Twins in 1970 when he accepted his release on the eve of the American League season. On April 1, 1970, the circuit transferred the Seattle Pilots to Milwaukee, and Merle was hired to broadcast for the team, which had been renamed the Brewers. The franchise shift was not without a barrage of legal confusion—as outfielder Steve Hovley remembers, "once the team bus got to Salt Lake City, we didn't even know whether to turn left [to Seattle] or turn right [to Milwaukee]." The bus headed right for the Badger State, leaving barely a week for professional seamstresses to remove the "Pilots" stitching from player uniforms and replace it with "Brewers." The first home game in Milwaukee on April 7 was a nightmare as Andy Messersmith of the Angels decimated the Brewers behind Gene Brabender by a margin of 12-0. Baseball would prove to be a difficult product to sell in Milwaukee the second time around. Only in 1973 did attendance top one million, and another five years would pass before the Brew Crew posted a winning record in 1978.

The early Brewers teams, however, were not without their share of characters and comic incidents, including the time relief pitcher Tom Murphy sent his identical twin brother Roger in uniform into Bud Selig's office to negotiate his contract. In 1971, Merle welcomed into the broadcast booth a Milwaukee native and former Braves catcher who would soon become a legend throughout Wisconsin.

"Merle Harmon helped me from the start," recalled Bob Uecker of his rookie season in the catbird seat—many years before playing Harry Doyle in *Major League.* "I'd never done baseball when I joined him in the booth, not unless you count my play-by-play into beer cups in the bullpen. Beer cups don't criticize, [but] people do…Merle and Tom Collins let me do color, then play-by-play, and saved me if I screwed up."

Uecker, already familiar with the bullpen as a player, achieved a save of his own on March 18, 1971. Visiting the Brewers at their spring training headquarters in Tempe, AZ, were the Tokyo Lotte Orions. As Merle looked at the lineup, bewildered by the unpronounceable last names, Uecker reassured him that he could handle the situation. After all, Uecker could speak Japanese. Or could he? When it came time to announce the batting order, Uecker introduced the leadoff hitter as center fielder Tom Toyota. Following him in the lineup were Nick Nissan, Sal Subaru, Paul Panasonic, Hank Honda, and Mike Mitsubishi. Merle recalled "Paul Panasonic had quite a day, hitting a three-run homer and belting a two-run double."

As the decade of the 1970s progressed, Merle explored a variety of business ventures while continuing to expand his versatility as a broadcaster. He was among the founders of a new broadcasting school in Milwaukee. In 1973, Merle had the privilege of broadcasting the World Games from Moscow. When he decided to photograph tourist scenes of the Soviet capital on his personal camera, it generated a skirmish with the KGB. Nevertheless, they were able to arrange a deal—"the KGB got the film and Merle got to go home." Departing Moscow at 9:00 on a Saturday morning, he called a baseball game in Minnesota that night. While broadcasting World Football League action on August 8 of the following year, Merle had the dubious distinction of introducing Richard Nixon for a speech on national television. The 37th president made it perfectly clear of his intent to resign the next day. Later on, Merle became an elder in the Reorganized Church of Latter Day Saints.

In 1977, Merle undertook perhaps the greatest risk of his career by establishing the first retail store to sell officially licensed merchandise of professional and collegiate sports teams—Merle Harmon's Fan Fair. The seed was planted in Merle's conscience over a decade earlier, when he broadcast for the New York Jets. After receiving a Jets desk clock as a Christmas present one year, Merle received dozens of accolades from people asking where they could buy one for themselves. To their chagrin, the answer was "nowhere." Similarly, fans could purchase Brewers caps only at stadium concession stands. Even then the caps were made from mesh as opposed to the wool hats worn by the players. Team executives were simply uninterested in the idea of allowing casual fans to wear official team property. Still, Merle knew that consumers were willing to purchase official Brewers caps or Jets desk clocks, and he sought to satisfy them. Following a family discussion, Merle's son Reid agreed to operate a "sports fan's gift shop" at a major shopping center in Milwaukee. Three of the other Harmon children followed Reid into the business, and the fans responded. Virtually the entire Brewers team showed up to meet legions of fans as they waited two hours to enter the store. Meanwhile, the dairy across the aisle sold "every scoop of ice cream in the place." Although the store grossed only $300 that initial day— "just enough to pay the electric bill"—it marked one small step for an enterprise which would eventually mushroom into 140 franchises. For his achievements Merle won the 1993 Graham McNamee Award as a broadcaster who excelled in a second endeavour.

Merle's final year with the Milwaukee Brewers was 1979. Led by manager George Bamberger, the "Brew Crew" won a franchise-record 95 games to finish in second place behind Baltimore. Despite the offensive juggernaut powered by Robin Yount, Paul Molitor, Gorman Thomas, and the rest of "Bambi's Bombers," it was time for Merle to move on. Having signed a broadcasting deal with NBC which included *Game of the Week,* the 1980 World Series, and a return trip to Moscow to call the Summer Olympics, he resigned from the Brewers. Alas, the Soviet Union invaded Afghanistan on December 27, 1979, prompting the United States to lead a boycott of the 1980 Olympiad. On a brighter side, at least Merle did not give the KGB another opportunity to confiscate additional rolls of photography.

Replaced at NBC by the youthful Bob Costas in 1982, Merle returned to the American League as a broadcaster for the Texas Rangers. In Arlington he was united with two old friends. Former Milwaukee Braves manager Bobby Bragan was now the director of the Rangers' speaking bureau, while the director of television planning was none other than the Wyoming Cowboy himself, Curt Gowdy. The crowning achievement of Merle's career behind the microphone occurred in his final year as a baseball broadcaster. On August 22, 1989, the Rangers' legendary right hander Nolan Ryan entered the game with 4,994 strikeouts. Five innings and five batters called out on strikes later, Oakland speedster Rickey Henderson stepped to the plate. When Henderson whiffed and the hometown crowd went wild, Merle used a technique demonstrating that at times, no man is greater than the event – not the broadcaster, not even the pitcher. He said absolutely nothing. "If the event warrants," he explained, "let the crowd and TV director take over to capture the emotion." Merle continued to broadcast freelance events before retiring from the profession altogether in 1995.

Merle is one of the most genuine individuals one could ask to work with. Despite several battles with adversity through poverty during the Depression, employment insecurity throughout his career, fan admonishment in Milwaukee, Charlie Finley in Kansas City, and the KGB in Moscow, one would never sense that his life was an obstacle course of unforeseen circumstances. Merle retained his cornerstone values of family and faith from his formative years to senior citizenhood. He would not forget the people he worked alongside, retaining friendships with players, writers, and other broadcasters, including Len Dawson, Bill Grigsby, Wes Stock, and the late Joe McGuff. Merle, who sold the Fan Fair conglomerate in 1996, was inducted into the Texas Baseball Hall of Fame that same year. In 2004, the Salem Community High School—his alma mater in Illinois—inducted him as a charter member in its Hall of Fame. Although Cooperstown has yet to acknowledge Merle with a Ford Frick Award, when his protégé Bob Uecker was so honoured in 2003, the Milwaukee broadcaster made certain to credit his mentor in his acceptance speech.

Merle and his wife Jeanette remained in the Metroplex after his retirement from the Rangers, and they continue to live in Arlington. He still conducts daily exercises on his treadmill, and he volunteers one day a week at a local soup kitchen. In an ironic turn of events, Merle may no longer be the second most famous sports personality named Harmon. Several years ago, when the great Harmon of Michigan appeared as a football coach on *Bizarre,* a variety series hosted by comedian John Byner, at least one spectator was heard asking, "Tom Harmon? Don't they mean Merle Harmon?" ∎

Sources

"Hall of Fame Candidates Selected," *Salem Times-Commoner,* April 16, 2004.

Aaron, Hank, and Lonnie Wheeler. *I Had a Hammer.* Scranton, PA: Harper Collins, 1991.

Bryant, Howard. *Shut Out: A Story of Race and Baseball in Boston.* New York: Routledge, 2002.

Buege, Bob. *The Milwaukee Braves: A Baseball Eulogy.* Milwaukee: Douglas American Sports Publications, 1988.

Dewey, Donald, and Nicholas Acocella. *Encyclopedia of Major League Teams.* New York: Harper Collins, 1993.

Harmon, Merle, and Sam Blair. *Merle Harmon Stories.* Arlington, TX: Reid Productions, 1998.

Hawkins, Burton, ed. *Texas Rangers 1982 Media Guide.* Arlington, TX: Texas Rangers Baseball Club, 1982.

Hoffmann, Gregg. *Down in the Valley: The History of Milwaukee County Stadium – The People, the Promise, the Passion.* Milwaukee: Journal-Sentinel and the Brewers Baseball Club, 2000.

Liberman, Adam, et al. *2004 Atlanta Braves Media Guide.* Atlanta: Braves Public Relations Department, 2004.

Sears, Bill. *The Milwaukee Brewers 1970 Inaugural Yearbook.* Milwaukee: Milwaukee Brewers, 1970.

Smith, Curt. *The Storytellers: From Mel Allen to Bob Costas – Sixty Years of Baseball Tales from the Broadcast Booth.* New York: Wiley, 1995.

Smith, Curt. *Voices of Summer: Ranking Baseball's 101 All-Time Best Announcers.* New York: Carroll & Graf, 2005.

Thornley, Stew. *Holy Cow! The Life and Times of Halsey Hall.* Minneapolis: Nodin Press, 1991.

Note

The author also wishes to acknowledge the following people for their contributions to this essay: Dave Baldwin, Bob Buege, Jeanette Harmon, Steve Hovley, Rich Klein, Bob Koehler, Nick Purdon, Rick Schabowski, Wes Stock, Stew Thornley, and especially Merle Harmon.

The Night Elrod Pitched

by Norman L. Macht

If Earl Weaver's retirement repose is ever disturbed by nightmares, chances are a recurring one bears the dateline: Toronto – June 26, 1978.

That night the fledgling Blue Jays, losers of 102 games in their second year of existence, handed Weaver the most humiliating loss of his career. The 24-10 rout also inscribed the late Orioles bullpen catcher Elrod Hendricks and outfielder Larry Harlow in the pitching ledgers of the record books.

Playing before 16,184 in Exhibition Stadium on a balmy Monday night, Weaver confidently sent southpaw Mike Flanagan (11-4) to the mound against the last-place Blue Jays, who had won 22 and lost 47.

Eddie Murray doubled Rich Dauer to third in the top of the first and Lee May's single gave the O's a quick 1-0 lead off lefty Tom Underwood. In the bottom of the first Flanagan fanned leadoff batter Willie Upshaw, which must have made the superstitious Weaver squirm, for it is common knowledge among those attuned to the baseball occult that striking out the first batter of the game is an omen of ill tidings to follow.

It didn't take long for the tide to turn. Flanagan faced six in the second and retired none. By the time reliever Joe Kerrigan could stop the flood, nine runs had scored.

The Birds scratched back with one in the third, but Kerrigan was roughed up for four runs on five hits in the last of the third before Tippy Martinez bailed him out.

Down 13-2 after three, the O's battled back with three in the fourth, but Martinez continued to throw batting

NORMAN MACHT*'s biography of Connie Mack (through 1914) was published in July. Now a resident of San Marcos, TX, he has begun writing "the rest of the story," which he hopes will not take another 22 years.*

practice for the Jays. It was man overboard for Tippy, who gave up six runs on five hits and two walks.

With the score 19-6 in the fifth, Weaver contemplated his rapidly depleting bullpen, the need for at least two rested arms to pitch a doubleheader in Toronto the next day, and the relative merits of a different line of work.

Meanwhile, to make sure there would be at least one survivor, bullpen catcher Elrod Hendricks had sent closer Don Stanhouse to the clubhouse, reasoning that if Earl saw him, he would use him. When Earl saw nobody in the bullpen but Elrod, he looked behind him in the dugout and saw his regular center fielder, Larry Harlow. Benched against a left-handed starter, Harlow hadn't pitched since his rookie pro season at Key West in the Florida State League.

Weaver asked if he would go in and pitch. Harlow said okay. He walked out to the mound and began warming up with catcher Rick Dempsey, while Toronto manager Roy Hartsfield engaged in a discussion with the quartet of umpires over how many warmup pitches are allowed for an outfielder coming off the bench to pitch. By the time the matter was peaceably resolved, Harlow's left arm was limber.

Weaver looked like a genius when Harlow disposed of catcher Brian Milner (a .444 lifetime hitter in two games) on a ground ball to second, and struck out Upshaw. Up stepped Bob Bailor, who had been Harlow's roommate for a half dozen years in the Baltimore organization. Bailor laughed as he stepped in to bat against his old roomie. Whether there is any connection between that outburst of hilarity and what happened next is left to the psychobabblists to unravel.

Bailor walked. Howell walked. With Rico Carty at the plate, Harlow threw a wild pitch that advanced the runners. A minute later he wished he'd thrown another one. Carty almost took his leg off with a line drive.

"I thought [shortstop] Kiko Garcia would get it," Harlow said. "When he didn't, I knew I was in trouble."

He was right. He walked Otto Velez, and John Mayberry hit a grand slam. The score was 24-6.

While Harlow was handing out his fourth free pass of the inning, to Dave McKay, Earl Weaver was on the phone to the bullpen.

"Can you throw strikes?" he said.

Elrod looked around him; there were no pitchers in the bullpen.

"You know you're speaking to Elrod," he said.

"I'm fully aware of that," Earl said. "Can you throw strikes?"

"Sure I can throw strikes," Elrod said, still wondering why Earl was asking the question.

"How long will it take you to get loose?"

"For what?"

Weaver said, "As soon as you can get loose, I'm gonna put you in the ball game."

"Well," Elrod said, "I warmed up all the pitchers who went into the game. I threw 40 minutes early hitting this afternoon. I like to think I'm pretty loose, as loose as I'm going to get."

"You're in the ball game," Weaver said, then hung up and walked to the mound.

"I knew Weaver was mad at me when he came out," Harlow recalled. "I told him it was tough to throw strikes when it was so long since the last time I pitched. He was pretty disgusted."

Elrod stood in the bullpen with his catchers' mitt and coaching shoes. "You gotta be kidding," he said to himself as he started "the longest walk of my life. On the way in I was thinking, 'What's the major league record for runs scored in a game?' I knew that after I got out there, unless I got hit with a line drive, they would break the record. I couldn't pitch with a catcher's mitt so Jim Palmer came out and threw me his glove and yelled, 'Hold 'em there, Rex.' The pitchers used to call each other Rex.

"It was scary. I had never been out there without a screen in front of me for batting practice."

Elrod told Dempsey there was no need to put down any signs. "Everything was going to be straightforward,

slower even than B.P. I didn't try to mix them up; there was nothing to mix."

He had so much "stuff" on his first few throws, the ball kept popping out of Dempsey's mitt. Dempsey took out his chewing gum and stuck it on the ball.

"He was having more fun out of it than I was," Hendricks said. "It was probably a joke to everybody else but Earl. He didn't think it was funny."

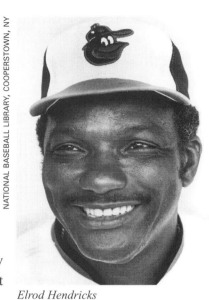

Elrod Hendricks

Rico Carty was standing near the dugout laughing. Elrod yelled at him, "If you or that big guy at the plate [Tim Johnson] hit one back at me, I'm going to come after one of you. You hit it too hard. I'm going to throw inside. You pull the ball." He was more concerned with survival than his earned run average.

Johnson hit what looked like a rocket right back at him. Elrod flinched and got out of the way. "But it was really an easy three-hopper I could have barehanded," he later recalled.

He got Milner on a fly ball to end the inning. He pitched 2.1 innings and retired with a career ERA of 0.00.

"I was surprised that I did as well as I did," he said later, "but they were probably tired by the time I got there."

Stanhouse volunteered to pitch the eighth to get some work.

"Nice going, way to go," Weaver told Hendricks. But he never asked Elrod to pitch again.

The Orioles scored three in the seventh and one in the eighth to pull within 14. That's how it ended, 24-10. The Blue Jays had 24 hits and eight walks. At least the Orioles made no errors, except for showing up that night. ∎

Note

This is slightly revised from its appearance July 22, 1994, in the now-defunct *Orioles Gazette.*

"Dirty Jack" Doyle

A Baseball Life

by Neal Mackertich

The Ball

It all started with a baseball. My wife Marilee's otherwise wonderful family are not big baseball fans. With the exception of my father-in-law Robert Belliveau's golf club and ball design expertise (he was an innovative design engineer with Spalding), sports are not typically the topic of conversation at family gatherings. Marilee's late grandmother Marion O'Connell was different. Marion, an avid golfer and big Tiger Woods fan, and I were known to sneak away from the dinner table to catch an ESPN update or two. Every now and then Marion would talk about the old days and how her late husband Sam was a big baseball fan. After learning about just how much I love baseball and the history of the game, Marion and her daughter Betty Anne (my mother-in-law) gave me an old signed ball of her late husband's as a gift. They said that they had looked for an old '27 Yankees ball that they used to have lying around but thought that Sam had given it away. Not only was I extremely grateful for the gift, but I was intrigued. What was my wife's family doing with an old signed ball and talking of the '27 Yankees? It turns out that Sam's best friend was an old scout for the Cubs named Jack Doyle. A quick inspection of the ball and reference to my handy *Baseball Encyclopedia* identified the ball to be signed by the '43 Cubs. I quickly looked up the career statistics of each player and bemoaned the fact that I missed Jimmie Foxx's signature by only a year. I then showed it off to all my baseball friends. For some reason, I didn't pursue more information involving Jack Doyle for another year or so. I even remember questioning why Jack Doyle, a

NEAL MACKERTICH *is a diehard Red Sox fan with a passion for the game, his family, and all things SABR.*

mere scout, put his signature on a ball signed by otherwise legitimate ballplayers. Little did I know at the time, Jack Doyle (a.k.a., "Dirty Jack" Doyle) was much more than just a legitimate ballplayer… but rather was one of the most interesting baseball characters of all time. His remarkable career as a player, manager, umpire and scout would span an incredible and entertaining 71 years!

Catcher on the Rise

John (Jack) Joseph Doyle was born October 25, 1869, in Killorglin, County Kerry, Ireland, on the Laune River, south of Tralee. The Doyles immigrated to Holyoke, MA, when Jack was but a child. Years later upon refusing to pay $1.50 for a hotel room, he quipped: "My father raised our whole family on $1.50 a day and gave us all a complete education, short and long division." Holyoke at that time was a bustling and growing mill town full of opportunities that Ireland could not provide.

Young Jack Doyle played New England semi-pro ball in 1887 before breaking into the professional ranks with Lynn in 1888. Amazingly, the box score from that initial game, May 3, 1888, Lynn at Portland, has survived. Jack Doyle batted eighth, going 2-for-4 with a run scored and 11 putouts from the catcher position (10 by strikeout), three assists and three errors (the other catcher had seven) in a 9-6 victory. In 80 games with Canton in 1889, Doyle impressed big league management both as a run producer (he stole 81 bases) and as Cy Young's battery mate. Inundated with offers from big league clubs, Jack Doyle signed with the Columbus Colts of the American Association for $2,500 in salary and a $1,000 signing bonus. In his first game with Columbus, Doyle put his exceptional speed to immediate use by stealing four bases off future Hall of Fame catcher Wilbert Robinson, then with the Philadelphia Athletics. At 19 years of age,

Jack Doyle was one of the youngest players in the major leagues.

"Just One Purpose: to Win"

"Dirty Jack" Doyle was an absolute terror on the base paths, stealing 518 bases in his career (tied for 30th all-time) averaging 53 steals per 162 games. Stealing bases at this rate over a lengthy career is remarkable for a catcher/first basemen even in those inside baseball days. Jack Doyle is arguably the greatest catcher/first baseman base stealer in major league baseball history. Some say his nickname derived from his uniform always being dirty; others point to his desire to win at all costs. They appear to both be contributors. Even in an exhibition game during his heyday with the Orioles, "Dirty Jack" slid face first into all four bases one trip around the diamond. Doyle himself said:

> I was a hard base-runner. You had to be those days. It wasn't a matter of being rough or dirty. With the dead ball, games were won by very small margins. As a result, a stolen base meant more than it does today. It often meant the difference between victory and defeat. And my base-running was for just one purpose: to win.

The First Pinch-Hitter and More

Jack Doyle spent his first couple of years in the major leagues learning the ropes primarily in a utility role. As one might expect of such a gamer, "Dirty Jack" began his penchant for being at the scene of baseball's most unusual and historically significant events. On June 7, 1892, at Brooklyn, Jack Doyle of Cleveland pinch-hit for pitcher George Davies with his team down a run in the ninth and promptly singled. It was long held that this was the first instance of pinch-hitting in major league baseball history. (Through SABR research, others have since been cited.) It was also during this period that Jack was reprimanded by the National League for dropping pebbles into the heel area of batters' shoes as they leaned forward to swing only to discover the discomfort as they attempted to run the bases. An edge to be gained was to be taken.

A Leader Among Giants

By 1894 Doyle was entering his prime and was one of the everyday leaders of the New York Giants. In 1894,
Doyle hit .368, scored 94 runs, drove in 103, and stole 44 bases in just 107 games while primarily serving as their starting first baseman. A great contact hitter, Jack Doyle also led the league in 1894 with an amazing at bats per strikeout ratio of 142.3. In those days, a World Series of sorts (The Temple Cup) existed between the top two teams in the National League. The Giants finished second in the National League in 1894 with a record of 88-44, a mere three games behind the 1890s dynasty that was the Baltimore Orioles. The big showdown was a mismatch this time, as Amos Rusie and Jouett Meekin limited the mighty Orioles to four runs in total with Doyle sparking the Giants by hitting .588.

During the 1895 campaign, Jack Doyle followed George Davis as player-manager as the Giants entered the infamous Andrew Freedman reign of terror. None of the Giant managers that season, Davis (16-17), Doyle (32-31), or Harvey Watkins (18-17) could rally the squad to their 1894 level. Turmoil and a revolving door of managers/players were to be a frequent occurrence during the Freedman era. (Doyle himself was to be traded to and from the Giants three times.) Frank Graham described Freedman as "coarse, vain, arrogant and abusive, he insulted, threatened, or assaulted any who opposed him and many who inadvertently, merely got in his way…For eight years Freedman ruled the Giants and almost completely wrecked them." Bill James famously described Freedman as "George Steinbrenner on quaaludes." At the end of the season, Jack Doyle would be on his way to the rival Orioles of Baltimore.

Birds of a Feather…

After two championship seasons, Oriole manager Ned Hanlon pulled off one of his trademark coups by trading Kid Gleason (a solid but unspectacular infielder who later went on to manage the infamous Chicago Black Sox) and cash for their fierce rival "Dirty Jack" Doyle. Other teams voiced their protest, as the mighty Orioles became even stronger. Despite their more than comfortable lead going into the final month, the Orioles of 1896 won 16 of their final 21 games. It was a natural fit. Doyle could be himself among this contentious band of characters loaded with future Hall of Famers: third baseman John McGraw, shortstop Hughie Jennings, right fielder

"Wee Willie" Keeler, center fielder Joe Kelley, and catcher Wilbert Robinson. Doyle was more than a nice addition to this squad; an old surviving scorecard has Doyle batting fifth in a powerful lineup that produced 995 runs (while yielding only 662) and stole 441 bases in only 132 games. Doyle himself had one of his best seasons, hitting .339 with 73 stolen bases and 29 doubles while scoring 116 runs and driving in 101 in only 118 games. The run barrage continued in 1897 with Doyle once again producing terrific results: hitting .354 with 62 stolen bases and 29 doubles while scoring 91 runs and driving 87 runs in only 114 games. Throughout his career Doyle was at best a mixed blessing in the field: while his speed and aggressiveness enabled above-average range, his below-average glove contributed to above average errors. Doyle would lead league first baseman in errors three times (1894, 1896, and 1900). But this was not the case with Doyle in 1897 (SABR fielding statistical statistics have him above average across the board), as he was clearly firing on all cylinders at the peak of his career.

On September 3, 1897, teammates "Wee Willie" Keeler and our man Jack Doyle went 6-for-6 during the same nine inning game for the Baltimore Orioles, reportedly the second time this had been accomplished in major league history. (Doyle would go on to record five hits in a game four times.) The Orioles would finish 50 games over .500 (90-40), but this time there would be significant competition from Boston. This was one of baseball's first great pennant races, culminating in a passionate final weekend series in Baltimore before the mighty Orioles were finally slayed. The Orioles had somewhat of the last laugh, however, as they drubbed Boston four games to one in the last Temple Cup ever played, with big-game Jack Doyle hitting .526. (Doyle is listed as the ex post facto MVP of the 1897 Temple Cup in the *ESPN 2005 Baseball Encyclopedia*). Doyle, who loved the spotlight, led his teams to blowout wins in all three Temple Cup series in which he participated, winning a remarkable 12 out of 13 contests. In these 13 showdown contests, Doyle hit .472 (25 for 53) and slugged .600. There are very few World Series and/or playoff performers of this caliber with 50+ at-bats across the history of baseball.

To say that the Old Orioles played with rare intensity is an understatement. Connie Mack is quoted as saying,

"The Orioles played the game like the gladiators in ancient Roman arenas…not as gentlemen." Boston sportswriter Tim Murnane called the Baltimore brand of baseball

> the dirtiest ball ever seen in this country… diving into the first baseman long after the ball is caught; throwing masks in front of the runner at home plate; catching them by their clothes at third base and interfering with the catcher, were only a few of the tricks performed by these young men from the South.

A famous quote from the voice of experience comes from Honus Wagner, regarding his first game against the Orioles:

> On my first time up, I got a single. The next time up, I might have had a triple but Jack Doyle gave me the hip at first, Hughie Jennings chased me wide around second, and John McGraw blocked me off at third, then jammed the ball into my belly, knocking the wind out of me.

Doyle fit right in with the Orioles and their style of play. At least until the tempers flared and their great run of championships was taken from them by Boston. Doyle and McGraw were said to have grown to truly dislike each other. One such flaring up was captured by Kavanagh and Macht:

> Some heads had become swollen with success. McGraw took to snarling and cussing at his teammates more than at the umpires, and became a royal pain in the neck to many of them. He rode Wee Willie Keeler to the point that they tangled naked in the clubhouse one day. Nobody moved to break it up. When McGraw was first to cry "enough," there were smiles among the onlookers. McGraw blamed "Dirty Jack" Doyle for stirring up trouble. Doyle blamed McGraw. They were probably both right.

McGraw insinuated that Doyle played more for his own stat line than to win. Having read much about Doyle and met with many who knew him personally, I am fairly certain that that nobody cared more about winning than Doyle did. Anger management issues: yes; interested in his numbers more than winning: no, definitely not. Having lost the pennant race, Hanlon decided to remake the team, and Doyle was moved to Washington in a six-player deal.

Doyle would stay connected with his famous Oriole teammates, attending reunions and the likes, including one put together by McGraw in 1922 that included old teammates: Sadie McMahon, Wilbert Robinson (in the middle of his own feud with McGraw), Steve Brodie, and manager Ned Hanlon. Jack Doyle along with the battery of Bill Hoffer and Bill Clarke would live long enough to enjoy the major league rebirth of the Baltimore Orioles in 1954 when the St. Louis Browns came to town. Both Doyle and Clarke were in attendance during the Opening Day festivities.

"Dirty Jack" Doyle during his playing days.

Fireworks in New York

After just 43 games of fairly typical play (including 17 games as player-manager) with Washington, New York Giants owner/president and resident madman Andrew Freedman was able to reacquire his former player during the summer of 1898 and reestablished him as the Giants' playing captain for the 1899 season. Doyle's second stint with the Giants would last through the 1900 season. Still a productive everyday player, Doyle suffered and fought along with the rest of his teammates through a particularly tumultuous period as the Giants bottomed out all the way to the cellar in 1900. As one might expect given this environment, cliques existed within the team. One clique included manager Buck Ewing and Jack Doyle. Another included George Davis and George Van Haltren. When the team got off to a slow start, Ewing was fired and replaced by Davis. Ewing blamed Davis, who supposedly had been home resting a sore knee (and "working" Freedman) while the team was on a long road trip. Doyle was subsequently traded before the 1901 season to the Chicago Cubs (for three players) after both he and Davis announced that it was impossible for them to get along. The saga would continue as Doyle would rejoin the Giants for the 1902 season as its captain and Davis would end up in Chicago (White Sox).

Fireworks in the clubhouse in 1900 for Doyle were matched on the field at least on one occasion. On Independence Day, "Dirty Jack" was called out in an attempt to steal second at Cincinnati and flew into a rage. He charged umpire Bob Emslie with such force that he pushed him to the ground. On the way down Emslie grabbed Doyle and they rolled over a couple of times in short center field before being separated by the other players. Both Doyle and umpire Emslie were arrested and charged with disorderly conduct. While Doyle was extremely apologetic regarding his behavior, the fact that both men were charged indicates some sort of mutual culpability. It was truly a different time.

A Reunion with Hanlon and a Shortstop Who Threw Spitters

In 1903 Ned Hanlon would trade for 33-year-old Jack Doyle to play first base and be the captain of his Brooklyn team. It would be one of the best years of his career, as Doyle led Brooklyn in almost every category. Playing in all 139 games, Doyle was all over the league leaderboard: putouts (1st), RBIs (3rd), singles (6th), at-bats and hits (7th), stolen bases (tied for 8th), times on base (tied for 10th). That was to be the swansong of his career, as Doyle tailed off in 1904.

In 1905, Jack Doyle came out of retirement to play in a single game for the New York Highlanders against the Tigers in Detroit. As recorded by Ernie Lanigan: "Clark Griffith sent him out to work at first in a game started by Jack Chesbro, whose spitball was real wet. In the final frame, a ball thrown from short took a freak jump as it neared Doyle and hit him in the jaw. Griffman lost the game, Doyle lost the job. Said it was time to quit when both the pitcher and shortstop threw spitters." Lanigan went on to interestingly comment: "Look up the games Chesbro pitched for New York and you'll find that he very seldom received errorless support."

The Reformation

Where would an aggressive, no-holds barred talented player go after his rabble-rousing days are over? Law enforcement, of course! Jack Doyle served as police commissioner of his hometown Holyoke in 1908 and '09. Perhaps even more ironically, Doyle came back to baseball in 1911 as an umpire. The great pitcher Christy Mathewson saw the irony in this reversal: "Umpire Bob Emslie is under cover. It is no secret, or I would not give way on him. But that luxuriant growth of hair apparently comes off at night like his collar and necktie… I had to laugh myself… when Mr. Lynch appointed Jack Doyle, formerly a first baseman and a hot-headed player, an umpire and scheduled him to work with Emslie. I remember the time several seasons ago when Doyle took offense at one of Bob's decisions and wrestled him all over the infield trying to get his wig off and show him up before the crowd. And then Emslie and he worked together like Damon and Pythias. This business makes strange bed-fellows."

On June 2, 1911, an announcement came from NL headquarters that umpire Jack Doyle had been temporarily relieved from duty "for not knowing the rules." After returning to the National League, Doyle had follow-up stints as an arbiter with the International League, PCL, Western League, and the American Association before hanging it up as an umpire.

According to a New York paper, Jack Doyle, by then the "ivory merchant of New York," was greatly enjoying the 1915 off-season until he was reminded that he still owned the remains of the Asbury club of the Atlantic League by a young prospect: Prospect: "You are Mr. Doyle, aren't you? Well, I'm a pitcher and I want you to give me a trial." Doyle: "I'll do ever better than that. I'll give you the club."

Bill Veeck, Gabby and the Hack

After bird-dogging as a scout for various clubs, including crosstown Chicago rivals, Doyle became the Cubs' head scout in 1920. It was a great run as the Cubs won pennants in '29, '32, '35, '38, and '45. Doyle has been personally credited with discovering numerous Cubs stars: Gabby Hartnett, Billy Herman, Riggs Stephenson, Phil Cavarretta, Guy Bush, Augie Galan, Charlie Root, Stan Hack, and others. Reportedly, it was upon Jack Doyle's recommendation that the Cubs acquired one of their greatest sluggers in Hack Wilson after the Giants failed to protect him against the draft. And there was great fun along the way, spring training on Catalina Island and countless cross-country trips in search of talent. A few interesting captured tales from the road:

Courtesy of Bill James:

John McGraw heard about Hartnett and sent Jesse Burkett to check him out, but Burkett reported that Hartnett would never make it as a catcher because his hands were too small. Hartnett disliked Burkett and would speak bitterly about him for many years after. He signed with Worcester of the Eastern League. He played fairly well and Jack Doyle, scouting for the Cubs, took a liking to him, reportedly because he has "a strong puss" and didn't back down on contact plays at the home plate. Doyle bought him for the Cubs.

Cubs president Bill Veeck Sr. once wired Doyle to head down to Fort Worth and take a look at a real prospect named George Washington. Doyle thought he was being kidded and telegraphed back: "Your wire received. Shall I detour via Springfield and catch Abe Lincoln?"

The aging, feisty Doyle still liked to mix it up with the players. The essence of this is nicely captured by Peter Golenbock in his description of a late night spring training poker game involving Gabby Hartnett, Doyle, and rookie Phil Cavarretta. After Cavarretta bluffed his

Jack Doyle (on left) dining with the O'Connells (the author's wife's grandparents).

NEAL MACKERTICH

way into a big final pot with only a pair of jacks to Doyle's three kings, a still fuming Doyle took the kid aside and said: "You only had a pair of jacks?... I could kill you…young man, you're a young player…we got good reports on you…if you play baseball the way you play poker, you're going to be an all-star."

Elder Statesman

Jack Doyle's commentary and charisma were not limited to the ball yard. In 1949, at the age of 79, Jack Doyle attended the wedding and reception of my future in-laws and slipped them five crisp hundred dollar bills (quite a sum in those days). Upon hearing a year later that Betty-Anne was with child, Doyle promised another five hundred if it was a boy and nothing if it was a girl. Alas, my future sister-in-law was off to an inauspicious start.

Two other lasting family memories of "Dirty Jack" from this era include visiting with old ChiSox manager "Pants" Rowland (where have all the great nicknames gone?) out in California and attending the first integrated World Series, as Jackie Robinson and the Dodgers hosted the Yankees of Joe DiMaggio at Ebbets Field. My mother-in-law Betty-Anne, then a freshman at the prestigious Pratt Institute in Brooklyn, recalls "people being pretty excited." For Betty-Anne, who is not much of a sports fan, it was her first and only baseball game. I haven't dared to take her to another, as that is a pretty high standard.

Even into his 80s, Doyle regularly traveled south for spring training, providing input for the Cubs, and on the game in general ("it's improved tremendously, just about everything has gotten better—pitching, infield play and hitting… baseball is the future of our country"), and participating in various first (the Orioles' return to Baltimore) and last pitch (the last game at the Polo Grounds) events.

John Joseph Doyle died of heart failure on New Year's Eve 1959 at the age of 89 in his hometown of Holyoke, MA. Active in the game to the end, Doyle was employed by the Cubs as either their head scout or as a scout/adviser for the final 38 years of his life. Amazingly, "Dirty Jack" Doyle was employed by professional baseball as player, manager, umpire, and scout for 71 years. A full and interesting baseball life led indeed. ∎

Bibliography

Bready, James. *Baseball in Baltimore.* Baltimore: Johns Hopkins, 1998.

Golenbock, Peter. *Wrigleyville.* New York: St. Martin's Griffin, 1999.

Green, Paul. *Forgotten Fields.* Milwaukee, Wisconsin: Parker Publications, 1984.

James, Bill. *Whatever Happened to the Hall of Fame?* New York: Simon & Schuster, 1994.

James, Bill. *The New Bill James Historical Abstract.* New York: Free Press, 2001.

Kavanagh, Jack. *Uncle Robbie.* Cleveland: SABR, 1999.

Palmer, Pete. *The 2005 ESPN Baseball Encyclopedia.* New York: Sterling, 2005.

Ritter, Lawrence. *The Glory of Their Times.* New York: Macmillan, 1966.

Shatzkin, Mike, and Jim Charlton. *The Ballplayers.* New York: Arbor House, 1990.

Schwarz, Alan. *The Numbers Game.* New York: St. Martin's Press, 2004.

The Library at the Baseball Hall of Fame, archived articles and photographs.

Tom Greenwade and His "007" Assignment

by Jim Kreuz

On April 24, 1943, Brooklyn Dodger president Branch Rickey sent a confidential memo to his top scout with instructions to begin searching for "colored" ballplayers, thus setting the wheels in motion that would result in the signing of Jackie Robinson. This document, and those that followed shortly thereafter, are historically significant yet have remained a secret until now. They read like an Ian Fleming novel, with Rickey cast as "M" and his scout, Tom Greenwade, as James Bond.

One has to be a hard-core baseball fan to recognize Greenwade's name, but you will recognize some of the ballplayers this scout has signed—Bill Virdon, Pee Wee Reese, Gil Hodges, George Kell, Hank Bauer, Tom Sturdivant, Elston Howard, Clete Boyer, Ralph Terry, Bobby Murcer, and Mickey Mantle. Yet the ballplayer he was probably most proud of recommending, but is least known for being associated with, is Jackie Robinson. Before telling the story behind this scout's search for Mr. Robinson, you need to hear about the first "colored" player the Dodgers tried to sign.

Silvio Garcia – Their First Choice

His name is Silvio Garcia, and when the Dodgers tried to sign this Cuban shortstop in 1943 he was playing in Mexico, which is one reason why Branch Rickey sent his top scout there in May 1943. Rickey was intent on keeping this scouting effort top-secret, so his first conversation with Greenwade was in person, prior to the April 24th memo. The two arranged to meet at the Biltmore

JIM KREUZ *was introduced to SABR by former ML pitcher Tim McNamara, whose high school catcher was a kid named Gabby Hartnett, his shortstop at Fordham was Frankie Frisch, and his best friend on the Boston Braves was an outfielder named Casey Stengel.*

Hotel in Kansas City, but Greenwade had trouble locating his boss because Rickey signed in at the hotel registry as Greenwade, not wanting the locals to know the Dodger president was in town and start asking why.

The why included a request to check out "colored" ballplayers in Mexico, and in particular Garcia, whom Dodger manager Leo Durocher had seen play in the Mexican League. The Brooklyn skipper claimed that Joe DiMaggio couldn't carry Garcia's glove. I'm assuming someone asked Leo if Garcia could carry DiMaggio's bat.

In a December 3, 1953, newspaper article, Greenwade described how their hotel meeting went. "All that secrecy had me buffaloed. And I got more curious after he sat and talked to me about things that had happened in his life. He told me one story about the time a hotel refused to allow the catcher of his Ohio Wesleyan team to have a room. The catcher was a Negro, and I began to get the idea."

Tom only had two problems with this trip. One, he didn't want to keep it a secret from his wife, Florence, and two, he didn't speak Spanish. True to form, Rickey quickly solved both by suggesting that he take his wife, and he provided a translator. Florence made it to Mexico, but the translator did not. It seems he went on a drinking binge in San Antonio and was left behind.

Where Did the Documents Come From?

I'm not your typical SABR researcher. If it isn't right underneath my nose, I'm not going to find it. It took a few subtle suggestions from editor Jim Charlton for me to finally pull the shovel out and start digging. A portion of the information for this article was handed to me by the Greenwade family. That was the easy part—no shovel required. While I was working on an earlier article about Greenwade's scouting career, I asked his son and daughter for copies of any documents that would add to the piece. What I received were confidential memos from Branch Rickey directing his number one scout to begin a clandestine search for ballplayers in Mexico in early 1943. I saved these gems for this article.

It's been widely assumed that the Brooklyn Dodgers' scouting of the first black major league ballplayer of the 20th century did not seriously begin until the spring of 1945. Jackie Robinson was signed by Rickey in October of that year to a Montreal Royals contract, and in 1947 became the man that "broke the color barrier." The Robinson signing in 1945 coincided with the death of baseball Commissioner Kenesaw Mountain Landis, a man many assumed to be against baseball integration, in the minor leagues as well as the majors. But was he?

Landis Wasn't the Entire Reason

According to David Pietrusza's well-written book on Landis, *Judge and Jury,* we shouldn't lump all the blame on the Judge for the lack of "colored" ballplayers in the majors. The remainder goes to the Jury (Major League Baseball and America). Quoting Pietrusza from page 406,

What share of the responsibility for baseball's Jim Crow status did Landis bear? What were his attitudes on race and how did he handle racial matters—both as arbiter of baseball and on the federal bench? The answers may never be really known, but the picture of Landis as an "openly biased" individual who almost single-handedly blocked baseball's integration clearly distorts the actual events, America's racial attitudes, and perhaps even the man himself. Landis certainly bears some responsibility for baseball's segregation. However, to imply that it was he—and he alone—who created or prolonged the situation whitewashes the attitudes and actions of much, if not most, of baseball's establishment.

Quoting Richard Dozer's 1983 *Baseball Digest* article on Leo Durocher and a meeting Durocher had with Commissioner Landis at his office,

Durocher recalled that he mentioned having played in an exhibition against Josh Gibson, the great Negro League catcher, and observed that even though Gibson had great talent he apparently was not welcome in the major leagues. "Landis looked down at me with that glare of his and said 'Bring me the man who says you can't have a colored player in the big leagues, and I'll take care of him real quick.' I believe to this day that

Landis would have accepted the black player if an owner had signed one, Leo said.

So why was Rickey so secretive? My guess is he assumed that if Landis wouldn't balk at the signing of a black ballplayer, the owners would. That's one secret Branch took with him to his grave.

The Search Begins

John Thorn and Jules Tygiel wrote an excellent piece on the Jackie Robinson signing, but could only find documentation on the search that went back to April 1945 when a handwritten memo uncovered in the Rickey Papers gives instructions to Dodger scouts to "Cover Negro teams for possible major league talent." The memo was signed "Chas. D. Clark." No one knows who this man was. It could have been a fictitious name.

We now have proof that the date the Dodgers' search began was on April 24, 1943, in the form of an inter-club communication from Rickey's office in Brooklyn to Tom Greenwade at his home in Willard, MO. It's titled, PERSONAL AND CONFIDENTIAL.

Dear Tom:

I am enclosing some very confidential material. In the newspaper you will see averages. I don't believe you can afford to show these to Tuero. You will have to work them out for yourself."

Tuero is possibly Oscar Tuero, a Cuban pitcher who had played with the St Louis Cardinals from 1918-1920.

In a follow-up memo dated April 29, 1943, Rickey mentions that,

I am very sure that his (Tuero's) services will not be required more than two to four weeks and not that long if you find that you can get along very nicely without him. Of course, at no time now or in the future will he know anything about part of the objective of your trip…

He later added,

Tuero is not at all above chiseling. He was a chiseler as a ball player, so far as that is concerned, and if he shows very decided tendencies to do the chiseling act with us, I am inclined to have you go on down on your health seeking job without him…. As a matter of fact, I don't trust him…

Rickey also gives some advice regarding Tom's upcoming scouting trip to Mexico. In the same note, the Dodger president mentions that he is "hoping that we will be able to get several of them signed to Durham or Olean contracts, or even Montreal if we can find one good enough." Of course, when Jackie Robinson was signed, he was sent to their top minor league club in Montreal. Notice he never mentions "colored" ballplayers, only referring to them as "them." That's because he'd already conveyed his intent during their Kansas City hotel meeting, and he didn't want to risk someone besides Greenwade reading the memos. Tom knew he was to focus on "colored" ballplayers.

By May 10, 1943, Tom Greenwade was receiving transmittals in Mexico City from Rickey in Brooklyn. You can feel his anticipation as he wrote:

> Dear Tom,
>
> I am enclosing some information herewith. Write me fully airmail and mark it personal and confidential on the outside of your envelope and give me all the dope on players. We can certainly use some good Mexican boys right now at both Durham and Olean. The Durham Club is terrible. I don't believe you should try to sign any boys until you get a full report on everybody and know exactly what you want to do with everybody before you start to work on anybody. I hope you will be able to work quietly without any newspaper publicity whatever.
>
> If you run into anything especially good I will send help to you or I might even come myself.

Greenwade also received detailed information prior to leaving his home on Silvio Garcia who was playing in Mexico at that time, and was considered the best ballplayer from his country. The two attached photos of Garcia that accompanied the report definitely would qualify him as a "colored ballplayer."

Silvio Garcia – The Attempted Signing

In an April 14, 1958, *Los Angeles Times* article written by Braven Dyer on Walter O'Malley, I found some interesting information on our subject. "O'Malley (and not Rickey) almost became the man to sign the first Negro for Major League Baseball. Early in his affiliation with the Dodgers O'Malley went to Havana, Cuba, to sign a Negro shortstop named Silvio Garcia. On arrival

he discovered Garcia with 49 other Cuban Army conscripts in a pup tent encampment.

"As a big sports hero, Garcia was the first man tapped by the military. Not hankering to tangle with the whole Cuban army, O'Malley staged a strategic retreat and Garcia never appeared in a major league line-up."

According to Murray Polner's well-written 1982 biography on Branch Rickey, "Walter O'Malley…went to Cuba in 1944 with a letter of credit for $25,000 with instructions from Rickey to sign Silvio Garcia, a black player, only to learn that Garcia had been drafted into the Cuban army." I spoke to Polner and he recounted the O'Malley interview. The author could find no other living source in the early 1980s who could corroborate O'Malley's story, yet portions are backed up by the Dodgers scouting report on Garcia, which mentions that he might be redrafted soon into the Cuban army.

The only thing that bothers me about O'Malley's statement is the year—1944. All the secret documents from the Greenwade family are from 1943, and yet in a December 3, 1953, newspaper article given to me by the Greenwades there is mention of Tom discussing his trip to Mexico to scout Silvio Garcia in 1944. One of three things happened: both Greenwade and O'Malley were either telling the truth, they were covering up the actual date, or, they both forgot the correct date/year.

I'm convinced they both simply forgot what year it was when telling their story. I'm certain that O'Malley made the offer in 1943, not 1944, because Garcia would have been back in the army by 1944. The clincher is the fact that Rickey was anxious to sign someone in 1943, as is evident by his tone in the Greenwade memos. Garcia was 28 at the time, two years older than Robinson was when signed by the Dodgers.

I don't think it's too much of a stretch to take O'Malley's story and add our report on Garcia to conclude that the Dodgers made an attempt to sign him in Cuba after the end of the 1943 season. Yet, based on the 1958 *Los Angeles Times* article, O'Malley never actually approached Silvio with the offer, thus allowing their search to remain a secret.

In an October 3, 1956, article in *The Sporting News* on our scout, this item came up. "On Greenwade's say-so, the Dodgers steered away from Garcia…" Quoting

George Weiss and Tom Greenwade.

Greenwade in this piece, "He couldn't pull the ball….He was a right handed hitter—everything went to right field." My conclusion—Greenwade wasn't high on Garcia, but Rickey was, based on Durocher's recommendation, and when the Cuban army stepped in and blocked the move, Tom convinced the Dodger brass to drop any future pursuit of the shortstop.

In Roberto Echevarria's book, *The Pride of Havana,* the author mentions the Dodgers' attempt at signing Silvio.

> Legend has it that Silvio Garcia was seriously considered by Branch Rickey to be the man to break the color barrier in the United States, but that when asked what he would do if a rival hurled racial slurs at him, the Cuban answered: "I would kill him." This ended his chances.

Unfortunately, Silvio Garcia passed away in 1978, so there is no way we can substantiate this story. When Roberto Echevarria mentioned to me that Garcia has a son living in Miami but did not know what his first name was, I realized my time playing detective Colombo on the Silvio Garcia story was over. The ballplayer thought to be one of the best shortstops in Cuban baseball history won two Mexican League batting titles and was considered a superb fielder, so he had the talent to possibly play

in the major leagues. Unfortunately, the closest he came was when he spent time in the USA playing in the Negro Leagues.

On a side note, there was some success in that Mexico trip. A 21-year-old catcher with the Monterrey club caught Greenwade's eye, and a recommendation was forwarded to the home office. A few years later the Dodgers signed him—Roy Campanella.

The Scouting of Jackie Robinson

In *The Sporting News* article of 1956, author Harold Rosenthal states, "He [Greenwade] was the only scout used on the Jackie Robinson job," a statement repeated by Tom's son and daughter to me. Quoting Greenwade from this article,

> I saw Jackie play about 20 times…but I never spoke to him once. When I finally did speak to him he had already made the Dodgers and I was scouting for the Yankees. John Griffin, the Brooklyn clubhouse man, introduced us in St Louis.

Tom Greenwade scouted for the Dodgers until December 1945, when he signed on with the Yankees. He conferred with his boss, Mr. Rickey, prior to making the decision to leave, and Rickey chose not to hold him back, knowing the Yankees would make Tom the highest-paid scout in baseball, which they did. His annual salary jumped from $3,600 to over $11,000 (including an annual bonus).

What we can't answer with certainty is why the Dodgers president waited two years after the attempted signing of Silvio Garcia before making the second attempt—with Jackie Robinson. Again, did he fear a backlash from Landis and the owners? My guess is, yes, he got cold feet until Landis passed away and our country was in a state of euphoria after winning the Second World War.

Greenwade described the task of following Robinson's 1945 Kansas City Monarch ball club in *The Sporting News* piece. "The war was still on, there wasn't much transportation available, and the Monarchs got around by bus. Most of the time I chased them...When I scouted Robinson, I told Mr. Rickey that he didn't have a shortstop's arm. It wasn't strong and he needed to dance a step and a half before cutting loose. Maybe he'd make a first baseman or second baseman, but never a shortstop."

To stress his singular effort one more time, "I want to make it very clear that I was the only scout used on Robinson. The only time Clyde Sukeforth went to see him it rained and they didn't play." My impression of Tom Greenwade, formed via research on this piece, was that he was a very modest man, did not go around bragging about his exploits, but wanted to keep the facts straight. Keep in mind that if his recommendation of Robinson had resulted in a bust, Greenwade's reputation would have been scarred. He had quite a bit riding on this and therefore should receive due credit.

Clyde Sukeforth – Robinson Recommendation

Clyde Sukeforth is credited by some as the scout who recommended Jackie Robinson, yet we now know he was used as a checker by the Dodgers to confirm Tom Greenwade's recommendation. In a November 28, 1993, phone interview, Clyde describes that day.

> I didn't see him play before we signed him. He [Rickey] knew a lot about Robinson. He just sent me down there to check out his arm. He [Robinson] naturally couldn't understand [why Clyde was there], was very interested in why Rickey was interested in his arm, and he developed that he had fallen on his shoulder the night before and was out of the lineup for a couple of days, maybe more.

So I asked him to meet me down at my hotel, and he did. He kept asking me [why], and I just told him, "I just work here. I can't tell you anything but I do know there is a lot of interest in you." There was a colored club in Brooklyn not affiliated with the Dodgers but you had a right to assume that it was. So I told him, "Mr. Rickey can answer your questions, why don't you come on back to Brooklyn with me?"

And the rest was history.

The Next Bob Feller

Tom Greenwade was not always perfect when projecting a player's future. Our scout's biggest disappointment in his talent-hunting career was the hard-throwing, hard-luck Dodger pitcher Rex Barney, who tossed a no-hitter and had a 15-win season with Brooklyn. Tom thought he was the second coming of Bob Feller, but Rex's control problems ended his short career.

Only Two Were Humming "Where Have You Gone, Mr. Robinson…"

The only two Dodgers that were in on the Jackie Robinson signing were Branch Rickey and Tom Greenwade. It was obvious Rickey wanted to keep things close to his vest, and he did so by only including his best scout. And his best scout was the best that ever scouted. Greenwade's major league ballplayers (over 40 of them) would agree with this. When Mickey Mantle was sent down to the Kansas City club in 1951, he didn't immediately call his father, Mutt Mantle. His first phone call was to his trusted friend and scout Tom Greenwade. The scout was close to all of his players, as should be his plaque in Cooperstown.

Where would the Dodgers and Yankees of the late 1940s to the mid 1960s be without the man that signed a majority of their stars? Probably watching the World Series from the stands.

In 1964, Tom Greenwade left the Yankees and his scouting career to live out the rest of his life in his hometown of Willard, MO. He passed away in 1986 at the age of 81. ∎

The Suspension of Leo Durocher

by David Mandell

"I never questioned the integrity of an umpire. Their eyesight, yes."
           – Leo Durocher

In September 1941 Brooklyn Dodger president Larry MacPhail was elated. His Dodgers had defeated the Boston Braves and were returning by train to New York City, the National League pennant safely in hand. To celebrate the Dodgers' triumph, MacPhail waited for them at the city's 125th Street railroad stop. MacPhail brought champagne for his victorious players and eagerly waited for their arrival. To his surprise, the train raced by without stopping, headed directly to Grand Central Station, 83 blocks south, and left MacPhail and his champagne buckets behind. MacPhail was convinced that his Dodger manager, Leo "the Lip" Durocher, son of a railroad engineer, had ordered the conductor not to stop. Durocher later maintained that he did not know MacPhail was even there. It did not matter to MacPhail. A major league feud was on. Six seasons later, MacPhail and Durocher met again, resulting in the suspension of Leo Durocher.

Born July 27, 1905, in West Springfield, MA, Durocher reached the majors in 1925, playing two games with the New York Yankees. Durocher spent the next two seasons in the minors, playing in Atlanta and St. Paul. In 1928, he rejoined the Yankees for two seasons, hitting .270 and .246. While teammate Babe Ruth shattered batting records, Durocher hit no home runs and picked up a reputation as a "good field no hit" player. In his memoirs Durocher recalled how the Babe labeled him the all-American Out. During his time with the Yankees rumors circulated that Durocher had stolen Babe Ruth's watch.

DAVID MANDELL *is an attorney in Connecticut and has followed the Giants since Herman Franks was the manager.*

Durocher angrily denied them and decades later he was still indignant. As he put it, "Fresh, yes, Pool hustler, yes. But steal the Babe's watch? Get out of here!" The Yanks sold Durocher to Cincinnati, where he spent three seasons before being sold to the St. Louis Cardinals. Playing with its famous Gashouse Gang for four seasons, Durocher hit his career-best batting average as a regular, .286 in 1936.

In 1938, he went to Brooklyn, and became player-manager in 1939, replacing Burleigh Grimes. Durocher's rival for the job was Babe Ruth, then a first base coach with the club. When Dodger boss Larry MacPhail selected Durocher, Ruth left the club. Durocher recalled his initial discussion with MacPhail about managing. MacPhail asked, "What makes you think you can manage?" When he replied that the only way he could prove it was on the ball field, MacPhail responded, "You a manager? That's the funniest thing I ever heard." The two tangled quickly over a bingo prize Durocher won at a pre-spring training workout in Hot Springs, AK. MacPhail ordered Durocher to turn over his $660 winnings and accused him of gambling. MacPhail "fired" Durocher, the beginning of a ritual where MacPhail would tell Durocher he was fired but never carry out the threat. By the end of his career Durocher joked that MacPhail had fired him 60 times.

Durocher phased down his playing time, becoming full-time manager in 1946. His 1941 team won the National League pennant, and the team finished the 1946 season two games behind the league champion St. Louis Cardinals. Durocher's tenure included an arrest for fighting with a heckler who accused him of throwing a game. The fan told reporters that a furious Durocher said, "You've got a mother, how would you like to call her names?" before striking him. In Durocher's version, the fan fell on wet cement.

Durocher became baseball's best-known manager, and rumors flew that he might switch to the Yankees. On October 3, 1946, Durocher denied them. His former president Larry MacPhail now ran and partly owned the Yankees. Durocher told reporters,

Larry MacPhail gave me my first chance to be a manager. He was a wonderful man to work for. Yes, I expect to see him now that the season is over. He is a good friend of mine and I expect to see him often.

Four weeks later Durocher arrived in Columbus, OH to meet Dodger president Branch Rickey and said no one had approached him about the Yankees job. Intrigue continued as Dodger coach Charlie Dressen resigned and joined the Yankee organization. In early November the Yankees settled the issue, naming Bucky Harris as manager. MacPhail decided against Durocher, saying, "I don't think Leo would have been the logical choice for this job. Don't get me wrong. I think he is a great manager, but there were other angles involved."

On November 25, Durocher signed a contract with the Dodgers reported to be $42,000 plus a $20,000 attendance bonus. Durocher denied even reading the contract, saying,

I can make more money next year than I did last season under the bonus plan. Believe it or not I actually signed the paper without turning it over to see how much the salary was. Why shouldn't I? Mr. Rickey has always been like a father to me.

Durocher naturally couldn't let Larry MacPhail have the last word. He added that MacPhail had called him three times, offering more money, but he had said no each time. With the managerial issues settled, baseball looked forward to the 1947 season and the arrival of Jackie Robinson with the Dodgers.

Durocher's offseason was one of the most memorable in baseball history. On January 21, 1947, his private life became very public. Durocher had developed a relationship with actress Laraine Day. Born in Roosevelt, UT, the 29-year-old beauty had already acted in 32 movies, beginning with a small part in the 1937 film *Stella Dallas*. She was best known for her role as a nurse in the *Dr. Kildare* series. The couple married in El Paso, TX. Marriage is normally a happy event, but Leo's had a

problem. In California, Day was still considered a married woman by Judge George A. Dockweller, who presided over her divorce case from her first husband, airport administrator Ray Hendricks. Unwilling to wait until California courts concluded her divorce, Day crossed the Mexican border and divorced in Juarez. After her Mexican divorce, Day and Durocher found a justice of the peace in El Paso to marry them.

Judge Dockweller was irate when he heard the news. Durocher phoned him twice, proclaiming his love for Day. Dockweller was skeptical, saying, "He is a very facile talker, but this is one umpire he will have a hard time convincing." The Durochers agreed not to live as husband and wife until Dockweller completed Day's marital litigation. The press reported that Durocher had moved to actor George Raft's home, but Durocher claimed to have checked into the Miramar Hotel in Santa Monica.

Day's lawyer, Isaac Pacht, demanded Dockweller's removal, accusing him of bias. Husband Ray Hendricks preferred to keep Dockweller. His attorney, Joseph Scott, told another California judge considering the matter, "This particular judge, [Dockweller], has serious and wholesome views on family life and the sanctity of marriage. I don't blame this wretched girl. I blame this Durocher—this long distance chatterbox." Compared to the other things he had been called, chatterbox was mild for the Lip. The divorce litigation eventually ended, and Durocher and Day married in California to avoid any further allegations of adultery or bigamy. The controversy continued to follow Durocher.

His boss, Branch Rickey, announced his support for Durocher. "Never for a moment have I considered the possibility that Leo might not continue as manager," he announced and denied that the Day marriage would have any bearing on his status. He emphasized, "We will talk about a dozen things, but not one of the dozen has to do with what happened in California."

Others were less forgiving. On February 28, the Catholic Youth Organization withdrew from the Brooklyn Dodger Knothole Club. The Dodgers feared the loss of its 125,000 members and fans. Reverend Vincent J. Powell of the Brooklyn Diocese accused Durocher of undermining the moral and spiritual training of youngsters. Powell said the "present manager of the Brooklyn baseball team is not the kind of leader we want for our young people."

Retired pitcher Harry Coveleski didn't even wait for the marriage controversy to become public. From his Pennsylvania tavern, Coveleski said, "Durocher's another smartie like John McGraw of the Giants. Durocher thinks he can win by out talking the other fellow." Coveleski wasn't finished. The "Giant Killer" added, "That bum, Durocher! He can't manage a coal mine team for my money."

Durocher soon had more problems than complaints from baseball's old-timers. He got an inkling of what was coming when commissioner A. B. "Happy" Chandler gave him a list of reputed gangsters and gamblers to avoid. Durocher agreed and considered the matter closed. Unfortunately for him, Larry MacPhail did not. MacPhail erupted over an article published under Durocher's name in the *Brooklyn Eagle* newspaper. Actually written by Dodger traveling secretary Harold Parrott, it teased MacPhail about his hiring of Dodger coach Charlie Dressen. With the Dodgers and Yankees playing in Havana, Cuba, confrontation was inevitable.

Dick Young, the sportswriter who went on to a long career covering or creating feuds, asked Durocher what he thought about two of the men that commissioner Chandler had ordered Durocher to avoid, appearing in MacPhail's box at the Dodger-Yankee games. Did he agree with Branch Rickey that baseball had different rules for MacPhail than it had for Durocher? Durocher proved his nickname Lippy was appropriate. In his memoirs he wrote, "Did I agree? Well, you know me. Ask me a question and you get an answer. You're damn right I agreed."

MacPhail announced that he would file a complaint with commissioner Chandler. Durocher learned of the complaint while he was in the Panama Canal Zone. Chandler asked MacPhail to think it over, but he was adamant. Durocher defended himself, telling reporters that MacPhail had tried to run him out of baseball for turning down his offer of $75,000 to manage the Yankees. The hearing was held in a Sarasota, FL, hotel with Yankees officials MacPhail and Dan Topping on one side and Dodger directors on the other. Durocher recalled that the most important Dodger official, Branch Rickey,

Durocher as manager of the Giants.

was away at a family funeral and Leo's request for a delay was denied.

As commissioner, Chandler had extraordinary powers. According to Professor Jeffrey Standen of Willamette University College of Law, an expert in sports law, Major League Baseball's constitution grants the commissioner authority over clubs and employees. The commissioner may take action that he finds is in the best interest of baseball. Baseball rules 21 and 21f allow the commissioner to discipline employees for misconduct. Chandler's decision would be final. Professor Standen points out that baseball's rules give its commissioner the power to suspend and courts will generally not intervene unless the commissioner's decision is arbitrary or capricious, a heavy burden to meet.

Durocher described the hearing room as resembling a courtroom, but his rights were limited. MacPhail recited the article that had infuriated him, and Durocher told him he hadn't meant anything by it. Durocher wrote that he thought he had patched things up with MacPhail when MacPhail ripped the article up and told him to forget it. Chandler's questioning focused on allegations that as manager he played high-stakes card games with a pitcher. Durocher denied it, saying he never collected anything from the player. Rickey spoke to Chandler several days later, and the hearings ended with the participants waiting for the decision.

The announcement came April 9 as Durocher and the Dodger management met at the team's Brooklyn office. Durocher was suspended for the season and the suspension was extended to cover the World Series. Major League Baseball secretary-treasurer Walter W. Mulbry defended the suspension saying, "A long time ago the commissioner told Durocher that he already had too much unfavorable publicity and that the next offense would be his last." Durocher spent Opening Day watching his wife act in the movie *Tycoon* at RKO Studios in Lone Pine, CA. He considered suing Major League baseball but decided against it. The Dodgers hired Burt Shotton to manage, and he directed the club to the National League pennant.

Durocher said little publicly during the season, playing golf in California and hoping for reinstatement. On September 25 he flew to New York to meet Branch Rickey during the World Series. Mulbry announced that once the series ended, Durocher's suspension was terminated and he could negotiate with any club. Rickey and the Dodgers would not rehire Durocher without a letter signed by Commissioner Chandler. In December, the Dodgers decided. Durocher was named manager again and Burt Shotton was appointed farm system director. Rickey stressed his objections to Durocher's suspension, after saying he did not want to re-open the controversy. "The Commissioner knows I felt that Durocher had not done wrong."

Durocher began the 1948 season with the Dodgers, but his tenure wasn't long. Despite Branch Rickey's restoring him as manager, Durocher suspected that Rickey wanted him out. Given Rickey's treatment of Dodger Eddie Stanky, Durocher had good reason to wonder about his loyalty. Stanky requested a salary increase to $20,000. Five days after signing Stanky for $18,000, Rickey traded him to the Boston Braves. After sending Durocher on a scouting trip to Canada during the All-Star break, Rickey summoned him to his office but refused to commit the Dodgers to retaining him for the season. Instead Rickey told Durocher that Giants owner Horace Stoneham wanted him to manage the Giants. Not getting a commitment from Rickey, Durocher met with Stoneham, and on July 16 he replaced Mel Ott as Giants manager. Burt Shotton returned to manage the Dodgers. Given the rivalry between the Dodgers and Giants, the swap was shocking. It was Mel Ott's Giants who were the object of Durocher's trademark remark that nice guys finish last. Durocher remained as Giants manager through 1955, winning two pennants and the 1954 World Series. His most memorable moment came when the Giants defeated the Dodgers on Bobby Thomson's home run in 1951.

Durocher left the Giants after the 1955 season, saying he was fired because owner Horace Stoneham knew he was quitting. He became a broadcaster and the host of *The NBC Comedy Hour* for three episodes in 1956. In 1961 he rejoined the Los Angeles Dodgers as one of manager Walt Alston's coaches. As a coach he remained as feisty as he had been as manager. It didn't take long for the old Durocher to surface. In his first week he got into a heated exchange with umpire Jocko Conlan, ending it with an exchange of kicks. Durocher ended up in a familiar place, under suspension, although only for three games.

Durocher stayed with the Dodgers to 1964 and then became Cubs manager in 1966. In midseason 1972 he was fired but soon became the Houston Astros manager for the remainder of 1972. He retired after the 1973 season. Throughout the 1960s and 70s Durocher regularly appeared in television shows, usually playing himself in episodes of *The Beverly Hillbillies, The Donna Reed Show, The Munsters,* and others. His final role came in a 1987 movie about the Yankees, once again acting as himself. He died October 7, 1991, in Palm Springs, CA. Three years later, Leo Durocher was admitted into the Baseball Hall of Fame.

Laraine Day and Durocher divorced in 1960. Day acted until her retirement in 1986, last appearing in a two-part episode of *Murder, She Wrote.* Larry MacPhail died October 1, 1975, in Miami, FL. MacPhail was elected into the Hall of Fame in 1978, and is remembered for introducing night games to baseball.

To paraphrase the Lip, nice guys end up in the Hall of Fame. ■

Ray Brown in Canada

His Forgotten Years

by Bill Young

Ray Brown: Hall of Famer

When Negro Leagues great Ray Brown was inducted posthumously into baseball's National Hall of Fame in 2006 as one of 17 individuals chosen for their essential contributions to "the history of blacks in the game," he also became the first player with links to the Quebec Provincial League ever to receive such an honor.

Thought by many to be the equal of Satchel Paige, Brown was recognized principally for his outstanding achievements with the legendary Homestead Grays of the 1930s and 1940s, although his Hall of Fame plaque does acknowledge "several standout seasons pitching in Cuba, Puerto Rico and Mexico." It makes no mention of Quebec.

That is unfortunate, for in the years Brown spent north of the border the burly right-hander lined up with three teams in three different leagues and helped each to a league championship. Although pretty much forgotten now, his story, and the impact he had on La Belle Province, form an important part of his legacy, and tell us much about the history of baseball in Quebec at that time.

Brown was born in Alger, OH, in 1908. By the early 1930s he had emerged as the ace of the Pittsburgh-based Homestead Grays' pitching staff, a role he maintained through 1945. The key to his success was always his uncanny ability to keep hitters off balance. "About the best pitcher in baseball at that time," is how Negro Leagues veteran Charlie Biot once described him. "He had control; he had a number of pitches."

BILL YOUNG *is a retired college dean and museum curator, and a founding member of the SABR-Quebec chapter. His main research interests pertain to the history of baseball in Quebec, especially the Quebec Provincial League and the Montreal Expos. He is the co-author (with Danny Gallagher) of the best-selling book,* Remembering the Montreal Expos.

Although primarily a curveballer, Brown's repertoire included a deceptive fastball and both a slider and a sinker. Later in his career he added a knuckleball. He accumulated great pitching statistics in his years with Homestead—his lifetime winning percentage (.704) ranks second all-time—and throughout the Gray's outstanding streak of eight pennants in nine years, he typically started a third or more of the team's league games.

Stanley "Doc" Glenn, a catcher with the Quebec Braves in 1952 and 1953, who put in seven seasons with the Philadelphia Stars at the start of his career, remembers Brown well. Although they never faced each other in the Provincial League, Glenn still recalls the years he endured batting against Brown in the Negro National League.

"He was a great pitcher—not a good pitcher—a great pitcher," said Glenn recently, speaking from his home in Pennsylvania. "He had all the tricks. He was number one for the Homestead Grays for a lot of years." Glenn characterized Brown as "a complete ballplayer. When he wasn't pitching he would play the outfield. I never knew him personally, only as a ballplayer, but he was a fine one." The former receiver considers Ray Brown's Hall of Fame selection to be "great news, an honour well deserved."

Josh Gibson Jr. played in the Provincial League himself in 1951, and he considers Brown to be one of the best pitchers he ever saw. "Number one is Satchel [Paige]," Gibson, the son of black baseball's greatest hitter, told diarist Brent Kelley, "then Ray Brown. I watched Ray pitch as a kid, but I batted against Satchel. Damn, Ray Brown was good."

But with time all things do change, and by the late 1940s, as the luster of black baseball had begun to fade, Brown discovered he was running out of places to play, especially with his own abilities now on the wane. He would have to seek out new and greener pastures. And he was all on his own. His extravagant marriage to the daughter of Grays' owner Cum Posey—it took place at home plate on the Fourth of July, 1935—had imploded some time before, done in by his hard drinking and the uncertainties that surround a life in baseball.

However, jobs were hard to find, especially for a black man who was pushing 40. Although baseball's racial barrier had been shattered five or so years earlier, there were still many towns where non-white players were not welcome. And so Brown headed for the Mexican League and Tampico, where matters of race had never been a problem. After several good years there, the rambling urge once more kicked in, and by 1950 he had packed his suitcase and set out on the road again.

Ray Brown: Heading for Quebec

This time Brown gravitated in the opposite direction, toward Sherbrooke in Quebec's Eastern Townships, where baseball was the summer game and the local entry in the Provincial League was one of the strongest in the circuit. He would have known about the league, la provinciale as it was called in French, from fellow travelers encountered in winter ball and elsewhere; he would have been aware of its readiness to sign players of whatever race or nationality as long as they could play.

The Provincial League had existed in various forms for much of the century, mostly as an independent, some would say outlaw, organization. It had a long history of finding spots for talented players of color. Indeed, as far back as the late 1800s there were recorded accounts of black players on local teams. In 1929, the peripatetic Chappie Johnson had placed a unit composed solely of black players in a local league. According to Quebec baseball historian Christian Trudeau, black men were a constant presence in Quebec baseball from those days forward. Ted Page, Alphonso Lattimore, Alfred Wilson, Ormond Sampson, are just some of the names which appear regularly in accounts of that time.

When baseball finally blew open the doors of integration in 1946 and six men of color inked contracts with clubs recognized by Organized Baseball, it was more than just a coincidence that four of the six played for Quebec-based teams in three different leagues, and one of them was Canadian-born.

By 1949, regarded by some as the golden year of Quebec baseball, the Provincial League had become famous (or infamous, depending on one's point of view) as a refuge for baseball's dispossessed. Former Negro League players [Terris McDuffie, Quincy Trouppe], young Latinos [Vic Power, Roberto Vargas], displaced major leaguers from the war years [Walter Brown, Tex Shirley], local home-grown talent [Roland Gladu, Paul Calvert]—all were welcome.

So too were those major leaguers who had jumped to the Mexican League in 1946, and now suspended, had exhausted all their options. Or almost. They were still welcome in Quebec, and they came: Sal Maglie, Max Lanier, Danny Gardella. It is generally agreed that during this period la provinciale provided some of the best baseball played anywhere in Canada. It was into this environment that Ray Brown stepped in 1950.

Normand Dussault, who still makes Sherbrooke his home, recalls this time with great affection. A two-sport athlete who spent his winters playing hockey, including several seasons with the fabled Montreal Canadiens, was the starting centerfielder for the Sherbrooke Athletics, and he remembers Ray Brown well. "Sure, I knew Ray Brown," Dussault said recently, "He was my teammate. He was from the States."

When told that Brown had been selected for Cooperstown, Dussault chuckled. "Imagine. Ray Brown! In the Hall of Fame! Good for him!" He then added, "Ray was an old fellow by the time he came up here, about 42, I think. He couldn't run, but he was still very good. We called him Poppa. He stayed around for at least four years, you know. He was a really good pitcher."

In 1950, the Athletics were managed by Roland Gladu, a Quebec-born baseballer whose own story merits special treatment. Many consider that Gladu more than anyone, was the driving force behind the early development of the Quebec game, to the point where it now produces the likes of an Eric Gagne and Russell Martin.

A power-hitting first baseman, Gladu had played everywhere, and for everyone from the Montreal Royals to London, England, in the 1930s. He played with Quebec City, then for a cup of coffee with the Boston Braves in 1944, back to the Royals, off to the Mexican League and banishment from the game, to stardom in the

Provincial League. When he retired, Gladu became a highly regarded scout for the Boston Braves. Some of his early signings included Claude Raymond, Georges Maranda, and Ron Piche.

As the 1950 season was winding down, the Sherbrooke club found itself fighting for first place, and looking for players to help make that final push. Since becoming manager of the Sherbrooke club in 1948, Gladu had imported a steady stream of performers from the winter leagues. He had already inked the likes of Claro Duany (the Puerto Rican Babe Ruth) and Silvio Garcia ("one of the best hitters who never played in the major leagues," or so said Tommy Lasorda.) When Ray Brown appeared on the horizon, Gladu did not hesitate to sign him up.

The announcement in Sherbrooke's *La Tribune* held a promise of great things to come. "Brown, a black player who stands more than six feet," it read, "has been pitching in Mexico and in Venezuela, where he had an excellent record." However, it took Brown the rest of the regular season to get untracked. He lost his first five decisions, and not until the very end of the campaign did he earn his sole victory, a 6-2 triumph over bitter rival St-Jean Braves. It was a "sensational performance," according to *La Tribune*. Brown even led the offense, driving home three of his team's six runs, and, "for once, his team-mates gave him adequate support, managing 10 hits and committing only one error behind him."

His timing was perfect: the playoffs were about to begin. It was here the lantern-jawed hurler truly showed his mettle. With Brown leading the way, the Athletics rolled over Drummondville in the semifinals and then took their nemesis, St-Jean, to seven games before collapsing in the last match of the championship series, 15-6. Although he was only one of four pitchers to work the game, Ray Brown took the loss, done in by fatigue and a couple of untimely errors behind him.

Nevertheless, the wily veteran with the bag of tricks had been the workhorse of the playoffs. He appeared in nine of the 13 games, recorded three victories against two losses, and at the plate, where he was often asked to pinch-hit, batted .353, with six hits in 17 at-bats, including one home run.

For some reason Brown's pitching record does not show in the 1950 official league statistics, but an unoffi-

Brown as player with the Homestead Grays.

cial count puts it at one victory and five losses. He also occasionally played the outfield and pinch-hit, batting .250, with two home runs and seven RBIs.

In sum, Ray Brown had shown enough to warrant an invitation to return in 1951, one he happily accepted. He was about to embark on a streak of three championships in three years, all with different teams, all in Quebec.

Ray Brown: A Champion

The banner headline across the top of the sports page read, "Ray Brown reaches terms with Sherbrooke Athletics."

It was March 20, 1951, and the *Sherbrooke Record* was confirming that last year's source of inspiration for the team's brilliant playoff run was coming back. A season of promise was at hand.

The veteran hurler compiled a solid 11-10 record and ERA of 3.31, while the team nailed down the pennant, though it took them until the final game of the season. They then went on to easily conquer both Drummondville and Quebec in the playoffs to claim the league title. While Brown had always been a career starting pitcher, he was called upon to fill any number of other roles as well. In fact, manager Gladu used him so much in relief that the *Record* took to calling him "Fireman" Brown. At other times he played the outfield or third base, and even stepped in for first baseman Gladu when the playing manager's bad back kept him out of the lineup.

Brown was also the club's go-to pinch-hitter. Although his batting average shows as a modest .193, including four home runs and six doubles, he always seemed to come up with the key hit when it was most needed. This was never more true than in the last game of the regular season.

With the Athletics down 4-0 to Granby in the sixth inning and needing a win to lock up first place, manager Gladu called on Brown to pinch-hit. The veteran did

not disappoint, blasting a two-run home run over the right-field fence and completely shifting the momentum of the game, as the Athletics went on to a 7-4 victory and top spot. The playoffs were almost an anticlimax, and on September 19, playing at home, Sherbrooke was crowned champion with a convincing win over the Braves from Quebec.

But then fortunes changed. Only hours after the team had carted off the league trophy, a fire swept through old Sherbrooke Stadium, leaving the stands in smoldering ruins and the team without a home field. Town authorities first attempted to have a new grandstand ready for the following season, but when this proved impossible the club was forced to release its players and disband. Baseball did return to Sherbrooke in 1953, but never again could it recreate the elan and excitement that had embraced the 1951 season.

In the meantime, Brown was once more left without a team. Faced with a long winter of uncertainty, he elected to stay on in Sherbrooke and work at the huge Ingersoll-Rand plant in that city, trusting that better things would appear in the spring, as they did. On April 16, *La Tribune* announced that Roland Gladu had signed to manage the Thetford Mines Miners of the Quebec Senior League. Then, in an aside, it added that Brown, whose "wine-red Buick convertible" had been seen around town all winter, "will follow his old manager, as they have become great friends." It was a wise decision.

The Quebec Senior League, and its companion Laurentian League, were similar in structure to the independent Provincial League of the 1940s. These secondary loops had grown increasingly popular in Quebec, for, unlike the "new" Provincial League of Organized Baseball, where every club was soon to become affiliated with a major league team, they had not lost their local touch: they still had room for both homegrown talent and the displaced.

Composed of teams from four towns located south of the St. Lawrence River and east of Sherbrooke, the league was well salted with Provincial League veterans. The Plessisville Braves, now counting Brown's old pal Norman Dussault in their midst, were considered the class of the circuit and expected to repeat as champions in 1952. But they had not counted on the surprising

Miners. With Gladu leading the league in hitting—his average flirted with the .400 mark for most of the season—and Brown chalking up a team-best 16 wins against five losses and batting over .300, Thetford walked away with first place.

Brown then added four more wins in the playoffs, bringing his total for the season to 20, as the club went on to take top laurels. "Four victories in as many matches is a feat to be celebrated," gushed the weekly newspaper, *La Canadien*, "and here the honours go to our veteran pitcher, Ray Brown," as it declared him the club's MVP, "without a doubt." So successful was the Thetford Mines baseball adventure that the town immediately sought and obtained a Provincial League franchise for the following year. Once again Ray Brown was left without a team. But not for long.

Early in 1953 the Lachine Indians of the Laurentian League began shopping around for a player-manager, and Brown leapt at the opportunity. With the omnipresent Normand Dussault now at his side, the veteran succeeded in leading the Indians to another championship—Brown's third in three years. The old pitcher opened the campaign with nine straight victories, finishing up at 13-5, and Dussault was dominant both at the plate and in center field.

After the final game of the season, local dignitaries held a celebration to honor the club. According to the *Lachine Messenger,*

> Ray Brown acted as spokesman for the Indians in thanking the directorate [of the club] for the manner in which the players had been treated throughout the season just ended, and he hoped that the same team would next year again represent Lachine.

Sadly, this was not to be. The club became involved in a dispute with league authorities and elected to withdraw. All of its players were let go.

For Brown, one last hurrah still awaited. Following the Lachine success, he was called back to Thetford Mines, where the Miners, now in the Provincial League, were hoping to make the playoffs. As *Le Canadien* noted, "Even at his age, Ray still possesses the stuff our club needs to create momentum and regain the desired heights."

And it worked. Columnist M. A. Simoneau affirmed, "Management could smile for having called on the services of [Brown] who helped to reduce the deficit, especially in the last weekend of the season." Brown's contribution enabled the Miners to eke out a fourth-place finish. But he was not in the lineup for the post-season. Because the team had signed Brown after the deadline by which its playoff roster needed to be deposited with the league, he was declared ineligible. The Miners were knocked out by Granby in the first round.

It is here that the trail of Ray Brown's baseball career in Quebec fades away. He had married a local woman whom Jeannine Dussault, Normand's wife, recalls was very good-looking. "She was a white woman, a French-Canadian, from around Sherbrooke, I think. I'm sorry, I can't tell you her name." Mme. Dussault recollects that at Lachine in 1954, "we would often sit together in the stands. She was very nice. But I never saw her again after that year."

Brown did eventually return to his native Ohio, where he died in 1965. He was 57 years old. While it is true that his years in La Belle Province would have little influence on his Cooperstown selection, certainly his presence made a difference to the game in Quebec. ∎

"I'm the Biggest Worrier in the World"

John Wesley Callison

by John Rossi

In December 1959 I was studying for my master's degree in history at Notre Dame. As a Phillies fan since 1946, I was starved for news about the team when one of my friends told me that they had traded Gene Freese to the Chicago White Sox for someone whose name he couldn't remember.

I was shocked. Freese had been one of the few positive players on a last-place 1959 Phillies team that won just 64 games, their lowest total since 1947.

Freese had hit 23 homers in 1959, including three grand slams and five pinch-hit home runs. He took over third base from the failing Whiz Kid, Willie Jones, early in the season and proceeded to provide the only excitement for a truly awful team. True, Freese was a terrible third baseman. Despite playing in only 109 games at third he led all National League third sackers with 22 errors. My friends and I would try to buy seats behind first base, as you could almost count on Freese throwing a ball into the stands either in infield practice or during the game.

Who did the Phillies get for Freese? I wondered. In those pre-Internet, pre-ESPN days sports news was hard to come by. I finally ran down a copy of the *Chicago Sun Times* and discovered that they had gotten someone named John Callison in the deal. Being a committed National League fan, I had never heard of him. The *Sun Times* article gloated that the White Sox had pulled one over on the hapless Phillies. The 1959 American League champs had filled their one big hole at third base while giving up little in return.

Little did the *Sun Times* and I know that the Phillies' new general manager, John Quinn, had pulled off a coup

in his first trade. Quinn had taken a major step in dismantling the old Whiz Kid team that owner Bob Carpenter hadn't the heart to break up.

John Wesley Callison was born in Oklahoma in 1939 and his family, like thousands of other Okies, migrated to California at the end of the Depression, in this case to Bakersfield. Callison was an outstanding high school athlete and was signed by the White Sox in 1957. In two years in the minors he showed signs of brilliance, hitting .340 in his first season in Bakersfield in the California League and then making the jump to Triple A Indianapolis in the American Association the next season. There he led the league in homers with 29. He got his first taste of the majors in a brief call-up by the White Sox in late 1958.

Callison's two sparkling minor league seasons earned him the label "the next Mickey Mantle" because of his power and great speed. It was a label that would haunt him for the rest of his career.

Callison was brought up to the pennant-winning White Sox in 1959 but got into just 49 games and hit a pathetic .173. Callison, who was always plagued with doubts, said he was "embarrassed" and "disgusted" to be a part of pennant-winning team and contribute so little. The White Sox soured on him. Their loss was the Phillie's gain.

I first saw Callison in the spring of 1960. Quinn and newly hired manager Gene Mauch were trying to rebuild a team that had grown old. To me Callison, who was 5' 10" and about 175 pounds, looked small, timid at the plate, and tentative in the field. However, I soon began to follow him closely. Over the next few years he became my favorite player on a Phillies team that gradually won the hearts of the city's fans.

Mauch played him in all three outfield positions in 1960, where he was part of an all left-handed platoon

JOHN ROSSI *is a Professor of History at La Salle University in Philadelphia. His most recent baseball book is:* The 1964 Phillies: The Story of Baseball's Most Memorable Collapse, *Macfarland & Co., 2005.*

Callison is congratulated by his teammates after hitting a 9th inning three-run homer off Dick Radatz to give the NL a 7-4 win in the 1964 All-Star Game at Shea Stadium.

that consisted of youngsters Tony Curry and Tony Gonzalez. Callison proved a mediocre left-fielder but Mauch saw something that the fans and the always tough Philadelphia sportswriters missed and moved him to right field in 1961. He blossomed there and became one of the best right fielders in the National League, no mean feat when you consider the competition: Roberto Clemente, Frank Robinson, and Hank Aaron.

From 1962 through 1965 Callison led all National League outfielders in assists, demonstrating a throwing arm that was both powerful and amazingly accurate. During those four seasons he totaled 91 assists. For comparison's sake, Aaron had 43, Robinson 35, while Clemente had 59 in those four years. Even the best American League outfielders couldn't come close to Callison's figures. Al Kaline had 21 in those four seasons while the Boston's Carl Yastrzemski totaled the most assists over that period, just 63.

Callison's was one of the first of the new faces that Quinn and Mauch developed in the awful 1960 and 1961 seasons, when the Phillies finished in the cellar with the worst record in baseball, including an infamous 23-game losing streak in 1961. In 1962 Callison, along with newcomers Gonzalez, catcher Clay Dalrymple, shortstop Ruben Amaro, second baseman Tony Taylor, and pitchers Jack Baldschun, Chris Short, and Art Mahaffey, pushed the Mauch-led Phillies over the .500 mark for the first time since 1953.

Callison was Mauch's pet. He helped turn Callison into a dangerous hitter while carefully protecting his sensitive ego. Mauch would tell anyone who would listen, knowing it would get back to Callison, about the right fielder's skills. "He can run, throw, field and hit with power," Mauch once bragged about Callison. "There's nothing he can't do well on the ball field."

Mauch benched Callison during the last game of the 1962 season to salvage a .300 average for him. Callison's 23 homers tied the record for any Phillies left-handed hitter in Shibe Park/Connie Mack Stadium. He broke that record each of the next three seasons, hitting 26, 31, and 32 homers. His 32 homers in the 1965 campaign was most any Phillie had hit since Stan Lopata clubbed that many in 1956 and the most of any Phillies left-handed hitter other than Hall of Famers Chuck Klein and Lefty O'Doul and Cy Williams up to that time. In fact, in the history of the Phillies only Ryan Howard, Jim Thome, Williams, and Klein have hit more homers left-handed than Callison in a season. His 185 homers is fourth highest of all Phillies left-handed hitters behind Klein, Williams and Bobby Abreu.

Callison's speed also flourished in the big spaces of Shibe Park/Connie Mack Stadium. He reached double figures in triples for five consecutive seasons, 1961 through 1965, once leading the National League and once tying.

Callison's greatest season was 1964, the "Year of Blue

Snow" when the Phillies blew a seemingly impossible six-game lead by losing 10 consecutive games with only 12 games remaining.

After starting slowly—he was hitting only .206 early in May—Callison got hot and along with rookie sensation Richie Allen and they provided the offense for a Phillies team that was picked to finish anywhere from fourth to sixth place. In July he won the All-Star game with a dramatic ninth-inning three run homer off Boston's premier reliever, Dick "the Monster" Radatz. This was only the third walk-off homer in All-Star history: the others were hit by two pretty good sluggers, Ted Williams and Stan Musial.

Callison said he didn't run around the bases after that homer, he just floated. Later he was asked about the feat so many times he said he felt like Bill Murray reliving the same day over and over in the movie *Groundhog Day.*

By August 1964, Callison had his average around the .300 mark, and he hit nine homers in the last five weeks of the season, including a three-home run game during the Phillies' losing streak. Handsome in a classic Hollywood manner, he was the Cinderella Man of the Phillies. *Sports Illustrated* and *The Sporting News* both featured him on their cover. With the Phillies seemingly destined to win the pennant, to the surprise of everyone, Callison was the consensus choice for National League MVP. But that was not to be. With a suddenness that was shocking, the Phillies' season unraveled.

The stress of the pennant race was taking its toll on Callison. A constant worrier, he was smoking heavily and acting as if he expected the Phillies' balloon soon would burst. By the end of September he had lost 10 pounds and came down with the flu. In a famous incident in a game in St. Louis toward the end of the losing streak, the sick Callison pinch-hit a single and then put on a warm-up jacket. He was so weak that the Cardinals first baseman, Bill White, had to button it for him.

Despite his illness Callison was one of the few positive forces, along with Allen, on the Phillies during the losing streak. He hit four homers and drove in 10 runs during those games.

Callison had one more outstanding season for the Phillies. In 1965 he clubbed 32 homers and drove in 101 runs and was regarded at 26 as one of the dominant power hitters in the National League. Then suddenly everything turned sour. In 1966 he hit just 11 home runs, not hitting his first until Memorial Day, and finished with only 55 RBIs. He led the National League in doubles with 40 but seemed to have lost his power stroke.

He also was feuding with Mauch, who was trying to unlock the key to a player he regarded as having all the tools for greatness but who seemed dogged by self-doubt. Callison did an article for *Sport* magazine around that time whose title summed up his problem: "I am the greatest worrier in the world."

As it turns out, after 1965 Callison was effectively finished as a great hitter. He never again hit 20 homers in a season or drove in 70 runs. It was said that he suffered from a series of nagging injuries, especially to his legs. He adopted the exercise regimen that had helped Carl Yastremski set records in 1967, but it didn't help. He began to wear glasses, but that proved useless also. In 1969 the Phillies gave up on Callison and traded him and a player to be named to the Chicago Cubs for pitcher Dick Selma and outfielder Oscar Gamble. After a couple of seasons with the Cubs, Callison was sent to the Yankees, where he finished his career in 1973.

Callison's post-baseball career was an unhappy one. He longed to get back to baseball in some capacity, especially with the Phillies, but never caught on with any team. He and his wife Diane and their two daughters continued to live in the Philadelphia area. Callison remained popular with the older generation of fans and in later years would often go to the Phillies fantasy camp to reminisce about his playing days.

His business investments turned sour and he turned to a series of unfullfilling jobs. In 1986 he was operated on for a bleeding ulcer and had a heart attack while in intensive care. He had to have a triple bypass. All this before the age of 50.

Callison died in October 2006 after a long bout with cancer. His career mirrored in many ways the fate of the team he was most associated with, the Phillies, especially the 1964 team. It was one of unfulfilled promise, a case of what could have been.

Still, for five or six years he was the most popular player on a developing Phillies team, an icon for victory-starved Philadelphia fans. That's not a bad epitaph. ∎

Debs Garms

1940 National League Batting Champion

by Greg Erion

If a baseball fan scanned the list of National League batting leaders in the *New York Times* on September 15, 1940, they would note a tight race among the top five hitters. Three points separated them with just two weeks left in the season:[1]

Cooney, Boston	.319
Mize, St. Louis	.318
Hack, Chicago	.317
Gleeson, Chicago	.316
Lombardi, Cincinnati	.316

This list contained several familiar names. Stan Hack was a solid .300 hitter. Ernie Lombardi led the league in 1938, and Johnny Mize, the 1939 batting leader was not only one hit away from the lead in average, but with 41 home runs and 120 runs batted in he was positioned to win the Triple Crown. Mize's hope to achieve the Triple Crown and the others' chances to win the batting title would be dashed the next day by the appearance of Pittsburgh Pirate third baseman-outfielder Debs Garms at the top of the list with a lead of more than 60 points.[2]

Except for the fact that Garms is the answer to a few trivia questions such as "Who broke up Johnny Vander Meer's string of hitless innings?" or "Who won the 1940 National League batting title?" his name today is fairly obscure to all but a few baseball historians.

There are several reasons for his anonymity. Garms was a journeyman ballplayer in an era sporting the likes of Foxx, Musial, and Ruth. He never made an All-Star team or exhibited the charisma of players like Dean or Reiser. Despite a seemingly undistinguished reputation,

GREG ERION *has a Master's Degree in History from San Francisco State University and teaches history at Skyline College. He would like to thank David Garms, David W. Smith, Jules Tygiel and Mary Waters for their contributions to this article. Any errors are the author's.*

however, teams always sought him for the attitude and hustle he brought to their roster. Of the teams Garms played for, his most notable years were with the Pittsburgh Pirates, where in 1940 he won the batting title.

The Pirates purchased Garms from the Boston Bees in 1940 as they attempted to rebuild their team after finishing sixth, a finish that cost manager Pie Traynor his job.[3] Frankie Frisch, hired to replace Traynor, inherited a team with poor morale, a team still fixated on the effects of losing the pennant during the last week of the 1938 season.

Frisch, who had managed the Gashouse Gang St. Louis Cardinals to the world championship in 1934, was an intense individual who hated the thought of losing and was considered an ideal hire to improve the Pirates' outlook. Prior to being hired by the Pirates, Frisch had broadcast games for the Boston Bees in 1939 and became particularly aware of the playing potential—and attitude various Bees possessed.

Early in January, Charles "Chilly" Doyle, a baseball writer with the *Pittsburgh Sun-Telegram,* interviewed Frisch about the Pirates' chances for 1940.[4] Frisch made it clear that he wanted to redesign the team with an emphasis on fight and hustle. Left unsaid was his suspicion that several Pirates, including Lloyd and Paul Waner, would have to improve their attitude or be replaced. Doyle noted that Frisch had made a few purchases from the Bees but was still looking to make other transactions to change the demeanor of the club. At the end of February, when spring training began, Frisch was still looking to make deals.

During the first week of March 1940, Garms drove his family from Texas to Bradenton, FL, for the Bees' spring training. Upon arrival, he was informed the Pirates had purchased his contract. The Pirates were holding spring training in San Bernardino, CA, clear across the continent. After spending a few hours resting, Garms packed his family back in the car and drove them to Texas, subsequently boarding a train for California to join his new team.[5]

Frisch had been impressed by Garms while broadcasting for the Bees and purchased his contract even though he did not have a particular spot in the lineup for Garms. Frisch told Doyle, "Garms will be available for infield and outfield duty. I like his style, especially his spirit." [6] In a series of articles written during spring training Doyle noted the positive attitude Garms would bring to the Pirates through his competitive play.

Garms hustled through spring training and hit .472. He would later recall, "That whole year, [1940] the baseball looked as big as a grapefruit coming up to the plate."[7] Based on his hitting, Garms was named starting right fielder replacing Paul Waner. The future Hall of Famer's diminishing skills at age 37, alleged drinking problems, and casual approach to preparing for the game irked Frisch.[8] Waner never got back into the lineup on a regular basis, playing in just 89 games before being released the following December.

Subsequent assessments of Garms' play during the 1940 season usually described him as a utility player, disregarding the fact that he had been a full-time player with the Bees. While Frisch experimented with various platoon options in the early stages of the 1940 season, Garms appeared in most of the early season games. Garms did go out of the lineup in early May, for the better part of two months, not because he was benched, but because of a knee injury he suffered in Boston.[9] He returned to the lineup in a game against the Giants on June 16 and got three hits, only to reinjure his knee the next day in Boston for a second time. Occasionally pinch-hitting the next several weeks, his injury gradually healed, allowing him to begin playing on a regular basis starting July 20.

By then the Pirates were halfway through the season in sixth place with a record of 33-44. Frisch, disconcerted because of indifferent play, made several changes to the lineup, including the replacement of Lee Handley at third with Garms. Making the most of his opportunity that day, Garms had four hits to drive in five runs as

the Pirates beat the Bees. Garms would be particularly effective against his former teammates that year, hitting .481, a performance based in part on how he was pitched to by the Bee staff.

Garms recalled in a conversation with his son that the Bees consistently pitched him low and away all season. He was mystified that they would continue pitching to his strength as an opposite-field hitter until he was approached one day by a Bee pitcher whom Garms had singled off the day before. He asked Garms the location of the pitch he had hit. Garms replied, "Low and away." The pitcher then told him that Bees manager Casey Stengel had jumped on him for *not* pitching low and away. Why Stengel persisted in making pitchers work toward Garms' strength seemed odd. Perhaps it was to prove a point. Stengel was apparently not happy that Bees general manager Bob Quinn had sold Garms to the Pirates in March.[10]

Garms continued his hot hitting the next several weeks, hitting .400 for July, and raised his average up to .345 by the end of the month as the Pirates began climbing out of the second division. Little notice was made at the time that Garms' average had passed that of Giants catcher Harry Danning, listed in newspapers as the league batting leader. At the beginning of August the Pirates dropped a doubleheader on August 1, then ran up an eight-game winning streak, moving into fourth place. Garms continued his hot pace, hitting .480 during this streak.

On August 21, Doyle noted that while Garms had the highest average in the league, he would have to amass 400 at-bats to win the title. It was the first time he was mentioned in connection with the batting race. At this point Frisch, thinking Garms needed 400 at-bats to qualify for the title, moved him up to leadoff in the batting order.

On August 31, Bama Rowell of the Bees was leading the league with a .328 average. Garms was hitting .369. Over the next several weeks Garms' average continued to improve as the listed leaders' average kept slipping. By September 11, Dixie Walker of the Dodgers led with a .320 average with Garms at .384. Although the lead would change almost daily between Jimmy Gleeson, Johnny Cooney, Lombardi, and Walker, none of them

Debs Garms as a member of the St. Louis Cardinals.

could push their average above .320, which at that time was the lowest average to ever lead the National League.[11] Observers of the game began to comment on the situation. Peter Hinkle, in a letter to the *New York Times,* observed:

> The way the percentages of the leaders are running now it appears that the man who eventually succeeds in hitting .325 will win the title. Normally it takes a mark of .350 or better to win the individual batting championship.[12]

In an interview appearing in the *Washington Post* on September 18, Dizzy Dean sounded off on various subjects including the National League batting race. Dean pointed out that Johnny Cooney, "an old converted pitcher is right up there for the batting title with .317 whereas back in the old days Frankie Frisch or Jim Bottomley would hit .350 and finish sixth."[13] *The Sporting News* also noted the low batting percentages, observing that Lombardi was leading the league with only a .319 average. "Not since 1919, when Edd Roush led with a .321 mark has the National League's top batter turned in a figure as low as that owned by Ernie Lombardi…"[14]

Garms' performance continued to contrast sharply with the low average leading the league. On the day

Hinkle's letter was written, Garms average reached a season-high .387. He was now 67 points ahead of Walker. Doyle's arguments in August about Garms deserving the title had made little impression at the time. Now others were beginning to appreciate Doyle's perspective. John Lardner wrote a column in the *San Francisco Chronicle* that argued Garms should be declared the champion. After noting that Walker was then leading the league at a .319 average Lardner asked, "So what would you say to a fellow in that same league, who is hitting .388? (sic)" Lardner extolled Garms' accomplishments, arguing that a near 70-point advantage "is too much difference."[15]

When the Reds were in New York a few days later, their manager, Bill McKechnie, who had managed Garms as a Bee in 1937, was asked if Garms was as good as his average reflected. While McKechnie observed Garms had not performed that well while playing for him, he conceded that Garms' high average "must account for something." McKechnie then asked, "What's this I hear about a batter having to be at bat 400 times to be eligible for the championship?" A reporter replied that this was erroneous. "That's all wrong. I asked Ford Frick [president of the National League] about that and he said that so far as he knows that is an American League rule and has not been adopted by the National League."[16] On September 16 the *Times* began to list Garms as the leader. Garms at .382 was 63 points ahead of Lombardi.

These observations culminated with an announcement released by the National League on September 19 that all Garms had to do was play 100 games to win the title. Frick, formally confirming what he had told reporters a few days before, stated there were no rules governing qualifications for the title. "The batting title is simply unofficial and never has been subject for league legislation." The article goes on to note, "It is apparent the whole batting championship situation is in a state of confusion and that Garms, with the only respectable average in the league, has a chance to be considered."[17] Bill Brandt, spokesperson for Frick said that while there were no rules governing qualifications, "he thought 100 games would be a sufficient prerequisite for the championship."

At the time of this announcement 11 games remained on the schedule and Garms needed to play in only seven. In a rather prescient comment, another article mentioned, "His [Garms] mark is so much better than any of the others it doesn't make much difference whether he gets a hit or not."[18] Virtually every comment on the subject noted the confusion about the requirement to attain 400 at-bats dated from the time the American League gave $500 to the batting leader based on a minimum of 400 at-bats. Not only did league presidents, managers and sportswriters chime in, but fans added their comments on the subject as well. Another reader wrote to the *New York Times* stating Garms should be declared winner because he "will lead the batters by a wide margin."[19]

Frick's opinion appeared in the news throughout the country on September 19. On the 21st Pittsburgh played the Reds. In the second game of a doubleheader, the Pirates filled the bases with two out in the bottom of the 10th inning. Garms came to bat and singled to drive in the winning run with his fifth hit of the game.

That game-winning blow was his last hit of the season as he went into a 0-for-23 slump. Garms ended the season playing 103 games with 127 hits in 358 at-bats finishing at .355, 36 points ahead of Lombardi and 38 points ahead of Chicago's Stan Hack, who played in 149 games. Garms' average also led the majors, as Yankee Joe DiMaggio led the American League with a .352 mark. Despite being considered a singles hitter, Garms finished sixth in the league with a .500 slugging average and struck out only six times the entire campaign to achieve a superlative ratio of one strikeout per 60 at-bats. The Pirates finished the second half with a 45-32 record, 78-76 overall to finish fourth.

While the season ended, controversy over Frick's decision continued. Though *The Sporting News* supported Garms as champion, it suggested qualifications for batting titles be made uniform throughout baseball. Specifically referring to Garms, they made note of the wide margin he enjoyed over his rivals despite being asked to play various positions.

The Sporting News editorial further noted, "There has never been a similar situation…when a player led the loop with such a high average and participated in a limited number of games…" This was not an accurate observation, as twice before batting titles were awarded to individuals with fewer at-bats than Garms. In 1926, Reds catcher Bubbles Hargrave was awarded the National League batting title despite having just 326 at-bats in 105 games, although his position as catcher probably worked in his favor in deciding whether he should be considered the leader. In 1914, Ty Cobb, who had been injured part of the year, was awarded the American League title despite having 345 at-bats in 97 games. Given the level of Cobb's sustained deeds over the years, there was little doubt he would have maintained his level of hitting over the full season. These instances were ignored in the controversy raised by Garms' performance.

Most of the opposition to Frick's decision centered on Garms not having the 400 at-bats required in the American League—that what was good for one league should be good for another. A good deal of the resentment centered in Chicago, where Cub fans felt that Hack should have been declared champion based on his full-season performance. Counter to that argument was an observation made by several, including columnist Bob Ray in the *Los Angeles Times,* that had Garms gone 0-for-42 and achieved the 400 at bats his "adjusted" average at .318, still would have been one point higher than Hack.[20]

Under modern standards, which call for 3.1 plate appearances per game, Garms was 92 plate appearances short of the requirement. Based on this measurement Garms would have needed just 16 hits in 92 at-bats, a .174 average to beat Hack.

In retrospect, the controversy over Garms' winning of the batting title was based on several factors. He was described as "coming out of nowhere" or being "a surprise champion." This is certainly justified by the manner in which he became eligible for consideration. Frick's announcement came with only 10 days left in the season. A second factor was Garms himself. Although Garms' prior performance with the Bees indicated he was a legitimate .300 hitter, he had not solidified his reputation as a proven hitting star, as had batting title predecessors Johnny Mize, Ernie Lombardi, and Joe Medwick.

Garms also won because of peculiar circumstances that existed at the time. Observations of those familiar with the game were correct; batting averages were declining. The National League batting average for 1939 was .272. In 1940 it was .264. It would shrink further to .258 in 1941, and over the next 20 years would never rise above .266. This trend was reflected in the performance of top hitters. For the 1937-1939 seasons, 24 full-time players hit .320 or better. From 1940 to 1942 only one full-time player, Pete Reiser, hit over .320 (.343).

By mid-September 1940 no one in the National League was at .320, which from perspectives of the time were unsettling to those interested in the game. Contrasting sharply with this was Garms' average then in the .380s range. The disparity between what was expected of a batting leader and what Garms was then hitting was too great to ignore.

One wonders whether Frick would have made the same ruling if Garms' average was in the .320-.330 range or if his hitting spree had occurred in the closing days of the season rather than early September. Garms' early September performance may have been enhanced by his early season injuries. His past history suggested a declining performance the last month of the season. Perhaps the time he was out of the lineup early in the season may have delayed onset of the slump he experienced the last days of the season.

Controversy over Garms' title did not immediately force a change in how batting championships were determined. His title, however, proved a sign of things to come. Two years later Ernie Lombardi was awarded the National League title based on less playing time than Garms. Although his position as catcher probably helped in being considered for the title, it is worthy of note, the closest mark to Lombardi's .330 leading average was Enos Slaughter's .318. If Slaughter had been recognized as champion, his mark would have been the lowest to ever lead the National League up to that time. Rules for qualifications were subsequently changed, initially to 400 at-bats, then to the present-day requirement of 3.1 plate appearances per game.

When queried about his father's attitude toward this controversy, David Garms related that he had an almost detached attitude about the matter. Aside from recalling that Frisch had moved Garms up to leadoff in the order to gain more at-bats the elder Garms said nothing about the controversy concerning his being awarded the championship. He seemed to be content to let others worry about the numbers while he concentrated on playing his game. Through it all, Garms was as calm as the center of a statistical hurricane, just hitting a ball that "looked as big as a grapefruit coming up to the plate." ∎

Notes

1. "Major League Leaders," *New York Times,* September 15, 1941.
2. "Major League Leaders," *New York Times,* September 16, 1941.
3. The Boston Braves were known as the Bees for the 1936-1940 seasons.
4. Charles J. Doyle, "Changes Already Made by Frisch Expected to Bolster Spirit," *The Sporting News,* January 4, 1940.
5. Interviews with David Garms, August 29 & 30, 2006.
6. Charles J. Doyle, "Buc Nemesis Bought from Boston," *Pittsburgh Sun-Telegram,* March 4, 1940.
7. Pete Kendall, "Ex-Major Leaguer Debs Garms Dies in Glen Rose," *Cleburne Times-Review,* December 17, 1984.
8. Parker, Clifton Blue. *Big and Little Poison: Paul and Lloyd Waner, Baseball's Brothers* (Jefferson, NC: McFarland, 2003).
9. Charles J. Doyle, various articles, *Pittsburgh Sun-Telegram,* June 19, July 5, 6, 21, 25, August 1, 1940.
10. Garms, August 29 & 30, 2006.
11. "Major League Leaders," *New York Times,* September 1-16, 1941. Larry Doyle led the league at .320 in 1915 and Tony Gwynn would subsequently lead the National League in batting in 1988 with a .313 average.
12. Peter D. Hinkle letter, "Low 1940 Batting Averages," *New York Times,* September 14, 1940.
13. "'Just a Joke,' Says Dizzy Dean of N.L.," *Washington Post,* September 18, 1940.
14. "Batting Slump Hits Both Majors," *The Sporting News,* September 20, 1940.
15. John Lardner, "Who's N.L.'s best hitter? Read on and be surprised," *San Francisco Chronicle,* September 14, 1940.
16. Harry Keck, "National League's Times-at-Bat Myth Exploded by McKechnie's Curiosity," *Pittsburg Sun-Telegram,* September 21, 1940.
17. "Garms Given O.K. in Batting Race," *Washington Post,* September 20, 1940.
18. "Hitting Crown: Garms May Beat Out Joe D'Mag," *San Francisco Chronicle,* September 20, 1940.
19. Ernest A. Kerstein, "Rule Which Denies Honors to Garms Is Hit by Reader," *New York Times,* September 16, 1941.
20. Bob Ray, "The Sports X-Ray," *Los Angeles Times,* December 30, 1940.

Once Around The Horn

by Thomas Perry

To see anybody in Shelby, NC, on a Saturday afternoon in the 1940s was easy enough: head toward one of the cotton mills that sponsored a baseball club. Folks packed the stands to talk about wars and depressions, family matters, and local politics. But it was baseball that commanded center stage.

Sometimes the game even had a hand in carrying on the family name.

"My father was a big baseball fan, and that's how I got my name." Roger McKee, actually Rogers Hornsby McKee, was born September 16, 1926, about the time the St. Louis Cardinals, managed by Rogers Hornsby, clinched the National League pennant and then beat the Yankees in the World Series. "Dad and a bunch of guys from the mill were listening to a game on the radio, and he told them he was gonna name his boy after Hornsby."

Young McKee did the name proud, and at 16 was pitching the local American Legion team into the 1943 state tournament semifinals. His battery mate was another future major leaguer, Smoky Burgess, and they batted third (Burgess) and fourth (McKee) in the lineup.

"Smoky was a great catcher, but he was an even better hitter." It was a five-game thriller against the Albemarle, NC, nine. McKee notched complete-game wins in the first and third contests, allowing one run in each game, and played the outfield in games two and four. In the fifth and deciding game at Shelby, he went the distance in 11 innings, but lost 7-4.

An older man made his way across the infield dirt and sought out the young man who had just given his arm and heart in a losing cause. He was a pitcher, too, from

THOMAS PERRY *has been a SABR member since 1985. His most recently published book is a novel whose narrator, Katie Jackson, is Shoeless Joe's wife.*

the rough-and-tumble days of the early 1900s. He came not to offer condolences. A big league scout has other things on his mind, and he wanted to talk with the kid about his future in baseball. They arranged to meet later that evening. McKee and his father walked downtown to the Hotel Charles and listened intently as Phillies scout Cy Morgan talked about the kid's future in the majors. A contract signed, a token bonus offered ("Small enough that I don't remember what it was"), and a handshake ended the evening.

"Oh, yeah," Morgan called after them, "we want you in Philadelphia within the week." It's the stuff dreams are made of.

The Phillies would gradually fit him in, they said, throwing batting practice, warming up on the sidelines, pitching an occasional exhibition game. That lasted until August 18 and a split doubleheader at Shibe Park with the Cardinals. In the first game, McKee was in the bullpen with the rest of the relievers, eating candy and having a good time. Merv Shea, bullpen coach and former catcher, looked toward the dugout and saw the manager waving his arms.

"They want you, Lefty."

"Me?" McKee wasn't sure he heard right, but with help from Shea he warmed up quickly and headed to the mound in the sixth inning. Things happened fast enough that he didn't have time to get scared, but still could give himself a pep talk.

"I thought back to my success in Legion and high school ball, and figured maybe I could get these guys out, too." He completed his relief stint, gave up three hits (one a bunt single) and two walks (one to Cards star Stan Musial). Reminded of that, he grins.

"Yeah. I hate that. Would have been nice to strike him out." It was a good outing, though the Phillies lost, 6-0,

PHOTOS COURTESY OF TOM MCKEE

McKee in Phillies uniform and in the Navy.

and a big thrill for the kid nearly a month shy of his 17th birthday.

By season's end, the Phillies were destined for a seventh-place finish, a distant 41 games out of first. The final two games were at Forbes Field against the Pirates, still in a fight for fourth place and the money that went along with it. Manager Freddie Fitzsimmons laid out the plan to his rookie left hander: if the Phillies took out Pittsburgh in the opener, McKee would start the second game; if the Bucs won the first and still had a chance at securing fourth place, Fitzsimmons would go with a regular starter. Philadelphia managed a 3-1 win behind Dick Barrett's fine effort. The kid got the ball for game 2, October 3, 1943.

The first inning went okay, but in the second a streak of wildness produced three walks. A couple of hits resulted in three runs, but that was all the scoring the home team could muster. Even a line drive off the bat of Tony Ordenana slamming into his knee couldn't derail the kid's magic that day—a five-hit, 11-3 complete-game win.

After a dismal strikeout in his first at-bat, McKee had an RBI single later in the game.

> My teammates scolded me because I never took the bat off my shoulder. "Can't hit it if you don't swing, rookie!" Of course, their words were a little stronger than that. Then they came through with 11 runs for me, and it was unheard of for the Phillies to score that many in a game. Guess they thought the poor little skinny boy was gonna need 'em.

Rogers Hornsby McKee, some two weeks past his 17th birthday, became the youngest pitcher since 1900 to start and win a major league baseball game. He remains so to this day.[1] Afterward, Pirates manager Frankie Frisch paid the young man a fine compliment, saying that he was one of the best looking young pitchers he'd seen come along in quite a while.

"Guess maybe I let him down, not sticking any longer than I did." It was the only major league game McKee would ever win, a promising career cut short by a mysterious arm ailment.

The Phillies stayed close to home for 1944 spring training, opting for Wilmington, DE, due to war-time travel restrictions. Ice and snow covered the ground the first few weeks of February, and workouts took place in a local gym.

> The first day we got outside, I threw quite a bit, and that might have been the finishing blow as far as the elasticity in my arm. From then on, any day I could go out and throw pretty good for a couple of innings; and then nothing.

The arm never hurt and he threw the same way, but the fastball just wasn't there. McKee believes the trouble began in that 1943 American Legion series, with three complete games in a five-day span. "That's a lot of stress on a young arm."

After spring training, the Phillies left him in Wilmington to finish the season with their Class B affiliate of the InterState League. McKee played first base after the regular sacker suffered a career-ending beaning, and still pitched on occasion. Connie Mack brought his Athletics down for an exhibition game early in the season, and Lefty was slated to battle Carl Scheib, another 17-year-old hurler. Wilmington topped the A's that day behind his complete-game effort, though he had not pitched for almost a month.

He did well enough to be called up at the end of the season, joining the last-place Phillies for two games. Pitching in one of those, he joined a line of relievers drubbed in a 15-0 loss to the Cubs at Shibe Park. And that was it—his last game in the Show.

> Thinking back to when I was hit by that line drive in the only game I won, I understand why I fought so hard to stay in there. I started that game and didn't want to come out, because I might not get back into another one. And really, I never did.

Tony Ordenana was part of the mystique of that game, too; In one game for the Pittsburgh Pirates, he had two hits in four at-bats, and never played another game in the majors.

The Navy made sure Lefty had little time to worry about his future in baseball, sending him a draft notice in December 1944. Boot camp was at Bainbridge, MD, and his assignment was in the Physical Instructor school. The base had a solid intramural program staffed by some good athletes—two barracks away from McKee was Stan Musial.

> We played basketball against one another, and of course we tried out for the team when baseball season started. You pitched against some pretty good major league material when you played service ball.

Both he and Musial shipped out to Pearl Harbor in the spring of 1945. The war was over in Europe that April, and the final Allied push would be in the South Pacific. Lefty pitched some during those months, but always with the same results: a good three or four innings, then nothing in the arm. His mound appearances, though, produced two great memories if no victories. Shortly after arriving at Pearl, the ball team was working out when one of the base commanders stopped by, donned the "tools of ignorance," and crouched behind the plate. Bill Dickey, Yankee great and future Hall of Famer, took the young man's offerings for about 15 minutes.

He'd stand up and throw a bullet back to me, and he was burning me up. I thought, "He's throwing harder than I am!" Come to find out, our shortstop was covering second, waiting for Dickey's throw down. That was part of his routine, but I didn't know that. I'd snag those smoking fast balls and throw it back to him, still not realizing what he was trying to do. Everybody got a good laugh at my expense.

Then there was Ted Williams. A Marine pilot, he flew into the naval station, and of course was asked to play ball. A member of the opposition that day, McKee went to warm up in the fifth inning; the makeshift bullpen was along the left-field foul line, a few yards from where Teddy Ballgame was playing.

"He watched every move I made, the way I threw, what I had. Lucky nobody hit anything his way. I went in to pitch the sixth inning, and he happens to come up." In the batter's box, Williams eyed the short porch in right field (only 220 feet away) topped by a high screen. Pacing on the mound, McKee had some disturbing thoughts.

"The greatest hitter in baseball already knew everything about my delivery and pitch selection, and I sure as heck couldn't fool him with anything. Figured I'd throw it as hard as I could, and see how far he could hit it." Williams jerked the ball down the right-field line, nearly taking the first baseman's glove and hand off. He recovered and tossed to Lefty for the out. Military personnel in the packed stands let out a collective, though good-natured, boo.

"Guess they wanted to see him hit, just like I did."

With victory in the Pacific secure in August 1945, men and women of the armed forces finished up tours of duty and came home. McKee went back to Philadelphia in early 1946, stayed a couple of weeks, and was informed by Phillies manager Ben Chapman to report to Terre Haute, IN, of the Class B Three-I League. Lefty never made his way back to the majors.

"They tried to pitch me one more time at Terre Haute, but I couldn't keep the ball in the park. I was fortunate to hit pretty well, and was given a chance to play first base and outfield for the rest of the year."

The switch began a solid minor league career that would take him from Terre Haute to Baton Rouge, LA, from Charlotte, NC, to Topeka, KS, with a lot of stops in between.

"Seems like I played ball in every city east of the Mississippi River. I had a good time, and enjoyed myself, but I don't think I realized fully that those days were the happiest of my life."

Some of those good times occurred during his stay with Baton Rouge of the Evangeline League. He did well enough in 1953, hitting .357 in 94 games (he had too few plate appearances to qualify for the batting title), but the next year he fashioned a true all-star season. In 140 games he hit .321 (with a .462 on-base average), had 12 triples, and stroked 33 home runs. Returning in 1956, he hit .307 in 75 games, and in 1957 posted .295 in 54 games before the team folded.

"Always liked the Evangeline League," he smiled.

After three games with Topeka of the Western League late in the 1957 season, he said good-bye to the nomadic life of a ballplayer.

"I remember it rained a lot right after I got there. Sitting in a hotel room while the rain beat against the window, I told myself I could be home with my family instead of sitting here alone in Topeka."

McKee put up solid numbers during his 12-year, 1,118 game minor league career: 1,115 hits, a .290 batting average, 115 home runs, and 702 RBIs.[2] He was one pitcher-turned-everyday player who knew how to hit.

From sandlot days on the cotton mill village to high school and American Legion ball, from triumph and heartbreak of a short major league career to hard-earned success in the minors, his life was a baseball journey.

"I lived the dream of about a million kids, being a major leaguer and all."

After his playing days ended, he settled down to a career with the U.S. Postal Service. And he found time to coach high school and American Legion teams with his good friend and former teammate Gene Kirkpatrick. It was a chance to give back, to pass on his deep love for the game, to help shape the lives of the young men who played for him.

"Some of the kids have told me years later that I helped them in some way, and I get a bigger kick out of that than I do anything."

He and his beloved wife of 60 years, Denice, never thought of leaving the familiar territory around Shelby, and joke that they never had enough money to get out of town, anyway. But after all the travels, all the places they have seen, and all the people they have come to know, there was just never anyplace better than home.

"It's all been so wonderful. I've been so fortunate in my life, and I've always felt lucky to have baseball." For Rogers Hornsby McKee, once around the horn has been a gracious plenty.

Notes

1. Documentation of this accomplishment is important enough to have independent verification. Jeff Chernow, Baseball Operations Manager of STATS, Inc., confirms that their research has shown Rogers Hornsby McKee to have been (and to this day, remains) the youngest pitcher since 1900 to have started and won a major league baseball game.
2. Mr. McKee's minor league statistics courtesy of Patric J. Doyle, Old-Time Data.

Jim Riley

A Unique Two-Sport Athlete

by Jeff Obermeyer

We always remember the exploits of our favorite sports stars. Their accomplishments are relived and dissected by casual fans and historians alike. The same holds true for those who reach a certain level of notoriety, that one great (or infamous) season, series, or moment that defines a career. For most players history is not so kind, as memories fade quickly and all that remains are a few lines of statistics.

There is another type of fame, however. Some players aren't remembered for what they accomplished as much as for just being in the right place at the right time, becoming a footnote in history and the answer to a trivia question. As a SABR member and a hockey fan, one of my all-time favorite questions is this: Who is the only man to play in both the National Hockey League (NHL) and in Major League Baseball? His name is Jim Riley, and the unique combination of these two very dissimilar sports begs a closer look at his career.[1]

James Norman Riley was born on May 25, 1895, in Bayfield, New Brunswick, to John Henry Riley and Margaret Byers. His father was American and his mother Canadian, both of English descent.[2] Not much is known of his early life.

Like many young Canadian men of the era, hockey exerted a strong pull on Riley, and he traveled east to Alberta to seek his fame and fortune. After playing one season of amateur hockey with the Calgary Victorias of the Alberta Senior Hockey League in 1914-15, Riley was ready to turn pro. During this era professional hockey was dominated by two leagues. In the east was the National Hockey Association (NHA), a six-team circuit

of Canadian clubs in Ontario and Quebec, while the west had the Pacific Coast Hockey Association (PCHA), a three-team league with member cities in British Columbia, Washington, and sometimes Oregon. Jim headed west, signing with the Victoria Aristocrats for the 1915-16 season.

In the summer following that first pro season, Riley picked up a bat and ball and got a tryout with the Tacoma Tigers of the Northwestern League, the earliest reference to his baseball career. At 5' 11" tall and 185 pounds Riley was a big man by the standards of the era, and while Tiger manager Russ Hall was impressed with his size, he felt the youngster needed a little more experience before making the move to professional ball, so it was back to the ice.

Riley remained in Washington that fall, joining the Seattle Metropolitans of the PCHA, and it was there that "Big" Jim really made a name for himself on the ice. Riley played seven seasons with the Metropolitans between 1916 and 1924, a run that included two league championships and four all-star team selections.[3] He also finished second in the league goal-scoring race twice, lighting the lamp 23 times in 1920-21 and 16 times in 1921-22.

In the spring of 1917 the Metropolitans hosted the Montreal Canadiens of the NHA in the Stanley Cup finals, taking the series in four games to become the first American-based team to win hockey's highest honor. Riley was kept off the score sheet in the series, though he did appear in all four games.

The 1917-18 PCHA season ended on March 13, 1918, and less than a month later Riley was married. He and his new wife, Myrtle Laura Riley, didn't have much time for a honeymoon, however. They wed on April 12 and just three days later Jim traveled north to Vancouver to be

JEFF OBERMEYER *works as a Subrogation Operations Manager for Farmers Insurance. During the off season he does hockey research, and his book* Hockey in Seattle *was published by Arcadia in 2004.*

The Seattle Metropolitans, circa 1921-23, featured three players who would go into the hockey Hall of Fame: Jack Walker (front row, far left), Frank Foyston (front row, second from left), and goalie Harry Holmes (back row, far right). Standing at the far left in the suit is Pete Muldoon, coach of the Metropolitans and the man who gave Riley his shot in the NHL (the other NHL coach Riley played for was his teammate in this photo, Frank Foyston). Jim Riley is in the front row, far right.

sworn in to the Canadian Army, serving in England for a year as part of an engineering detachment and quickly being promoted to sergeant. While he couldn't find an ice rink overseas, he did play baseball and quickly made a name for himself as one of the top third basemen among the military teams.

Riley's baseball career really took off in 1921, opening the season at second base with the Vancouver Beavers of the Pacific Coast International League and terrorizing opposing pitchers. By late June he was drawing rave reviews in the press, including this mention in *The Sporting News*:

> Jim Riley, the famous Seattle hockey star, is another slated for promotion. Riley is the Babe Ruth of the circuit and let it be mentioned also that at the keystone bag he has no peer in this company, although only breaking

in this season. Riley started the season batting just above the pitchers. Today he's in the clean-up hole on the Vancouver squad and delivering all the time.[4]

His .303 average and nine homers in 56 games caught the attention of the scouts as well, and on June 28 the St. Louis Browns acquired his rights. Less than a week later the struggling Browns called him up.

His major league debut came on July 3, 1921, in St. Louis during a matchup with the Chicago White Sox, replacing Jimmy Austin late in the game. Austin started the game at shortstop, and when he came out second baseman Marty McManus moved to short and Riley took over at second. Big Jim failed to get a hit in his lone plate appearance and the Browns fell, 5-1.

Riley started at second in both ends of a July 4 doubleheader against Detroit, going 0-for-6 at the plate and committing an error in the second game. The following day Tiger pitching again kept him off the bases and he picked up another error. In the wake of his hitless four-game performance Jim was sent back down to the minors, finishing out the season with the Terre Haute Tots of the Three-I League. He quickly got back on track, hitting .296 with the third-place Tots.

Fortunately for Riley, the hockey and baseball seasons did not overlap, so he still had a stable hockey career to fall back on while his baseball skills developed. In 1922, after finishing second in goal scoring in the PCHA, he reported back to Terre Haute and hit .313 over 114 games before being sent to Salt Lake City in the PCL, where he batted a respectable .268 against much stiffer competition.

In 1923, Jim got another shot at the majors. Though he was a right-handed fielder (he hit left), he was moved to first base while with the Shreveport Gassers of the Texas League. Though the Gassers finished at the bottom of the standings, Riley had a great year, batting .328 with 11 homers and 74 RBIs. His play again attracted the scouts, and this time it was the Washington Senators who came calling, sending two players to Shreveport for his rights. He was called up late in the year to fill in for an injured Joe Judge at first base, appearing in the last two games of the season and going 0-for-2 with a run scored and two errors. It was his last appearance in the majors.

At the close of the 1923-24 PCHA season Riley retired from professional hockey. While in Shreveport in 1923 he met a woman named Martha Baker, the widowed mother of the team's batboy, whom he eventually married sometime in late 1924 or early 1925.[5] It's likely that this relationship was a factor in his choice to concentrate on baseball and not return north to play hockey. After another outstanding season in Shreveport

(.312-26-127), Riley moved to the Southern Association to play with the Mobile Bears in 1925. His numbers in Mobile were almost identical to those he put up in Shreveport (.320-27-125) and his future looked bright.

In 1926, Riley was acquired by the Dallas Steers of the Texas League, replacing youngster Swede Lind at first base. He didn't disappoint, hitting .329 in an impressive 626 at-bats, driving in 111 runs. The Steers were the class of the league, finishing atop the standings at 89-66 and eventually knocking off the New Orleans Pelicans of the Southern League in the Dixie Series, four games to two (with one tie). It was Riley's first baseball championship, and he now had a title in each sport.

Once the baseball season ended, Riley once again heard the call of the ice, lacing up his skates for a couple of exhibition games with a team called the Dallas Texans. The PCHA had folded in 1925 and its players were scattered throughout hockey, so it didn't appear that Jim would have an opportunity to play professionally again.

When Riley played hockey in Seattle, the Metropolitans had been managed by Pete Muldoon. Muldoon was a sportsman through and through—a former professional boxer and lacrosse player, he also was an accomplished skater who often amazed crowds by skating

COURTESY OF DAVID ESHKANAZI

1921 Vancouver team. Riley is sitting in the second row, far left.

on stilts. Shortly after the demise of the PCHA, he moved to the NHL as the coach of its newest franchise, the Chicago Black Hawks. When Muldoon heard that one of the players from his 1917 Stanley Cup team was skating again, he came calling with a contract in hand.

Riley signed with the Black Hawks and made his NHL debut on January 19, 1927, against the Toronto Maple Leafs, a game won by Chicago in overtime, 4-3. He only lasted three games with the Black Hawks, but his return impressed one of his former teammates who was also coaching in the NHL, Frank Foyston. Foyston and Muldoon worked out a cash deal that sent Jim to the Detroit Cougars on January 31. In Detroit he was reunited with four of his former Seattle teammates and played in six games with the Cougars, picking up a pair of assists and 14 penalty minutes.

Riley retired from hockey again[6] and spent the next three seasons in the Texas League, splitting time between Dallas, Fort Worth, and San Antonio. He also played with Lincoln of the Nebraska State League in 1928 and 1929. His average and home run totals steadily diminished, and he was shipped off to Topeka of the Western League partway through the 1930 season. He sat out in 1931 before returning to the field with the Baton Rouge Senators of the Class D Cotton States League in 1932. There he had a bit of a resurgence, hitting .284 with the first-place Senators until the league folded on July 13, ending both his season and his professional baseball career.

With his playing days behind him, Riley and his family remained in the Dallas area, where he worked in a public relations capacity with a distillery. He was said to be a scratch golfer and remained so in his later years. The family moved to Seguin, TX, in the early 1960s, where they remained until Jim's passing on May 25, 1969, his 74th birthday, of lung and stomach cancer. He is buried at Guadalupe Valley Memorial Park in New Braunfels, TX. His wife Martha passed away in 1973.

As is often the case, our sports heroes are not always recognized for their accomplishments while they are alive, and the same holds true for Jim Riley. In 2000, 31 years after his death, Riley was inducted into the New Brunswick Sports Hall of Fame in the special "Sports Pioneer" category for his accomplishments on the ice and in the field, a fitting tribute to one of the first two-sport athletes.

Sources

Chicago Daily Tribune
LostHockey–www.losthockey.com
The Encyclopedia of Minor League Baseball
Seattle Hockey home page–www.seattlehockey.net
The Sporting News
Total Baseball, 8th Edition
Total Hockey, 2nd Edition
Washington Post

Notes

1. Andrew Kyle appeared in the major leagues in 1912 with Cincinnati and played professional hockey in the National Hockey Association (NHA) in 1917 with Toronto. While the NHL grew out of the NHA in 1918, the two leagues were not the same. The NHA folded prior to the creation of the NHL. The NHL does not recognize any statistics or records from the NHA period as being "official."
2. This is per Riley's description of their heritage during the 1930 census, taken while he was living in Texas. Riley listed his profession as "Ball Player."
3. Riley was named a PCHA Second Team All-Star three times between 1920-22 and a First Team All-Star in 1923.
4. Garvey, A.P. "A Tale of Baseball Breaks," *The Sporting News,* June 30, 1921.
5. The fate of Riley's first marriage to Myrtle is unknown.
6. Riley appeared in a handful of hockey games in California with the Cal-Pro League in 1928-29.

Joe E. Brown

A Clown Prince of Baseball

by Rob Edelman

You will not find Joe E. Brown's name in a major league box score. But in his way, he is as much a part of baseball lore as the Gas House Gang, the Whiz Kids, and the House That Ruth Built.

Joe E. Brown was a movie star: a wide-mouthed comedian whose face was his fortune. The zenith of his popularity came in the 1930s, when he appeared in a series of hit comedies produced by Warner Bros. Three of them—*Fireman, Save My Child* (1932), *Elmer the Great* (1933), and *Alibi Ike* (1935)—featured Joe E. as comical baseball players. Moreover, Brown was around the game all his life. He played baseball. He loved baseball. And he was a vigorous proponent of the game.

Joseph Evan Brown was born on July 28, 1892, in Holgate, a small town in northwestern Ohio. His parents were warm and loving but desperately poor, and young Joe E. was determined to abandon his roots and embrace a life of adventure. "I remember when I was a little guy going to school, stopping to look at a big 24-inch sheet announcing the arrival of the circus," he recalled in 1963. "Another boy was with me. I pointed to the aerial act and said, 'That's what I'm gonna be.' I remember it clearly. I didn't say, 'That's what I want to be.' I said, 'That's what I'm gonna be.'"

And so, at the age of nine, Joe E. lived out what for other youngsters would be a storybook fantasy as he left home to join the circus. He became the junior member of The Five Marvelous Ashtons, an acrobatic act that toured the country performing under big tops and in vaudeville

ROB EDELMAN *most recently authored the box liner notes and an essay on early baseball films included on the DVD compilation* Reel Baseball: Baseball Films from the Silent Era, 1899-1926. *He also is an interviewee on several documentaries included on the DVD re-release of* The Natural.

theaters. He earned $1.50 a week for the honor of being tossed through the air, and often being bloodied. As he grew into adolescence, Brown developed into a solidly proficient acrobat. While playing a date in San Francisco, he experienced firsthand the 1906 earthquake. It was around this time that he linked up with acrobats Tommy Bell and Frank Prevost and became the junior member of the Bell-Prevost Trio, a vaudeville act.

During this period Brown managed to play baseball whenever he could. He wrote in his autobiography, *Laughter Is a Wonderful Thing,* that his passion for the game "predates my first days at school, of that I'm sure, so it probably began when I learned to walk." In his youth, he explained, he

> began haunting the knotholes around big league ball parks when I wasn't on stage or practicing. And in the spring, after a season of sore ankles, skinned wrists, and broken legs, baseball as a career held more than a casual interest for me.

In 1908, Brown decided that he would seek summer employment as a ballplayer. Tim Flood, manager of the St. Paul Saints in the American Association, signed him as a second sacker, but his season ended abruptly when he broke his leg while sliding into third base. During the next few summers he played for various semipro teams in the Toledo, OH, area, including the Crowley All-Stars, Young Avondales, and Needham's All-Stars. One of the many baseball-related photos printed in his autobiography features a serious-looking Brown, with arms folded, garbed in a Crowley All-Stars uniform and posing with a dozen teammates.

In 1911, when he was 19, Brown was offered a Boston Red Sox contract. At the time, he also had a lucrative offer to appear in a burlesque show. He already had spent a decade in show business, and realized that his best chance for long-term success was on the stage. So burlesque won out over baseball.

On Christmas Eve, 1915, Brown wed Kathryn Frances McGraw. The couple eventually became the parents of two sons and two adopted daughters. As Joe E. now had a family to support, his career choice was appropriate given his now-steady employment on the stage. By this time, he had morphed from acrobat to comic actor. On occasion, he even incorporated baseball into his stage act. The *New York Times* described one such routine, in which "a young pitcher [is] harried by batters, umpires and base runners." Brown often quipped that he

> once had a major league job. The manager wanted me to play third base. He said that if I couldn't reach the ball with my hands, I would open my mouth and catch it between my teeth. I tried it once and darn near swallowed the ball.

His Great White Way debut came in *Jim Jam Jems* (1920), and he spent the decade as a headliner appearing on Broadway and touring in stage shows. But he was not through playing baseball. In 1920, Brown worked out and appeared in exhibition games with the Red Sox.

Throughout his career, newspaper or magazine profiles of Brown invariably cited his love of baseball—and his talent for playing the game. As far back as March 1921, the *Boston Globe* reported that Brown "has recently received an offer from the New York Americans to play with the team this year." The actor added,

> At one time I played [semipro ball in Toledo], but an accident to my arm made it necessary for me to give it up. Since then I have received many offers to go back into baseball but it would be rather foolish after I had started a successful career on the stage.

While a fine athlete—his athleticism is ever apparent in his baseball films, as he tosses balls and belts line drives without the aid of special effects or body doubles—it is debatable whether Brown possessed the talent to sustain a major league career. During a moment of candor in a 1937 interview, he even admitted, "[There] are a lot of stories about my baseball playing, but most of my big-league experiences happened in the imagination of various writers."

Brown's celebrity status, however, did allow him to maintain his insider access to major leaguers. On April 18, 1922, the *Boston Globe* reported, "The Red Sox and Yankees occupied boxes last night at 'Greenwich Village Follies' at the Shubert Theatre as guests of Joe E. Brown, the principal comedian in the show." The item concluded by noting that Brown "was formerly a professional baseball player."

By this time Brown's calling card was his face rather than his physical aptitude. A *Boston Globe* profile of the comic began: "'Did you ever see anything so funny as that man's expression,' exclaimed a woman in the audience at the Wilbur Theatre...as she gazed upward at Joe E. Brown, comedian of 'Jim Jam Jems.'" The article continued, "He has a comic style particularly his own, and not the least part of his success is the expression of his countenance. He doesn't have to say a word to get a laugh."

Nevertheless, the nature of Brown's comedy primarily was physical—and it was a wonder that he did not become a silent cinema comedian. His screen debut did not come until the dawn of the sound era, in *Crooks Can't Win* (1928), an inauspicious melodrama. He quickly established himself, however, upon signing a Warner Bros. contract and appearing in a series of comedies in which he alternately played two character types, both of whom were rubes. One was self-centered, with a mouth that was figuratively and literally big. The other was more shy and naïve.

Brown's three baseball films were especially popular. The first was *Fireman, Save My Child,* in which he starred as "Smokey" Joe Grant, an absentminded, Rube Waddell-like small-town firefighter whose pitching prowess earns him a spot with the St. Louis Cardinals. Just as he was starting his screen career, Brown had been cast in the road production of *Elmer the Great,* Ring Lardner and George M. Cohan's stage comedy about a none-too-bright hurler (originally played by Walter Huston) which opened on Broadway in 1928. Jack Oakie starred in the first screen version, titled *Fast Company* (1929). Brown was tapped for the remake, in which his character, Elmer Kane, is a small-town rube/home run hitter who plays for the Chicago Cubs and falls for a flighty actress. Finally, in *Alibi Ike,* Brown played Frank X. Farrell, a fireballing Cubs rookie right hander who is as brash and overconfident as he is talented.

When Warner Bros. decided to sign him to a contract, Brown asked the studio to provide him with his own baseball team. It was written into his contract that Warner Bros. would pay for the team's uniforms, equipment, and travel expenses. The ball club was named Joe E. Brown's First National All-Stars; it consisted of studio employees and former professional players, and was pitted against all-star, semipro, college, and Negro League nines up and down the Pacific Coast. Decades later, Brown described the contract as a "pip."

As he settled into his Hollywood lifestyle, the comedian was at the epicenter of Southern California baseball. In February 1932, he and Buster Keaton—another screen star whose love for baseball was legendary—were involved in an all-star fund-raiser for the Los Angeles Olympic games. Over 8,500 fans packed Wrigley Field to see the Joe E. Browns defeat the Buster Keatons, 10-3. Rogers Hornsby, Gabby Hartnett, Paul and Lloyd Waner, Sam Crawford, Billy Jurges, Stan Hack, Tris Speaker, Dave Bancroft, Carl Hubbell, Charlie Root, Pat Malone, Johnny Moore, and Pie Traynor were a few of the big leaguers who participated.

Brown also was instrumental in getting his baseball pals parts in movies. Frank Shellenback had a supporting role in *Fireman, Save My Child;* Shellenback and a roster full of ballplayers (Herman "Hi" Bell, Guy Cantrell, Dick Cox, Cedric Durst, Ray French, Mike Gazella, Wally Hebert, Wally Hood, Don Hurst, Smead Jolley, Lou Koupal, Wes Kingdon, Jim Levey, Bob Meusel, Wally Rehg, Jim Thorpe, and Ed Wells) appear as big leaguers in *Alibi Ike.*

In 1934, a *Los Angeles Times* reporter asked Brown, "You didn't really ask Dizzy and Daffy Dean to accept a picture contract, did you?" His response:

Why not? They're fine boys, interesting, natural, lovely characters. When I was sitting next to Dizzy in Detroit [during the World Series], with the fans swarming around him for autographs, he whispered, "Funny, isn't it? Five years ago I didn't even own a pair of shoes." They're not swell-headed. Besides, Warners wired me to ask them...

The Dean boys soon were starring in *Dizzy and Daffy* (1934), a Warner Bros. two-reel comedy short in which Shemp Howard (of the Three Stooges fame) remarks, "The only Dean I ever heard of is Gunga."

Brown also reportedly—and inadvertently—played a more direct role in the '34 series. According to the *Los Angeles Times,* Detroit hurler Schoolboy Rowe "caught part of his pitching hand in a door jamb...and subsequently had the bruise aggravated by a hearty good-luck hand-shake from Joe E. Brown, the film comedian."

From 1932 through 1935, Brown was a part owner of the American Association Kansas City Blues. In 1935, the rumor circulated that he was considering purchasing the Boston Braves, but this came to naught. Brown organized a semi pro basketball team whose roster was stocked with ex-UCLA Bruins. He owned racehorses, and often could be found at Santa Anita, Hollywood Park, and other Southern California racetracks. His Beverly Hills home housed a trophy room for his rapidly growing collection of autographed baseballs, bats, caps, and other sports memorabilia. He accumulated hundreds of items, from lumber used by Babe Ruth and Nap Lajoie and a cap worn by Eddie Collins to a baseball autographed by England's King George V, a football jersey worn by Red Grange, Gene Tunney's and James J. Braddock's boxing trunks, and a first-edition copy of Henry Chadwick's 1868 book, *The Game of Base Ball,* the initial hardcover baseball tome. Alas, most of the memorabilia was destroyed later in a house fire.

Decades later, Brown recalled that upon learning that Lou Gehrig was about to retire, he wrote the Iron Horse to request the ballplayer's first baseman's glove for his collection. "Lou wrote back, asking me to name anything but that, and I understood but I felt bad about having asked," he explained.

Not long afterward, he retired. In the fall of that year [1939] I went to New York to see the Yankees play in the World Series. Just before gametime a batboy came up to me and asked me to come to the Yankees' bench. Well—Lou was waiting there. He was very ill, by then, so thin and gaunt that I was startled at his appearance. But he smiled and held something out to me—it was his first baseman's glove. "Here it is, pal," he said.

By the late 1930s, Brown's popularity was waning. He left Warner Bros., appeared in some independent movies, and concluded his starring career in a series of low-budget Columbia Pictures comedies released in the late 1930s and early 1940s.

William Frawley restrains rookie Francis "Ike" Farrell, played by Joe E. Brown in the 1935 movie Alibi Ike.

But Brown did not fade from the public eye. During World War II, he proved that his heart was as big as his mouth as he became one of the first Hollywood celebrities to volunteer to entertain the troops. Brown trekked to combat zones from North Africa to Italy, the Pacific islands to Australia and New Zealand, bringing laughter to the GIs. He once estimated that he had traveled over 200,000 air miles during the war. Ever the jokester, he quipped, "When I opened my mouth in the South Pacific, 8,000 mosquitoes flew in." Even though he was a civilian, Brown reportedly was allowed to pack a carbine and ride in a tank while on Luzon, the Philippine island.

For his tirelessness in entertaining the troops, Brown was given a Bronze Star as well as a special citation, voted by the Military Order of the Purple Heart, for his "meritorious service." However, he and Kathryn personally felt the brunt of the war. Their eldest son, Don Evan Brown, a captain in the Army Air Corps, died at age 25 in October 1942, when his plane crashed near Palm Springs during a training exercise.

In 1945, as the war wound down, Brown signed to tour as Elwood P. Dowd in *Harvey,* Mary Chase's Pulitzer Prize-winning comedy. He opened in Chicago and eventually appeared in the play well over 1,000 times on stages from Broadway to Australia. He also returned to the screen, and gave a highly regarded dramatic performance as a small-town minister in *The Tender Years* (1947). He was ideally cast as Cap'n Andy in the second remake of *Show Boat* (1951), and gave what easily is his best-remembered performance as a loony millionaire in Billy Wilder's *Some Like It Hot* (1959). Here, as he slyly winks at the camera, Brown ardently romances Jack Lemmon's jazz musician-in-drag. His closing line— "Nobody's perfect"—is one of the more famous in film history.

Baseball, of course, remained an intrinsic part of his life. "Whenever he doesn't have a matinee, he's at some sports event," noted sports columnist Braven Dyer in 1946, while Brown was performing *Harvey* in Chicago. From 1953 to 1964, he served as first president of the PONY League, comprising teams made up of 13- and 14-year-olds. Long a supporter of the UCLA Bruins baseball team, the school's Westwood ballyard was named "Joe E. Brown Field."

During the 1953 season, Brown conducted pre- and post-game interviews for the New York Yankees and did five innings of play-by-play—three on television, and two on the radio. Radio-television critic Warren Bennett wrote that Brown was "as relaxed before the cameras as an old shoe. Shy, diffident ball players loosen up for him as they never did for his predecessor, the illustrious Joe DiMaggio." Brown told Bennett, "What I want to do is talk to the baseball fan who loves the game so much he stands in line to get a good seat."

In 1955, his 37-year-old son, Joe L. Brown, replaced Branch Rickey as general manager of the Pittsburgh Pirates. But Joe E. remained firmly rooted in Southern California—and as the Dodgers abandoned Brooklyn for Los Angeles, he was well-suited to become a high-profile promoter of West Coast baseball. In October 1957, not long after the team played its final game at Ebbets Field, Brown was the master of ceremonies of a star-studded luncheon at Los Angeles' Statler Hotel, held in honor of the team.

Brown was among the leaders in the battle for the "Yes" vote that would approve the Dodgers' contract with the city of Los Angeles, and result in the construction of Dodger Stadium. He became general chairman of the Taxpayers Committee on Yes for Baseball, and predicted that the Dodgers would lure baseball fans from far across the region—particularly if they competed in a spanking-new ballyard. The actor clearly was jockeying for support when he observed, near the start of the 1958 season, "Dodger President Walter O'Malley hopes to admit 300,000 youngsters [free of charge] to Coliseum games this season, and will up the figure to 600,000 when the club builds its own stadium in Chavez Ravine." He added, "The boy whose idol is Duke Snider or Junior Gilliam can't go very far wrong in his future life."

Joe E. Brown quietly lived out the rest of his life. He died at age 81 on July 6, 1973, of pneumonia and heart failure. Kathryn, his wife of 58 years, survived him. Brown was buried at Forest Lawn Memorial Park in Glendale, which houses the remains of entertainment industry legends from George Burns and Gracie Allen to Humphrey Bogart, James Stewart, and Spencer Tracy.

Brown's life may be summed up by the title of a classic Hollywood film, albeit one in which he did not appear: *It's a Wonderful Life*. "There's been tragedy, when we lost our boy," he recalled in 1963. "But I've had the chance given every other citizen in a free country of living my life as I wanted to live it and becoming what I wanted to become." ∎

Bibliography

Books

Bronner, Edwin J. *The Encyclopedia of the American Theatre, 1900-1975.* New York: A.S. Barnes, 1980.

Brown, Joe E., as told to Ralph Hancock. *Laughter Is a Wonderful Thing.* New York: A.S. Barnes, 1956.

Edelman, Rob. *Great Baseball Films.* New York: Citadel Press, 1994.

Newspapers

Bennett, Warren. "Joe E. Brown Bobs Up As Baseball Commentator." *Washington Post,* May 7, 1953.

Browning, Norma Lee. "Baseball Is Still the Big Love of Joe E. Brown." *Chicago Tribune,* September 28, 1966.

Davis, Jr., Charles. "Relives Baseball, Movies: Joe E. Brown Celebrates His 72nd Birthday as Past Meets Present." *Los Angeles Times,* July 28, 1963.

Dyer, Braven. "The Sports Parade." *Los Angeles Times,* August 16, 1946.

Gould, Alan. "Dizzy Dean Pitches for Cards Today." *Los Angeles Times,* October 9, 1934.

Henry, Bill, "Hollywood in Sport: Joe E. Brown Most Beloved Sportsman." *Los Angeles Times,* February 28, 1937.

Meagher, Ed. "Joe E. Brown Dies at Age of 81 at His Home in Brentwood." *Los Angeles Times,* July 6, 1973.

Millones, Peter. "Joe E. Brown, Comedian of Movies and Stage, Dies." *New York Times,* July 7, 1973.

Redfield, Margaret. "Joe E. Brown—That's Saying a Mouthful." *Los Angeles Times,* April 24, 1966.

Remenih, Anton. "Joe E. Brown Adds New Zest to Radio Show." *Chicago Tribune,* August 11, 1951.

Webb, Jr., Melville E. "Weather Man Plays Mean Trick on Boston Teams, Robbing Sox of Apparent Victory, Keeping Braves Idle." *Boston Globe,* April 18, 1922.

Wolters, Larry. "Where to Dial Today." *Chicago Tribune,* August 6, 1954.

Zimmerman, Paul. "Joe E. Brown to MC Affair for Dodgers." *Los Angeles Times,* October 22, 1957.

"Art of Comic Facial Expression." *Boston Globe,* March 6, 1921.

"Dodger Youth Program Lauded by Joe E. Brown." *Los Angeles Times,* May 2, 1958.

"Dodgers Will Bring Visitors from Far Away, Joe E. Brown Declares." *Los Angeles Times,* April 4, 1958.

"Does Filmdom Give Athletes Swelled Head?" *Los Angeles Times,* November 11, 1934.

"Durable comedian Joe E. Brown dies." *Chicago Tribune,* July 7, 1973.

"Joe E. Brown Gets Citation." *New York Times,* May 5, 1946.

"Joe E. Brown Loses Home and Mementoes." *Los Angeles Times,* November 7, 1961.

"Joe E. Brown May Buy Interest in Braves." *Los Angeles Times,* June 23, 1935.

"Joe E. Brown Nine Wins Olympic Benefit Tilt." *Los Angeles Times,* February 29, 1932.

"Joe E. Brown Target of the Circus Saints." *New York Times,* November 27, 1948.

Billy Harrell

Two Careers of "Helping the Kids"

by Brian C. Engelhardt

Billy Harrell has had two careers: his first started in 1952, when he signed with Cleveland and lasted for the next 15 years, during which he played for the Indians', Red Sox's, and Cardinals' organizations. His second career began immediately after his 1967 retirement from baseball, when he took a position as a juvenile probation officer with the New York Department of Corrections and extended for 25 years until he retired in 1992. In both of these careers he made a real difference with the people he dealt with on a daily basis: in the first career it was his teammates; in the second career the young men and women who were assigned to him as a juvenile officer.

Over the course of his time in baseball he appeared in 173 major league games, compiled in three tours of duty with the Indians and one with the Red Sox. He had a modest .231 lifetime average, eight home runs, and 26 RBIs. At Triple A, where he spent most of his time, he was a productive hitter, usually hitting around .280 as well as being a slick fielder, at one time or another having played every position except pitcher and catcher. Kerby Farrell, who managed Harrell in 1953 with the Class A Reading Indians, then later at Cleveland in 1957, described him as having "such tremendous hands, he could play the infield without a glove." Harrell's .330 average and 84 RBIs with Reading in 1953 resulted in his winning the Eastern League MVP award. All of this does not reflect the most lasting contribution he made to the teams he played for as well as to his teammates. Harrell is a

remarkably unselfish, patient man who led and motivated teammates in his own very quiet but effective way.

These qualities are apparent when meeting Harrell for the first time. He still exudes a warmth in his personality and sense of humor that teammates enjoyed more than 40 years ago. An example of this is in Harrell's reaction in September 2005, when he learned that the Reading franchise record of 170 base hits he set in 1953 had been broken by Chris Roberson (of the 2006 Philadelphia Phillies). Harrell immediately responded, "You tell Chris Roberson, 'Congratulations.' What was it anyway? Fifty-two years? … I am surprised it held up that long."

The Footsteps of Jackie Robinson

Harrell began his baseball career at a historic time, five years after Jackie Robinson had broken the color line. Racial equality was anything but the reality in baseball at the time when Harrell signed in 1952. African Americans had played only for Cleveland, Chicago, and the St. Louis Browns in the American League, and on only three teams in the National League. Spring training facilities were segregated as well as outright barring black players from certain minor league teams in the South. Harrell, like other black players entering the game at the time, would find his good nature and patience tested on a regular basis by such practices.

Like Robinson, an All-American in football as well a star in basketball and track during his collegiate career at UCLA, Harrell enjoyed a standout athletic career in college: in his case, basketball. Named Honorable Mention All-American in his senior year at Siena University in Albany, NY, Harrell received offers to play professionally from the Minneapolis Lakers and the Harlem Globetrotters after his graduation. Harrell's impact on Siena basketball is apparent in the annual presentation

BRIAN C. ENGELHARDT *is a SABR member who lives in Reading, PA. His promising basketball career ended abruptly at age 13 when the collapse of the 1964 Phillies stunted his growth. He has written several articles for the Reading Phillies web site, the* Berks Barrister, *and the* Berks County Historical Review.

of the "Billy Harrell Award" to the men's team leader in rebounds. Also like Robinson, who played in the Negro Leagues with the Kansas City Monarchs before signing a contract with the Brooklyn Dodgers, Harrell played briefly with the Negro League Birmingham Black Barons. Although his entry into baseball did not come with the fanfare that accompanied Robinson, Harrell was featured in a 1952 *Ebony* Magazine article titled "Future Jackie Robinsons: Amateur Teams will Supply Major Leagues With New Crop of Negro Stars" along with future African American major leaguers Earl Wilson, Dave and Dick Ricketts, and Johnny Lewis.

Harrell was assigned by the Indians to Cedar Rapids in the Three-I League (Illinois-Indiana-Iowa), so he was spared playing in the South. His wife was pregnant at the time, and he would have preferred to be playing closer to his home in Troy, NY. Florida was his first experience with institutionalized segregation. He recalled, "I had heard of drinking at 'colored' water fountains and those kinds of things, but when I came there and experienced them—it was so strange." In Winter Garden, FL, a city ordinance forbidding black ballplayers playing with white players prevented Harrell and future major leaguer Brooks Lawrence, then members of the Reading Indians, from playing an exhibition with their team. Harrell found it to be "really a strange experience."

Harrell also recalled the difficulty of having to deal with comments from the stands at certain stops in spring training. How he dealt with them is an indication of the strength of his character: "I heard them. It was a bad deal. But I just ignored it and tried to hit the ball. The guys on the team were behind me 100 per cent. You get base hits and that's what I did. That's how I handled it."

After hitting .325 at Cedar Rapids in 1952, Harrell enjoyed his MVP season with the Reading Indians, then of the Class A Eastern League. The team was a remarkable collection of future major league talent, winning a league-record 101 games. In addition to Harrell, there were 11 future major leaguers on the team, including Brooks Lawrence, Rocky Colavito, Herb Score, Rudy Regalado, Joe Caffie, Earl Averill Jr., Bud Daley, Joe Altobelli, Gordie Coleman, Doug Hansen, and Rod Graber. Reading manager Kerby Farrell went on to manage Cleveland in 1957. Harrell still has special memories of that team: "When I won the MVP award the fellas on the team, they really, really congratulated me. There was no big problem. No jealousy. It was a great group."

In 1954, Harrell was promoted to Triple A Indianapolis, where he hit .307, playing at shortstop, third base, and the outfield. Things looked promising for the next year, since Cleveland shortstop George Strickland hit only .213 that season. During spring training Cleveland manager Al Lopez had described Harrell as "a cinch to become a big league shortstop." Nonetheless, Harrell was back in Indianapolis when the 1955 season started.

After yet another solid season at Indianapolis (and after George Strickland's average dropped to an even lower to .209), Harrell was promoted to Cleveland for the last month of the 1955 season, where he appeared to make the most of his opportunities, hitting .421, with a .500 on-base percentage in 13 games. Harrell humorously recounts the events of first big league at-bat on September 2, 1955:

I was sitting on the bench and [Manager Al] Lopez is calling my name. Except he's calling, "Farrell" and I'm not paying any attention. I still hear, "Farrell, Farrell"— so then they said—"Hey, Billy, that's you." So I went up to hit. Virgil Trucks was the pitcher, and after two strikes and butterflies—I hit the ball, but it went right back to Trucks—an "at 'em" ball.

He looked forward to the next season:

I was excited after the end of 1955. The next year— George Strickland was having problems at shortstop— they told me they thought things would be really great for me. I had my hopes up.

George Strickland's Hot Spring

The Indians appeared to have other ideas than to give Harrell a full shot, as that off-season they traded Larry Doby to the White Sox for veteran shortstop Chico Carrasquel—an All-Star in four of the last five seasons. As if the team's acquisition of an all-star shortstop didn't create enough of a problem for Harrell's advancement, George Strickland hit .372 in spring training in 1956, so Harrell was sent back to Indianapolis, disappointed but characteristically taking things in stride: "After George had his hot spring, I went back to Indianapolis and I said to myself, 'Well you know, it's part of the game, part of life.'" Despite hitting .279 at Triple A Indianapolis in 1956 and .276 at Triple A San Diego in 1957, Harrell did not get back to the Indians until late in the 1957 season, when he hit .263, playing three infield positions.

The failure of the Indians to advance Harrell after the successful years on Triple A distressed several of his teammates, including Jim "Mudcat" Grant, who not only played with Harrell at Triple A San Diego in 1957 and with Cleveland in 1958, but also shared accommodations with him when they were housed together in a separate barracks facility for black players used by Cleveland over several spring training sessions. Grant, who pitched for seven teams in his 14-year major league career (numbering among his accomplishments that he was the first African American pitcher to win 20 games in the American League) respected Harrell's fielding ability—recalling Harrell as "a talented man…[who] could really pick it." His respect also reached to Harrell's character and the way Harrell handled the Indians' failure to advance him, remarking:

> I'm sure [Billy] was disappointed about the situation, but he never showed it. People talked about that it was a shame [that the Indians continued to keep Harrell at AAA], but unlike a lot of players where although they wouldn't talk about things in public, in private there would have been yelling and screaming, in private conversation that wasn't the case with Billy. He kept it to himself.

Grant, author of the recently published *Thirteen Black Aces*, described Harrell as quiet, but as a teammate "with a lot to offer." He added, "If you came to Bill he would always give you good advice—'cool down' kind of advice." He also explained how Harrell helped young African American teammates deal with the racial discrimination that they encountered in the 1950s and early 1960s:

> Coming out of the east like he did, there was a lot that [Harrell] didn't understand [about discrimination suffered by African American players] but he still was very helpful at times whenever you had a problem and went to him.

Grant compared Harrell to other African American players who helped him at that time: " Bill gave you advice to cool down—he was calming." Grant described teammate Larry Doby as "hotter," while he described Monte Irvin and Joe Black as "kind of in between."

The 30-year-old Harrell played the entire 1958 season with the Indians but hit only .218 in a reserve role. He was then placed on waivers, where he was claimed by the Cardinals and assigned to their Triple A team in Rochester, where he played in 1959 and 1960. Clearly his most vivid memory of his time with the Red Wings or, for that matter, of his entire baseball career was a regular season International League game between the Red Wings and the Cuban Sugar Kings played in Havana on July 25, 1959, which ended in a tie early in the morning on July 26, when stray gunshots fired by the crowd in celebration of the anniversary of Fidel Castro's Cuban revolution grazed two of the participants. (See inset). In a unique set of events immediately following the "gunfire" game in Havana, a few hours after the game ended, Harrell caught a plane from Havana to Toronto, where he played that night in the International League All-Star Game. The next day he flew back to Rochester in time for the July 27 regular season game that evening, resulting in Harrell playing in three games in three countries in a space of two days.

"A Gentleman and a Scholar"

Before the 1961 season Harrell was acquired by Boston in the Rule V draft. He laughs about the transaction:

> Maybe the Red Sox got me for $3 or $4 (under Rule V Draft rules at that time the price was considerably higher.) It's funny, my wife and family were living in Troy, and we had another baby and I said, 'Oh good, I'm in Boston'—it was pretty close by. I played one year (1961) in Boston, but then got sent out to Seattle (Rainiers, Boston's Triple A Pacific Coast League team). I wasn't close by anymore.

Harrell, now 34, assumed a role as a player-coach with Seattle, beyond the unofficial role of helpful teammate he had filled in prior years. One of his teammates on Seattle in 1962 was Dave Mann, also an African American, now sports editor of Seattle's "The Facts Newspaper." Mann's career paralleled that of Harrell, in that both played for a number of years in the Cleveland organization before moving over to the Red Sox organization. (Unlike Harrell, Mann never got to the majors despite occasionally hitting .300 or better and being among the league leaders in stolen bases in any league in which he played.) What impressed Mann most about Harrell was his attitude on returning to the minor leagues after having played for Boston the previous season:

Bill had been to the major leagues and now was down to show us how to go about getting there. On the field he was all baseball, all business. In the clubhouse he could have a lot of fun and laugh with the rest of us. Besides being a fine player, he was a teacher and instructor— when he took infield practice he was very explicit as to what he thought the right things were to work on. And if you wanted to learn something, you were smart to see the way he went about things.

Mann added: "Billy was very unassuming, even though he had been to the major leagues. Not everyone that comes down is like that, I assure you." Despite hitting .294 with 17 home runs with Seattle in 1962, Harrell did not earn a return trip to Boston.

For the next four seasons, Harrell continued to play with Boston's Triple A teams—at Seattle through 1964, then with Toronto in 1965 and 1966. Several of his younger teammates at Toronto in 1966 would go on to highly successful major league careers and, like Mudcat Grant, would later attribute a good deal of their success to Harrell's guidance. One such teammate was Reggie Smith, who starred for the Red Sox, Cardinals, Dodgers, and Giants over the course of a 17-year career. Smith credits Harrell as providing a " tremendous influence" on his development. He relates that Harrell "taught me how to become a professional in that he provided the stability necessary that I needed as a young player. He taught me the ropes more or less." He added,

At that time people thought I had a so-called chip on my shoulder—which I didn't—it's just that I was a fierce competitor. Billy taught me how to channel my energy, and had a very calming influence on me. He had always an anecdote or a story which managed to take a lot of tension out of certain situations. It really helped me keep things under control.

Notably, Smith won the International League batting crown the year Harrell worked with him.

In Harrell's own recollections of the young Reggie Smith what impressed him most was Smith's arm. Harrell remembers that, "[Smith] could fire it. Nobody ever had seen that kind of arm—he couldn't play the infield— he threw the ball too hard at first base. They had to put Reggie in the outfield. He could hum it, I'm telling you." Harrell also remembers how he worked to calm down a rivalry that Smith had with yet another budding star on the 1966 Toronto team—future 1975 American League home run champion George "Boomer" Scott. Harrell remembers the raw talent of each player:

Scotty and Reggie both wanted to hit the most home runs, and they were in competition with each other. George would go off like a volcano and I'd calm 'em both down, and I'd tell 'em we're all part of the same team, and it would help. They had so much talent and I felt good for both of them.

Also at Toronto was Mike Andrews, who was a member of the American League champion 1967 "Impossible Dream" Red Sox, an All-Star with the White Sox, and member of the world champion 1973 Oakland A's. (Andrews was the focus of a clubhouse mutiny staged during the World Series by his teammates after he was disabled by owner Charles O. Finley following two plays questionably designated as errors. The team rallied behind Andrews and threatened to boycott the next game until Finley restored Andrews to the active roster.) Andrews has been the chairman of the immensely successful Boston-based Jimmy Fund cancer research foundation since 1979.

He recalls Harrell as being "like a father" to the younger players," adding:

I personally learned so much from Bill—not only playing infield, but the way he carried himself off the field as well. He was a stabilizing influence with a young team plus he was the consummate pro and was always so positive. People would get upset at times, but Billy would just say, 'Now don't get excited.' It would settle things down.

Andrews noted in particular that the "calming influence" that Harrell brought with him not only benefited the players on the team, but at times helped calm the team's manager, a young Dick Williams (who the next year would go on to manage Boston to the American League pennant, and later in his career would guide Oakland to two world championships and San Diego to a pennant). Andrews recalls Williams as "sometimes being pretty brash." Andrews added: "Billy could still hit well too—even at that stage of his career."

Reflecting his role as a "player-coach" with the various Triple A teams, Harrell laughed and said, "I was the team grand pop. I've always felt that the older fellows should be helping the younger guys. I was there to help the kids—I was there to set an example—keep them calm." Mudcat Grant refers to Harrell with a term Grant says he reserves only for select individuals, explaining, "We used to have a term for a special kind of guy— the kind of guy Billy was— we called that kind of guy a 'gentleman and a scholar.'"

Helping the Kids: Part II

When he retired from baseball following the 1966 season at Toronto, the same qualities of unselfishness and a desire to help that led to his success with his baseball teammates led him to take a position with the New York Department of Corrections in Albany and begin a new career of "helping the kids," and specializing in working with juveniles. For the next 25 years, Harrell worked with youth, trying to help them to participate in sports and other activities, seeing them in his office once a week, while also going out to see them in their homes. Harrell took special care to "see that they got into school." He also worked to commence and administer an after care program, where he arranged to have baseball teams for boys in group homes. Harrell was proud of the success achieved, recalling, "After they moved on, a number of them came back, and they played against the institution. The kids then saw they could play ball so they could get straightened up and get a chance." Harrell saw baseball as a great vehicle to teach the youths assigned to him. In Harrell's view, "Baseball is a team sport." Teaching the young men he worked with the value of working on the team was something Harrell viewed as an important lesson and a key to success. He concluded his thoughts on the matter, saying, "I think I've always been that way with the way I played, and that's the way I look at life, being part of a team—I call it 'being responsible.'"

Harrell and his wife Miriam live in Albany. He spends time working for his church, and bowls in his spare time. He has a son, three daughters, five grandchildren, and three great grandchildren. The year 2006 was a big year for recognition of Harrell's accomplishments: Siena retired his jersey in January and he was inducted into the Reading Baseball Hall of Fame in July. Harrell enjoys seeing his children and counts his blessings: "I'm lucky. My children are spread out all over—Chicago, Las Vegas, and Rochester—so I always got places to go— like a free vacation." ∎

"Game Called on Account of Gunfire"

One of the oddest occurences in baseball began shortly after midnight on July 26, 1959, during an International League game between the Rochester Red Wings and the home Havana Sugar Kings. The game was called a tie due to gunfire from the crowd because a member of each team had been grazed by stray bullets. (Presumably the game was called a tie and not a forfeit because the umpires didn't want to anger already excited heat-packing home fans.) The story that ran on the AP wire dryly noted that it was possibly the first time in baseball history that a game was called on account of gunfire.

The crowd that night was particularly excited because it was the eve of the sixth anniversary of the July 26, 1953, storming of the Moncada Barracks by Fidel Castro and a group of his followers. That event, although unsuccessful in achieving its goal at the time (Castro ended up in prison as a result of the skirmish) marked the beginning of the "26th of July Movement," the name of Castro's revolutionary organization that eventually took control of the country on December 31, 1958.

Despite the political change in Cuba, the Sugar Kings continued to play in the International league. They were stocked predominantly with players from the Cincinnati organization, who comprised an interesting mix of former major leaguers like Lou Skizas, Carlos Paula, Yo Yo Davalillo, and Raul Sanchez, plus a number of future major leaguers including Mike Cuellar, Cookie Rojas, Leo Cardenas, Tony González, Jesse Gonder, and Elio Chacón. The Sugar Kings were managed by Preston Gomez, who would go on to manage in the major leagues with the Padres, Astros, and Cubs. The Red Wings roster included former major leaguers Billy Harrell, Luke Easter, B. G. Smith, and Gene Green, along with future prospects that included Duke Carmel and Charley James. They were managed by Ellis "Cot" Deal, who had as an assistant future Yankee coach Frank Verdi.

Harrell vividly remembers the excitement in the air that night at Havana's La Gran Stadium, as he recalled that not only was there a large crowd, but that Castro himself was expected at the game. As a result, events of the evening were held up until Castro's arrival. Harrell also noted, with a laugh, that while everyone was waiting for Castro's arrival, "Castro's son was down in the [Red Wings] dugout with us."

Following Castro's late arrival, the start of the regular game was further delayed as Castro pitched in a short preliminary exhibition for an army team. In addition, an earlier suspended game between the Sugar Kings and the Red Wings was completed. With the late start of the regularly scheduled game, it was close to midnight when the game went to extra innings. In the top of the 11th inning, Harrell hit a home run giving the Red Wings the lead, but the game was tied in the bottom of the 11th on a disputed play where the Red Wings argued that Havana's Jesse Gonder failed to touch a base. The ensuing argument resulted in the ejection of Red Wings manager Deal, which may have saved his life.

A few minutes later, at midnight, gunfire erupted both inside and outside the ballpark as soldiers carrying tommy guns and civilians with private sidearms all began to fire into the air in celebration of the July 26 anniversary. As Harrell described the scene: "Everybody was yelling, 'Cuba Libre!', and they were shooting guns and everything. It was pretty scary." At that point, both Red Wings coach Frank Verdi, coaching at third base in place of the departed Deal, as well as Sugar Kings shortstop Leo Cardenas were grazed by stray bullets. The umpires immediately took the teams off the field. Verdi, who was wearing a helmet liner, which caused the bullet to only graze his head, said to reporters at the time, "It felt like I got hit with a blackjack. I don't know if I would be talking to you had the bullet hit squarely." Speculation was that if Deal, who didn't wear a helmet liner under his cap, had been coaching instead of Verdi, the bullet would have caused serious injury.

The bullet that hit Cardenas went through his uniform, but didn't penetrate his skin.

An international incident ensued. The Red Wings refused to play in Havana for the remaining games of the series. Frank Horton, Red Wings president, called the United States ambassador to Cuba and arranged an immediate exit. The Cuban management called Rochester's refusal to play "absurd." Harrell related: "We had a tough time getting on the plane that night." (Actually, it was the next morning.) After a few days, matters settled and all other games in Havana that season were played as scheduled. In fact, the Sugar Kings won the 1959 Minor League "Junior World Series." The next season the International League again tried to play a schedule with a team in Havana, but on July 13, 1960, the Havana franchise was shifted to Jersey City due to the political climate at the time.

The bullets that flew during the 1959 anniversary celebration of the "July 26th Movement" certainly cause those events to take a place at or near the top of the list of bizarre circumstances that have ended baseball games. ■

Sources

Books

Moffi, Larry & Jonathan Kronstadt. *Crossing the Line,* Iowa City, IA, University of Iowa Press, 1994.

Swank, Bill. *Echos from Lane Field: A History of the San Diego Padres 1936-1957,* Paducah, KY; Turner Publishing, 1997.

Articles

Bennett, Brian A., "On a Silver Diamond," Scottsville, NY, Triphammer Publishing, 1997.

Doyle, Pat, "Gunfire in the Ballpark," *Baseball Almanac,* February, 2003. www.baseball-almanac.com/minor-league/minor2.shtml

"Future Jackie Robinsons': Amateur Teams will Supply Major Leagues With New Crop of Negro Stars," *Ebony,* vol. 7, issue 7, May 1952.

Pitoniak, Scott, "The night bullets replaced cigar smoke in the Cuban air," *Rochester Democrat and Chronicle,* March 28, 1999.

"Wings Refuse to Play After Havana Gunfire; Shanghnessy Gives OK," *Rochester Democrat and Chronicle,* July 26, 1959.

Interviews

Dave Mann, interview with the author, September 15, 2005.

James "Mudcat" Grant, interview with the author, January 8, 2006.

Mike Andrews, interview with the author, October 15, 2005.

Reggie Smith, interview with the author, January 12, 2006.

Billy Harrell interviews with the author, September 10, 2005; January 13, 2006; July 2, 2006.

Acknowledgment

A special thank-you to Susan A. Washington of the Rochester Public Library for her assistance in researching the events of July 1959.

The Magician

Don Mueller and the New York Giants

by J. A. Petterchak

As outfielder for the New York Giants in the 1950s, Donald Frederick Mueller played in some of the most memorable games of the era. Now approaching his 80th birthday, he reflected on a career of some 50 years ago.

Born in the St. Louis suburb of Mount Pleasant (now Creve Coeur), the young Mueller learned hitting from his father, Walter "Heinie" Mueller, who played for four years in the 1920s with the Pittsburgh Pirates. "He taught me an awful lot," said his son,

> because he picked the minds of a lot of the good ballplayers, what made them good hitters. He showed me how to grip the bat, to use pressure on one hand or the other to hit where you want to hit. He also had me focus on the ball by pitching corn kernels that I would hit with a broomstick. Concentrating on such a small object improved my depth perception, so in comparison, the baseball would seem a large object.

Mueller played two years of American Legion baseball, against larger, older boys. "I realized I couldn't overpower what those pitchers were throwing," he recalled. "I didn't have the strength. Just naturally, I guess, I didn't choke the bat, but just met the ball instead of trying to kill it."

At Pattonville High School, he won a spot on the baseball team, batting left-handed and throwing right-handed. As a junior he joined his older brother, Leroy, as athletes at the high school of Christian Brothers College in the St. Louis suburb of Richmond Heights. (Leroy would go on to a minor league stint with the Red Sox and Yankees in the mid-1940s.)

J. A. PETTERCHAK, *a Little League scorekeeper at age 13, was the director of the Illinois State Historical Library in Springfield. He now researches and writes biographies as well as business and organization histories.*

Developing into the caliber of a professional ballplayer while still in high school, Don received offers from several teams, including the Chicago Cubs, "except," he said, "my dad didn't like the contract they offered me." Walter Mueller's choice was the New York Giants, whose scout Gordon Maguire brought Mueller to Sportsman's Park in 1944, when the Cardinals were playing the Giants. Manager Mel Ott, who had been Don's favorite professional player, approved signing the 17-year-old for the Giants' Triple A farm team in Jersey City, managed by the great Chicago Cubs catcher Gabby Hartnett. Mueller played three games that season, driving in three runs with one hit in seven at-bats.[1]

The following year, as a high school senior, Mueller was invited to the Giants' spring training, "with permission from the CBC Brothers to have my lessons mailed to me." Observers would later credit Mueller's keen eye and excellent coordination for his hitting success. He credits his father's tutelage with the corn kernels.

During those World War II years, transportation restrictions confined spring workouts to the northern states. The Giants and Jersey City players practiced on the grounds of the John D. Rockefeller mansion in Lakewood, NJ. Even though the house was a distance from the ball field, the lanky Mueller smashed a hit through the front window, observed by astonished New York sportswriters. Reporting his feat, they predicted that the teenager would become a figure at the Polo Grounds.

He played only five games for Jersey City before joining the Merchant Marines.[2] In the service for two years, during 30-day shore leaves he returned to the team. Expected to become a slugger, he instead developed a controlled swing, choking up on the bat a bit, and meeting the ball rather than trying for power.[3]

Don Mueller of the Giants.

Mueller became the regular right fielder for the 1950 season, after slugger Willard Marshall was traded to Boston. Durocher, who on his selection as manager had announced, "I come to win," confidently predicted a pennant that year. Batting third in the lineup, Mueller's job was to drive leadoff hitter Eddie Stanky home and Alvin Dark to third, so that, theoretically, the Giants would have scored a run, with two men on and none out, and sluggers Monte Irvin and Whitey Lockman coming to the plate.

Early in the season, however, the team played mediocre ball, with poor hitting and worse pitching. By June, Mueller was batting an anemic .185, causing Durocher to drop him to seventh in the order and then to bench him.[5] But in early August as a pinch-hitter, Mueller began lifting his average, with soft bounders and line drives. Returned to the lineup, he responded by hitting well over .300 during the final two months, as did Stanky, Irvin, Dark, Lockman, and Henry Thompson.[6] Had the season lasted another week, the improved Giants might have swept past both the Phillies and the Dodgers to take the pennant.

Mueller ended the season with a .291 average, earning the reputation of a scrappy place hitter. Sports writers named him Mandrake the Magician for his ability to stroke the ball through holes in the defense.

His confidence restored, Durocher told reporters in the spring of 1951 that the Giants would "take it all." Many agreed, including a writer for the *Times*:

> For the first time since their last pennant-winning days in '36 and '37, the Giants toe the mark a definite pennant contender. Durocher, in the face of severe criticism from all sides, does seem to have achieved the objective he had in mind when he dismantled the power-laden but otherwise inept array that for so long failed to bring a pennant to the Polo Grounds. In its place he has developed a talented, fine-spirited group of players. The Polo Grounders do look primed for a quick get-away this spring.[7]

After his Merchant Marines discharge in mid-1946, Mueller battled .359 for Jersey City during the final weeks of the season. The next year Mueller hit .348 in a full season at Jacksonville, played in 99 games at Jersey City in 1948, then batted .358 in 36 major league games at the Polo Grounds. After a brief stay in Minneapolis, hitting .311, he was brought back to New York.[4]

Giants owners had replaced Ott as manager in 1948 with the fiercely competitive Leo Durocher. The offense under Ott had been known as the National League's "lumberjacks," for the number of big, slow power hitters. "The team did not have a good won-loss record," Mueller explained. "Leo got rid of the home run hitters. He wanted base hits, with good pitching. I got the job because I was his kind of ballplayer: hit, advance the runner."

Unfortunately, the Giants lost 11 games straight after opening with two wins in three games. After a particularly bad loss, Durocher berated each of the players, surprising even veterans by his foul-language tirade.[8] "It was a turning point," recalled one teammate. "You could feel the tension and pressure of those first dismal two weeks lift—like breaking through the clouds into clear sky when you're in an airplane. From the next day on we played fantastic baseball," a winning stretch that would continue through the season, aided by the talent and enthusiasm of 20-year-old rookie Willie Mays.

Mueller, who had been among the slumping hitters, saw his average improve over the summer. Of his 65 careers home runs, five came in two consecutive games on September 1 and 2, 1951, against the Dodgers at the Polo Grounds. "The count was one ball and no strikes," he recalled of a memorable at-bat in the first game. "Monte Irvin was on deck. He shouted to me, 'We got a call in the dugout. Your wife just had a baby boy.' I hit the next pitch, out of the park," for his second homer of the game. The new arrival was the first of three sons born to Don and Genevieve Babor Mueller, who had met as Pattonville High School and married in 1949.

The day following three home runs, Mueller was retired by big Don Newcombe in three consecutive at-bats. Then in both the sixth and eighth innings, Mueller hit the ball into the stands. Five homers in two games, tying a record achieved at that time only by Adrian Anson, Ty Cobb, Tony Lazzeri, and Ralph Kiner.[9]

Trailing the Dodgers by 13½ games in August, the Giants won 39 of their final 47 games to end the season in a first-place tie. With the Dodgers leading 4-1 in the bottom of the ninth inning of the third and final playoff game, leadoff Giant Alvin Dark singled off Newcombe. Mueller took the first pitch for a ball and noticed that Dark was being held close to the bag. The Magician hit the next pitch sharply to the left of first base, out of reach of first baseman Gil Hodges.

"I knew what I wanted to do," Mueller said later. "If he would have been playing back and not holding Dark, I would have tried to go up the middle. I always favored the middle."[10] On the single, Dark raced to third. Monte Irvin, representing the tying run, popped up for the first out. Then, with men on first and third, Whitey Lockman lined the ball into left field for a double. Dark crossed home plate, and Mueller, scrambling for third, slid past the bag and tore the tendons on both sides of his ankle. Writhing in pain, he was carried off the field on a stretcher into the clubhouse.

His roommate, Clint Hartung, called in as the pinch runner, was about to become a footnote to history. The Dodgers brought in Ralph Branca in relief of the tiring Newcombe. Bobby Thomson, a shy journeyman outfielder in the biggest spot of his career, stepped to the plate. Giants players and fans hoped for a single to tie the game, but Thomson delivered with a walk-off three-run homer into the left-field stands.[11] "I played the whole game and got a big hit in the ninth inning," Mueller recalled. "When Bobby Thomson hit his home run—The Shot Heard 'Round the World—I was the only one in the clubhouse, listening to it on the radio."

Mueller's injury kept him from playing in the World Series, in which Casey Stengel's Yankees won their third straight championship, four games to two. Some writers believe that had Mueller been in the lineup, the Giants might have won the Series. Indeed, his right-field replacement, Henry Thompson, hit only .143 in the four games and committed two errors.[12]

Giants fans anticipated another good year for 1952, with a 17-5 start. But they soon felt the loss of power hitter Mays, who left in May for military service, while Irvin was out with a broken ankle. The other hitters, including Mueller, felt pressure to attempt hitting for home runs. His ineffectiveness, however, caused Durocher to bench him for 28 games. Mueller also had to prove his ability in right field, vying with both Bobby Thomson and Hank Thompson, Hartung, and others, but played more games than any of them, ending the season with a .281 batting average.

In 1953, after being benched again for lack of home-run power, he decided to forgo any attempts at power hitting. "My chance of hitting a single is very good," he explained to a writer. "My chance of clouting a homer is very poor. It is certainly better for the team this way. If I am on base, I save a chance for Mays, Irvin, Thompson or somebody to knock me in."[13]

As proof of his theory, Mueller finished fifth in the National League with a .333 batting average. And, with only 13 strikeouts, he was the most difficult batter to fan that year. The team, however, finished in the second division.

In the first five games of 1954, Mueller found himself benched twice in favor of long-ball hitters. Then he hit a pinch single during an eighth-inning rally and played in every game for the rest of the season.[14]

On May 2, he "stood in right field and watched five balls go over my head" at Busch Stadium when Stan Musial hit five homers in a Giants-Cardinals double-header, all into the right-field seats. Although Mueller had hit five home runs in two consecutive games in 1951, Musial became the first player in baseball history with five in one day.

Mueller contributed to the Giants win in the second game, going five for five, including a double and a triple, producing two RBIs. "My five for five got exactly two lines in the paper the next day," referring to the extensive coverage of Musial's feat.

National League All-Star team manager Walter Alston, the Dodgers skipper, selected Mueller for the 1954 team. Pinch-hitting for pitcher Robin Roberts in a five-run fourth inning, Mueller came through with a clutch double, but the Nationals lost the game, 11-9.

Nearly all season, he made at least one hit per game, and on July 11, against four Pirates pitchers, he hit for the cycle: a double to left field, triple to right-center, and single to center. At his final at-bat, he sank one into the right-field seats off left-hander Paul LaPalme, his first homer of the season. As a left-handed batter, Mueller explained, "Normally, I didn't try to pull left-handers. I took them the other way. But I was a situation hitter and this was a situation. So I pulled him over the right-field wall for the home run."[15]

The homer was one of four that Mueller hit that year. He was the first Giant to hit for the cycle since Harry Danning in 1940 and the only major leaguer to accomplish the feat in 1954.

Willie Mays, who had returned from two years of military service, hit 41 home runs to lead the Giants to the 1954 League championship. On the last day of the regular season he and Mueller were tied for the batting title. Mueller singled twice, but Mays, with three hits, won the crown with a mark of .345. Mueller, who

throughout the season was close in average to Mays, finished at .342. Though runner-up in the batting race, Mueller accumulated 212 hits, most in the league that year, and 17 more than Mays.[16]

Entering the 1954 fall classic, the heavily favored Cleveland Indians, boasting four Hall of Fame pitchers and a then league-record 111 wins, had ended the New York Yankees' five consecutive years as World Champions. But the Series was brief, with Durocher managing a four-game sweep. Mueller, described by a *Time* magazine reporter as "a quiet, conscientious competitor," and "always a power at the plate," played right field in each of the games and batted a composite .389. His team's batting average totaled .254, while the Indians managed only .190.[17]

Mueller surmised that the Indians' quest for the American League win record hurt their chances in the Series. "They captured the pennant real early that year, but manager Al Lopez continued playing all of the regulars seeking the win record."[18] The 1954 Series was the most lucrative to that time, a record pool of $881,763.72, with full portions for each Giant of $11,147.90. The attendance of 251,507 also set a four-game Series record.[19]

In early 1955, with the Giants playing the Reds, the two teams went 16 innings, combining for a record-tying 10 double plays. Mueller started a rally in the 16th, hitting an outside fourth-ball pitch for a pop single that led to a 2-1 Giants victory.

That summer Mueller was again selected for the National League All-Star team. Batting twice, he garnered a hit off Early Wynn, the Indians' star right hander, in the fifth inning. The Braves' Henry Aaron ran for Mueller, then replaced him in right field for the remainder of the game, as the Nationals won in 12 innings, 6-5.[20]

Mueller's batting average began declining from .306 in 1955 to .269 in 1956 and .258 in 1957. The Giants finished third in 1955 and sixth in both 1956 and 1957. Mueller and his family looked forward to the Giants' move to San Francisco in 1958, but in March the team sold him to the Chicago White Sox. He saw limited playing time that year, with 166 at-bats and hitting for a .253 average. The following year, suffering from gout and arthritis, the 32-year-old retired from baseball, with a lifetime .296 batting average.

An avid outdoorsman, in the off-seasons Mueller, his brother, and fellow players often spent time together fishing and hunting. After his playing days, Mueller raised cattle on the family farm and for a few years scouted for the Giants in Missouri and Illinois. Then he began a lengthy career as an insurance company investigator.

In 2001, he was elected to the Brooklyn Dodgers Hall of Fame. Why the Dodgers? "Well, the Giants didn't have a Hall of Fame, and I guess the Dodgers were acknowledging that I was a pain in their butts."

In St. Louis County, Mueller's neighbors may be unaware that they reside near a two-time All-Star with a World Series ring, but they might notice the baseball bat he hangs in front of his home for first-time visitors. Occasionally attending Cardinals games at Busch Stadium, these days he and Genevieve prefer family activities. Their three grandsons attend college on athletic scholarships, while their granddaughter is a high school athlete in track and softball. When they were youngsters, Mueller taught each of them to hit corn kernels, with a wiffle-ball bat in place of the broomstick. ■

Notes

1. Tom Meany. *The Incredible Giants.* New York: A.S. Barnes, 1955, 93.
2. Meany, p. 93.
3. Bob Brian, "'Hitting' the High Spots," *Scholastic Coach,* March, 1965, 13.
4. Thomas Kiernan. *The Miracle at Coogan's Bluff.* New York: Thomas Y. Crowell, 1975, 237.
5. Kiernan, 35.
6. Kiernan, 57.
7. Kiernan, 24.
8. Kiernan, 65-66.
9. Meany, 90; *The Sporting News,* May 10, 1961, 8.
10. *St. Louis Post-Dispatch,* October 3, 2001, B5.
11. David S. Neft and Richard M. Cohen. *The Sports Encyclopedia: Baseball.* New York: St. Martin's/Marek, 1985, 286.
12. Meany, 94.
13. Meany, 90.
14. Meany, 91.
15. John C. Skipper. *Inside Pitch; A Closer Look at Classic Baseball Moments.* Jefferson, NC: McFarland, 1996, 77.
16. Neft and Cohen, 298-301.
17. *Time,* October 4, 1954, 71.
18. Skipper, 79.
19. *The Sporting News, Official World Series Records, 1903-1978.* St. Louis: The Sporting News, 1978, 199.
20. *The New York Times Book of Baseball History,* New York: Quadrangle, 1975, 182.

"Van Lingle Mungo"

by Dave Frishberg

In 1969, I was working as a pianist in New York City and beginning to write songs. I composed a rather brooding piece in what I considered a bossa nova style—a wide-ranging melodic line and a wandering tonal center. I had equipped the melody with two different lyrics. One was an angry satirical verse titled "Dear Mister Nixon;" the other was called "Don't Look Behind You" and soberly implored the listener to face the future. Neither lyric seemed to match the ambitious melody line.

One night I was paging through the newly published Macmillan's *Baseball Encyclopedia* by and my eyes fell on the name Van Lingle Mungo. "VAN LINGLE MUNGO"—the name scanned perfectly with a recurring melodic figure in my song, and I instantly sang it out loud. I knew then that the lyric would be only names—not names of famous stars, but names that evoked my childhood memories and, incidentally, illuminated some fragments of forgotten baseball history. I dived into the book assembling names that scanned, rhymed and related loosely to those years, the years of my childhood passion for the game.

Within an hour or so I had a complete lyric. About a month later I recorded an album of my songs including "Mungo," and that turned out to be the only track that got any airplay.

I was surprised. But I always felt the lyric wasn't finished, it wasn't doing the job and I kept tinkering with it. In my opinion I improved the song. I took out certain names from the original lyric and replaced them with

names from an earlier (wartime) era so that the nostalgic focus might be sharper.

Johnny Kucks and his rhyme mate Virgil Trucks had to go and were replaced by Lou Boudreau and Claude Passeau, whose names certainly sang better. The replacement of Roy Campanella's conveniently rhyming name was necessary because he was too recent. So I changed it to Art Passarella (an umpire), and that seemed to do the job: Gardella, Passarella, and Estalella.

Then I learned that Bob Estalella's name didn't rhyme in the first place, because it was pronounced as in Spanish: Esta-leya. So the whole rhyme scheme should have been scrapped, starting with "Danny Gardella," and now I stand forever humiliated in Baseball Songland. What did I know? I grew up in a minor league town and never heard Estalella's name uttered, only saw it in print. Same goes for Johnny Gee, whose name I mangled on the record with a soft "g." There may be other names I'm mispronouncing, but at this stage further corrections would only confuse me. In my search for relevant names that scanned, "John Antonelli" was an unfortunate choice, and it's annoying that he's in the song, because there turns out to be two John Antonellis whose major league careers nearly overlapped. I was thinking of the third baseman who was up with the Cardinals and Phillies during the war; I had seen him play with Columbus. I wasn't even aware of the more famous Johnny Antonelli, the left hander for the Giants. By the time Antonelli #2 came along I had already traded Duke Snider for Duke Ellington.

If you are keeping track, there are currently four surviving players from the Mungo song. I confirmed the dates of demise on a website called *The Baseball Almanac*, wherein biographical and statistical data claimed to be updated as of March 1, 2005. Of the original

DAVE FRISHBERG, *pianist, songwriter, and recording artist, grew up in St. Paul and was an avid follower of the St. Paul Saints during the 1940s. He hasn't followed current baseball since then, but he is a member of SABR and a collector of antique baseball periodicals and books.*

37 names, the surviving Mungolians are: Joost, Pesky, and Basinski. I'm positive Eddie Basinski is still alive and well, because he lives here in Portland and enjoys considerable celebrity and adulation as a Portland Beaver immortal. I had occasion to meet him once, and I excitedly told him how I used to watch him with the St. Paul Saints in 1946.

"You and Gene Mauch were a great double-play combination," I blurted. Basinski frowned and said, "Mauch wasn't much help."

Then I told him, "You're in my song, you know."

"Your song?"

"Yes, have you ever heard my song, 'Van Lingle Mungo?'"

Basinski stepped back, stared at me as if I were from Mars, excused himself, and walked off to chat with someone else.

The only other guy from the song I ever met was Mungo himself, who arrived from Pageland, South Carolina, to be on the *Dick Cavett Show* and listen to me sing the song. This was 1969, when Cavett had a nightly show in New York. Backstage, Mungo asked me, "When do I get the first check?"

When he heard my explanation about how there was unlikely to be any remuneration for anyone connected with the song, least of all him, he was genuinely downcast. "But it's my name," he said.

I told him, "The only way you can get even is to go home and write a song called 'Dave Frishberg.'"

He laughed, and when we said goodbye he said, "I'm gonna do it! I'm gonna do it!" If he did it, *The Baseball Almanac* doesn't mention it. ∎

VAN LINGLE MUNGO
Words and music by Dave Frishberg (1969)

Heeney Majeski, Johnny Gee
Eddie Joost, Johnny Pesky, Thornton Lee
Danny Gardella
Van Lingle Mungo

Whitey Kurowski, Max Lanier
Eddie Waitkus and Johnny Vander Meer
Bob Estalella
Van Lingle Mungo

Augie Bergamo, Sigmund Jakucki
Big Johnny Mize and Barney McCosky
Hal Trosky
Augie Galan and Pinky May
Stan Hack and Frenchy Bordagaray
Phil Cavarretta, George McQuinn
Howie Pollet and Early Wynn
Art Passarella
Van Lingle Mungo

John Antonelli, Ferris Fain
Frankie Crosetti, Johnny Sain
Harry Brecheen and Lou Boudreau
Frankie Gustine and Claude Passeau
Eddie Basinski
Ernie Lombardi
Hughie Mulcahy
Van Lingle...Van Lingle Mungo

Van Lingle Mungo